MW00786995

DEVILS DEN
THE RECKONING

TERRY LOVELACE, ESQ

Devils Den: The Reckoning

Copyright © 2020 by Terry Lovelace

All rights reserved. No part of this book may be reproduced or transmitted in any form or by any means, electronic or mechanical, including photocopying, recording, or by any information storage and retrieval system without the written permission of the author, except where permitted by law.

ISBN: 978-0-578-61023-8

For Sheila.

ACKNOWLEDGEMENTS

Since publishing *Incident at Devils Den, a true story ...* on March 10, 2018, I have been touched by so many people who have become colleagues and friends. Gratitude belongs first to those who read my book or listened to my audiobook. I appreciate your candid reviews, comments, and criticisms.

2020 saw a year where UFO conferences nationwide were cancelled due to the COVID-19 outbreak. I would prefer to share these stories with you in person, rather than just in print. I miss the conversations, handshakes, and hugs that are a part of every conference.

These friendships have been my greatest reward. If I have forgotten someone, I sincerely apologize for my oversight but know you're truly not forgotten.

My sincere thanks and gratitude for becoming a part of my life and sharing your own amazing stories.

Presented in no particular order:

George Verongos, my editor, mentor and friend. Special thanks to Sheila for her patience and kind support. Thanks to my loyal cat Murray who lovingly lay on my feet and purred throughout my many weeks of writing.

Thanks to Greg Shepard, Robert Schwartz, Jr., Robert Hastings, Dr. Bruce Solheim, Sharon Komorn, Comrade Mike Cleland, Dr. Jeff Kripal and staff at Rice University, Joseph and Alice Boeringa, Les Velez and the fine folks at OPUS including Garrett, Jason Bland and

Jamie and the gang at Paranormal Soup, Leslie Kean, Whitley Strieber, Kat from FATE Radio, Nancy Tremaine, Sev Tok, Doug Auld, Aurora, Yvonne Smith, Albert Wacha, Simeon Hein PhD, David Whitecrow, Lue Elizondo, James and Martha Lough, Linda Moulton Howe, Jimmy Church, Grant Cameron, Kris from VTSolution, Melinda, Maggie Dyer, Paranormal Zone TV with Norene Balovich, Lorien Fenton, the UFO Congress 2018, Agnes in Austria, Lorie Wagner, Lucinda Laughing Eagle, Deb Kauble and all of my CERO brothers and sisters, Chief Dallas Eagle, Mark @ PAUK Radio, Scotty at Artist First, Bruce Leininger, Alexander Boeringa, Lisa Honeywell/Greg and Leslie, Dr. "J," Alan B. Smith from Paranormal Now and KGRA, Chip in Florida, Kevin Estralla, Earl Grey, Dean Alioto, Chris Bledsoe, Kevin Day, Matthew Roberts, Scott at Parabnormal Radio, KMOX FM in St. Louis, very special thanks to Scott and Forest from ASTONISHING LEGENDS, Alexis Brooks, Dean Caporella, Steve, Mary and Matt, Steve Bates and the Houston MUFON, Daniel Alan Jones, Heather Wade, Kathleen Marden, Curry Stegan, Paul "Arizona" Barrett and the band ONE WORLD GOVERNMENT, Night Dreams Radio with Gary Anderson and James Chreachbaum, EERT RADIO, George Knapp, George Noory, Todd from Reality Unhinged, The Travel Channel for my appearance on "My Horror Story," Sheila Gay and Kerby from Rogue Talk Radio, Tim and Michelle from Midnight in the Dessert, Mike Vara, Lisa O'Hara, Cookie, Constable Extraordinaire Chris DePerno, Christian Uncut on UK Radio, Philip and Ronnie Kinsella, David Young, James Streble from Universal Secrets, KCMO Radio in Kansas City, Dave Emmons, Dave Scott, the guys from UFO Garage,

Bob Brown at Paranormal UK (PAUK) Radio, Allan Smith, Mark Watson and his show from London "Peer Beyond the Veil," Roswell UFO Festival 2018 and 2019, Barbara Jean Lindsey and the Cosmic Oracle, Veritas Radio with Mel, Erin Montgomery, Lenny Mandel, Miesha Starseed Awakening, Dion Mitchell, Robert Yocum and the talented script writer Carol Chrest, Cameron Braur, Rozanne Barone, Kerry Cassidy, Charles Rivers Productions, Mark Johnson PAUK Radio, Solaris Blue Raven, Kit, The Kingdom of Nye, Rex with the Leak Project, Into the Fire with Bear and Eric, Melisa Kennedy and the management and members of "UFO HUNTERS OF AMERICA," Ozark Publishing and Janet and Brandy, my friend Stephan from San Antonio MUFON, Tom Bowden and the nice folks at Oregon MUFON, Stargate to the Cosmos with Janet Kira Lessin and Dr. Sasha Alex, Victoria and Crystal from Contact in The Desert 2019 and 2021, Unknown Universe Radio with Wendy, John Baptist with End Times Ministry, Martin Willis at KGRA, David Noble, Kevin Randall, in memorial for Rick Bunch, and all of my dear friends from social media.

Thank you for the hundreds of candid reviews left on Amazon. I appreciate every single one.

Sincere thanks to the 1,341 kind folks who took time to email me and candidly share your amazing encounters. I regret that I could only include a handful of your stories, but collectively they are an impressive representative sample.

All stories in this book have been deidentified and your anonymity has been respected, unless otherwise requested. If you have a story you'd like to share, or comments, I can be reached at:

lovelace.landpope@gmail.com.

Lastly, to those of you who have always wanted to write a book, I encourage you to begin immediately. Remember, you're only responsible for the effort, not the outcome.

TABLE OF CONTENTS

PREFACE

The history of Toby and his decline deserves a deeper explanation. At conferences and by email the number one question I am asked is, "Whatever happened to your friend, Toby?"

It requires a look into the backstory of *Incident at Devils Den, a true story* .... I apologize to some of you who have heard this story before. But it deserves to be briefly revisited because it dovetails so nicely with the later years, and the improbable events that kept Toby and I needlessly apart.

I've also included facts that were left out of *Incident at Devils Den*. The sad story of my cousin Gerald and my friend Ernie deserve to be fully told. A complete telling of my messages from Betty, that I previously withheld due to their content, are likewise important and worthy of inclusion.

Before Chapter #1, an update on two stories as promised in *Incident at Devils Den*. In my first book I told the story of Rodney Letterman's bizarre disappearance from Devil's Den State Park in August of 2017. I published the book on Amazon on March 10, 2018, when Rodney was still classified as "missing." I promised to update you if things changed. They have.

Let me briefly review the facts for you. Rodney Letterman was a 32-year-old man from Bartlesville, Oklahoma. In August 2017, Rodney and a friend were walking the Butterfield Trail in Devil's Den State Park in NW Arkansas. It is a pleasant walk and appropriate for inexperienced hikers and others that might be less fit or have a disability.

Rodney Letterman had a medical condition. I would not call it a disability. He suffered from asthma according to a deputy sheriff from the Russellville Arkansas Sheriff's Department. His name is withheld under an agreement to respect his anonymity.

He told me that about a mile into their hike, Rodney began wheezing. He and his friend sat down on the side of the trail. Rodney admitted to his friend he had foolishly left his inhaler in the truck. There were other hikers about that day, so it was not like Rodney was abandoned when his friend offered to run back to the truck and retrieve his inhaler. The friend left and was back with Rodney's medicine in less than a half hour.

When he returned there was no trace of Rodney Letterman, except for his cell phone left on the ground where they had stopped. The friend thought maybe Rodney took a few steps into the forest to relieve himself and would return any minute. He called out for Rodney and waited. When Rodney still hadn't returned after fifteen minutes of calling his name, the friend called the ranger station. They responded immediately.

What followed was the biggest rescue mission of 2017. Over 1,500 volunteers including police and rangers from the adjacent Ozark

National Forest. Police helicopters with forward-looking infrared radar or "FLIR" crisscrossed 2,500 acres of dense forest looking for a heat signature. They came up empty. So did the Russellville PD's tracking dogs. According to the deputy, they sniffed the phone and sat down. I asked, "What does that mean?" He told me it meant the dogs could find no scent except for the phone. I asked the deputy if that was unusual. "Oh yeah," was his answer.

The official search was halted after a week. Rodney's family continued the search with friends and paid trackers until the funds and their hopes ran out in October 2017. And nothing was ever found of Rodney Letterman.

Until March of 2019 that is. A young couple strolling along the Butterfield Trail on a cool March day spotted something conspicuously sitting atop a log just off the trail. They thought at first it was an albino turtle. It was not. It was the crown, the very top of Rodney's skull, bleached bright white by the sun. This was sitting in an open and obvious place not far from where Rodney had vanished. It was an area that had been exhaustively searched before.

The medical examiner from Bartlesville conclusively determined the remains to be Rodney's based on DNA evidence. No other remains were ever found. Nor were any of Rodney's shoes, clothing, or personal effects.

2017 was an unusual year for deaths in Devil's Den State Park. Maybe. Deaths and disappearances are difficult to verify as the State Park's Department in Little Rock claims to have no records. In David

Paulides' *Missing 411* book series he reveals state and national parks claim to keep no records of the missing or the dead. His Freedom of Information Act (FOIA) request was not honored, claiming "no records were kept." That is awfully hard to believe.

The truth is thousands of people disappear under strange conditions and end up deceased or never found. I encourage you to read Mr. Paulides' books.

Earlier that summer, a 28-year-old women named Monica Murphy fell over a hundred feet to her death from a limestone bluff in the park. The park rangers had no comment. The death was ruled a suicide by the medical examiner according to the *Arkansas Gazette*. The link will take you to Northwest Arkansas On-Line News. Both Mr. Letterman and Ms. Murphy's death notices can be found here:

https://www.nwaonline.com/news/2017/oct/04/woman-who-died-at-devil-s-den-state-par/

In early 2020, a young man claiming to be Monica Murphy's son contacted me by email. He could not have been much older than 12 if he were really the son of Monica Murphy. It is possible the newspaper incorrectly cited Ms. Murphy's age and she was much older, but I have nothing to lead me down that path. Several internet sources also stated her age as 28 years at the time of her death.

He told the story of living near the park and his family camping there often. He said he hated the place. He described it as "spooky as hell," a feeling he claims to have experienced there long before his mother took her life. When I asked him to "describe spooky" he told me he had seen "glowing orbs of light" and "weird lights in the night sky."

I replied, "Yeah, I get that." I truly do. The truth is, I have only been camping once in my life. *Incident at Devils Den* is the story about my camping trip to the same park back in 1977.

But Monica's son declined my invitation to discuss the matter by telephone. That and the age discrepancy left me in doubt that Monica Murphy was his mother. But it is indisputable that a woman named Monica Murphy died in Devil's Den State Park from a fall off a limestone ledge in 2017.

It is true that anyone can create an online persona. In the case studies created from emails I received; I did my best to validate the individual sending me the story. The veracity of the story is outside my ability to debunk or verify, but if I believe the person sending me their story is a real person and not something sent through an alias, I am inclined to think their story has some validity. Especially when the facts align.

Since 2018, I have spoken at a dozen or more UFO conferences. The number one question people ask is "Whatever became of Toby?" That is why I devote chapter #1 to the task. For those of you who have read *Incident at Devils Den, a true story* ... some of this will be repetitious, but much of it is information that has never been released. I hope you enjoy.

Chapter #1

WHATEVER BECAME OF TOBY?

In late August of 1977, Toby was transferred to an air base in Japan. They processed his papers at light speed, and he was gone in a matter of weeks.

If you have read my first book, you will recall that after our trip to Devil's Den we returned to Whiteman Air Force Base, hurting and severely burned. We suffered second-degree burns over every inch of our bodies. We never blistered and our skin never peeled, but we were sick as dogs. Both of us were acutely dehydrated and diagnosed with "flash burns" to our eyes. It is an injury arc welders get if they don't wear eye protection. Essentially, it is a bad sunburn to the cornea. It is incredibly painful, like having sand rubbed in your eyes. I was also photophobic. The light was intolerable and made for a painful drive back home the following day in bright sunshine. It took a week for my eyes to heal in a dark room with sunglasses.

After we arrived back on base and went to our respective homes that day, we were both simultaneously taken to the Whiteman Air Force Base Hospital by our wives and were admitted. Curiously, the USAF kept us separated. According to researcher Grant Cameron, separating witnesses is common in the military when two or more service members have a UFO encounter. Especially one that involves abduction, injury, or proximity to nuclear weapons.

As the doctor finished my 1977 examination, the base commander, the hospital commander (who I knew well), and two guys I did not recognize in casual civilian clothes came into the exam room. The base commander asked the doctor to excuse himself. He shut the door on his way out.

My boss, the hospital commander, was the only one who spoke to me. He said, "Sergeant Lovelace, you're to have no contact with Sergeant Tobias. That means you will not speak with him by phone or in person, you will not attempt to contact him in writing or through a third party. You are to give him nothing and you will not accept anything he may try to give you. If you run into one another anywhere by chance you are to walk away immediately and without comment. That is an order Sergeant, if you violate my order there will be severe consequences. Do you read me?"

I answered, "Yes sir! Loud and clear."

But honestly, no. I did not understand. I was in so much pain and still frightened from our encounter, I really did not care. Clearly, they did not want us to communicate with one another. I am certain they knew what we saw.

Toby and I agreed on the drive back to base we would not tell a soul we were abducted and taken aboard a triangular spacecraft the size of a Walmart. The result of that disclosure would likely have been a psych evaluation followed by a discharge from the Air Force. Something neither of us wanted.

We were off duty for 30 days to recover. When we were cleared to return to duty, Toby continued to work at the hospital, but on the day shift. I was temporarily transferred to a supply squadron where they had no work for a trained EMT. I did busy work there for 90 days until Toby's orders for Japan came through.

MY FRIENDSHIP WITH TOBY

Before I travel deeper into Toby's story after our abduction, let me explain our friendship prior to June 1977 and the event that changed our lives. We worked together in the Whiteman Air Force Base emergency room. Toby and I were both trained medics and certified EMTs. We worked as first responders driving an ambulance on the midnight shift from 11:00 PM to 8:00 AM. If there was a plane crash, an auto accident, or a heart attack... we were the guys in the ambulance.

We worked together for three years. We enjoyed working the graveyard shift. There were very few officers around and there were many nights we never received a single call. We were both taking college classes towards undergraduate degrees. Working the night shift gave us plenty of time to study, complete homework assignments, play cards or sit outside in nice weather waiting for the crash phone to ring.

We enjoyed being first responders. Sure, we weren't fighter pilots, but driving an ambulance with a big eight-cylinder fuel-injected Detroit engine was fun. Especially with siren wailing, lights blazing, and no speed limit. It is pretty damn cool when you're 22 years old. It beat being assigned to a typewriter and a file cabinet.

But this was not a career for me. I was in the Air Force for the GI Bill, period. It was never a career; it was my ticket to a college degree so I could apply to law school.

My friend Toby had similar plans. Unlike me, Toby was a math genius. He had taken and aced a calculus class and two physics classes at Central Missouri State's campus in Warrensburg, Missouri, a short drive from the base. His ambition was to attend the University of Michigan to complete an undergraduate degree in physics and then onto a PhD in astronomy or cosmology.

Toby lived to watch the night sky. That was another reason for Toby to work the night shift. On pleasant evenings we could sit outside on the ambulance ramp in our lawn chairs, watch the stars and share a pot of coffee. We were in a remote part of rural Missouri, so light pollution was negligible. Toby could point out constellations and time when a satellite would pass over the base. This was the 70s and there were very few satellites in the sky compared to today. Our joke was to raise our hands and waive to the Russian satellites as they flew over the base taking photographs.

After everything that happened to us, I am left wondering where Toby's obsession with the night sky originated? It was an opportunity lost that we never discussed it. But UFOs were a taboo topic in the Air Force. It just was not discussed. I hope that has changed today with the formation of the Space Force, SpaceX, and talk in the *New York Times*

10

about "imminent UFO disclosure." I am writing this in 2020 and we are all still waiting.

The fallout from what we experienced was sad. We not only lost our sweet job that we enjoyed; I also lost my best friend. It is difficult for me to reconcile everything that happened to us, even today after 40 years it is still tough to integrate. This ill-fated, ill-conceived camping trip we made to Devil's Den in June 1977 was Toby's idea. I laughed when he approached me with the plan one evening.

LET'S GO CAMPING

In casual conversation at work one evening, Toby said, "Hey, I've got an idea. On our next long weekend, let's go camping. What do you think? Sound like fun?"

With all the sarcasm I could muster, I said, "No, why not just spend the night in your garage and eat bugs, that way we save the gas."

Toby was annoyed. "Get serious, this is a good idea, and we could have a blast."

I told him, "We're city kids Toby, what do either one of us know about camping? I know I've never been camping in my life and I'm pretty certain neither have you."

Like always, Toby was prepared with a counter argument. He explained, "Look, you enjoy photography, you have your little dark room set up and a nice new camera you can't use. We live in NCO housing *on base*. A base with enough plutonium to take out all of

11

Europe. If you stroll around snapping pictures of the anything, they'll lock you up."

Toby was correct in that regard. I was stationed there from 1973 until 1979, when my enlistment ended. Back then, Whiteman was a strategic air command base (SAC). There was a squadron of nuclear armed B-52 bombers and their accompanying KC135 tankers, sometimes called "flying gas stations." The 135s were there to provide the B52s with the inflight refueling necessary to make it to their targets and hopefully back home. Assuming there was a home left to return to.

There was also a squadron of Minuteman II ICBMs (intercontinental ballistic missiles). Each missile held five independently-targeted re-entry vehicles and were referred to as MIRVs. In civilian speak, each missile carried five nuclear warheads, each with a different city or military site programed as the target. The missiles were spread out over hundreds of acres of farmland, in hardened underground launch control facilities to make them difficult targets.

Whiteman Air Force Base is still a nuclear base today, but the missiles and B52s are long gone. It is now home of the nation's new generation of bombers, the B2. So, yes, photography was prohibited, and Toby knew I wanted to photograph wildlife and scenery.

How do a couple of guys like Toby and I prepare for something we have never done before? First know that we were known as the nerds in the hospital squadron. The word "nerd" was not a part of the American vocabulary yet. The closest thing at the time was "book worms" or just "bookish." We considered those nicknames as complimentary. Both of us were certain our hard academic work would pay future dividends. It would for one of us at least.

We prepared by doing some research, obviously. In the days before the internet, our research sources were limited. We had the base library. It was disappointingly inadequate. The closest thing we could find about camping was a 1958 Boy Scout Manual. It offered little insight. It explained how to snare and skin rabbits, taxidermy techniques, and tying various nautical knots. Not helpful.

Next, we asked a couple of the "outdoorsy types" for some camping tips. They looked at us like we were nuts. "It's not rocket science" was the standard answer. It became our mantra. Their suggestion was to, "Buy a cheap tent, take some air mattresses, a cooler of food and beer, some matches and you're good to go."

We made lists of things to bring and thought we had covered all the bases.

My interest was in photography, so I focused on buying some new filters for my camera and assorted black and white film. I was stocked and ready to take some great photographs. Toby's interest in this misadventure was the opportunity to do some sky watching in a light-pollution-free environment on this high plateau. It did seem like Devil's Den offered something unique for both of us.

It is notable that Devil's Den was a six-and-a-half-hour drive from Whiteman AFB. We were an hour or less away from a half dozen beautiful parks with camping facilities. Knob Noster State Park is just across from the main gate of the base. But Toby was fixated, almost obsessed with making the trip to Devil's Den for some reason.

Toby claimed Devil's Den State Park was perfect because of a unique plateau feature he had heard about. He discovered it through a mutual friend who had visited the park the previous summer. He gave Toby a map of the park and told him all about this high ground and approximately where we could find it. It was not on the map of the park available from the kiosk in the park's welcoming center.

From Toby's perspective it was a natural planetarium, an ideal platform for watching the night sky. By daylight, we would have a great view of the forest below us and an opportunity for me to photograph eagles, scenery and other wildlife.

There was just one tiny logistical problem. The plateau was in a part of the park that was off limits. We had no idea at the time, but the spot Toby chose for our campsite was not even inside Devil's Den State Park. It was on federal land and access was restricted as we discovered. But I thought, *What's the worst that can happen? They can throw us out of the park.*

I never made the connection to the warning sign. We were violating federal law by trespassing onto land that was clearly posted, "No Admittance, No Trespassing, No Camping, Hiking, Hunting, etc." There was a chain across the road connected to a post on either side. I was ready to turn back when Toby spotted a lock on the chain. It had been looped around and fastened with a padlock to form a noose that was draped over the opposite post and hung on a nail. He hopped out, lifted the chain from the post and it dropped to the ground. No campground for us.

On our trip down I suggested to Toby, "Why don't we just spend the night in the camping area for comfort and visit this spot in the daytime?"

Toby just looked at me and rolled his eyes. I forgot. I thought to myself, "Oh yeah, his view of the night sky was kind of the point of this exercise."

We found that plateau around 3:00 PM back in June 1977. I admit it was spectacular when we crested to top of the incline and the meadow opened in front of us. We both looked at one another as if to say, "Yeah, this is the place!"

Following are recent aerial photographs of the site where we camped. The guys from *Astonishing Legends* podcast, went through the trouble of looking for the high ground where we camped via Google Earth, albeit 40 years after the trip. I had never bothered to locate it. I was certain it would be covered with 40-year-old mature trees by now.

Latitude:	35°47'52.14"N
Longitude:	94°16'17.04"W

Map coordinates to campsite. Property of Terry Lovelace.

View of the plateau where we made camp. Property of Terry Lovelace.

An aerial view shows a roughly triangular shape top of the plateau. An area that's clear-cut so it remains unforested.

When we walked the summit's perimeter in 1977, from our perspective on the ground it seemed "horseshoe shaped," as I describe in my first book. But seeing the photographs from above today, I realize it is triangular and just large enough to accommodate what we witnessed.

It was covered in knee high grass and late-blooming wildflowers in '77. The view of the forest below from atop the meadow was spectacular. It was stunning. When I saw the aerial photographs, I could not believe my eyes. Amazingly, it is still there as of 2020, and still a grassy meadow.

When you enlarge the image, you can see that someone cuts the grass with a tractor on the top of this plateau in the middle of a federally managed wildlife preserve. There is still a single dirt road for access and thick forest all around. Why would the Bureau of Land Management, or whoever, go through the trouble and expense of cutting the grass and keeping it deforested? That is a lot of taxpayer dollars in gas over 40 years. For what purpose?

Despite my initial reluctance I soon found myself obsessed with this camping trip idea of Toby's. Within 48 hours it was all I could think of. We arranged our work schedule for a four-day weekend in June. Just enough for a two-night camping trip to Devil's Den.

We did not golf, participate in sports, or drink ourselves into oblivion on our days off. Toby and I were both married. At the ages of 22 and 23, respectively, we embraced family life. Our idea of a party was for the four of us to barbeque some chicken at one or the other's home and play cards afterward. Toby had two small children we were very fond of. Sheila and I would not start our family for a couple years yet. Toby's wife, Tammy, and my wife, Sheila, were also the best of friends. Because we both lived on base in NCO family housing units, we were only a few blocks away from each other. The hospital was an easy walk or bicycle ride from our homes.

A little more about Toby's personality and some comparisons. Toby was from a lower middle-class family from Flint, Michigan. I grew up in St. Louis, Missouri in about the same socioeconomic bracket. Both are "rust belt" communities today but enjoyed their share of prosperity in the decade of the 1960s. Toby's dad drove a bus; my dad drove a truck. Our mothers were both housewives as was the custom for the era. We both married young and to our high school girlfriends. We shared the same taste in music, mostly. At least we could tolerate it. Our contraband portable eight track player in the ambulance was equipped to play The Commodores and Stevie Wonder for Toby. My taste ran more toward the Beatles and Rolling Stones. We both enjoyed reading. Many nights in the emergency room we would pass the time by reading and drinking coffee.

We were dissimilar in ways too. We both had clearly defined but different career goals. Toby wanted to study astronomy and was a gifted mathematician. My skill set was the written word. I loathed math and planned to be a trial lawyer. Toby was meticulous about his appearance. Me, not so much. Toby was in excellent physical condition. I struggled with my weight. At a barbeque, I would enjoy a few beers with our meal and card game. Toby was a near teetotaler, never drinking more than a single can of beer, at worst, a can and a half. But other than those opposites, we were like brothers and genuinely enjoyed working together and socializing. I never expected that to change.

As the big day approached, I had some misgivings about our preparation. Misgivings about the entire trip now and then. Toby must have sensed my anxiety, he both admonished and reassured me. "Hey man, this is spending two nights in the woods, it ain't rocket science, remember?" He was half right.

Here is where the wheels started to fall off. We planned and purchased everything on our lists. I borrowed a nice camping lantern, fuel, and an axe from my neighbor. The food was stored at Toby's place, since he already had a large cooler. I bought a variety of 35mm black and white film from the base exchange and carefully packed my camera bag.

When the day of our trip finally arrived, we were over the moon with excitement. We were confident we had everything we needed, and we knew how to do this. The first leg of the trip down was full of exuberance and hilarity. We were having fun.

Until the half-way point in our road trip. Then a nagging thought crossed my mind, *Did I pack my camera bag?* We pulled over and unpacked the trunk and looked everywhere. There was no camera to be found. Of course not, it was not there. The camera was on my kitchen counter, exactly where I had left it. We were already invested in a three-hour drive. Turning around was not an option.

Toby did his best to lighten my mood. He promised he had his camera in his backpack. A 120 Kodak Instamatic camera better suited for birthday parties than soaring eagles, but it was a kind gesture. I agreed this would be a trip to reconnoiter. Like Toby said, "Those eagles will still be there next time." I tried to roll with it and not be a buzzkill.

When we finally arrived and unpacked the car, I discovered I had left the lantern, fuel and hand axe in my garage. I laughed. But I was also troubled. We restocked our ambulance after every shift. We know how to do this. We made careful lists and followed them. But here we were, far less prepared than we should have been. I was puzzled too; we were not this inept.

As soon as we arrived, we enjoyed a nice hike, mostly. By the time we returned to our campsite, we were losing daylight and had to scramble to set up camp as twilight encroached. Toby assembled our 10-dollar tent while I gathered firewood. A task that would have been much easier with a lantern and an axe. Most of what I collected were twigs, damp tree bark, and dead grass. It would make for a roaring yet short-lived bonfire. But it was adequate for our needs.

With the aid of the car headlamps on high beam, we finished setting up our camp and began preparing dinner. This is when we discovered Toby had been equally inept. He forgot most of the beer, brining just five cans instead of ten. Thankfully, our wives had packed some hot dogs and chips. Toby forgot the can opener for the beans. He forgot the beans. Apples, oranges, and candy bars also never made it into the cooler. I looked at him like, "What the hell?" He returned my look.

Finally, we managed to burn four hot dogs and split a bag of chip. A cold beer was icing on the cake. After dinner I told Toby, "Man, I can see how people would think this is pretty cool. Stuff, even hot dogs, taste better roasted over a campfire." I remember thinking, *this is pleasant.* The heat of the day was gone, and we had a nice mild breeze.

But the pleasantness would not last. Shortly after I made that remark came a lull in our conversation. That is when I noticed the sounds of the forest, the crickets and tree frogs, had fallen silent. I know this sounds cliché, but it's true. Many people have told me they experienced the same thing just before things got "weird." Even the gentle breeze we enjoyed earlier had ceased. The forest sounds had been loud enough to interfere with our conversation just minutes earlier. It unnerved me.

I asked Toby, like he would know, right? "Man, can you believe how quiet it got?"

He shot back with, "Relax, we've been laughing and making noise, the crickets will be back, just wait, they'll be back. We spooked them with *our* noise."

I felt more spooked than the damn bugs. Toby was wrong. The forest sounds and our cool breeze never returned.

Here is where things got very strange. Toby was looking to his left at something. I was just about to ask, "Hey, what're you looking at?"

ALIEN ABDUCTION

He spoke first and asked me, "Hey Terry, were those lights there before?"

21

I asked, "What lights?" Toby's torso blocked my view. Leaning back and half standing I saw what he was talking about. On the horizon was a set of three stars. Each about as bright as the North Star. They sat in a tight little triangle formation.

I saw that they were sitting too far above the horizon to have been lights from a train or a parking lot. Besides, we were miles from anything like civilization. Toby suggested maybe it was an aircraft, but we couldn't imagine any aircraft with that kind of light configuration.

After a few minutes, Toby suggested, "If this thing is on a steady course and headed directly toward us, it might give the illusion it's immobile until it changes course or gets closer so we can see movement." We just watched in silence.

About this time, I first noticed an inexplicable feeling of calm wash over me. I would experience the same phenomena in 2017. It was a discernible feeling of light sedation. Toby must have been affected similarly because there was hardly a word spoken between us.

The thing finally moved after a few minutes. It rotated once as if on an axis and oriented itself with the base of the triangle parallel to the horizon. Still, our reactions were muted. We were subdued considering what was playing out in front of our eyes.

Then it started climbing straight up at a slow but steady pace. It sped up a little as it climbed. It was a beautiful clear evening with a trillion stars visible; so many, the sky was dark blue. Not enough starlight to cast a shadow, but the sky was ablaze with stars. We noticed, as it traveled across the sky, that the stars would blink out for a moment and then pop back into view once it moved past. This answered the question, "Are we seeing three lights moving in perfect synchronization or is this a single solid object?" It was obviously the latter.

While we watched, it climbed to what I call its "ceiling" before beginning a steady descent. It was clear this thing was on a trajectory straight for our campsite. It also got bigger. Much bigger. The points of light spread apart but always remained equidistant to one another. It also made a tumbling-like maneuver. We saw it summersault, head over heels. I had the feeling this thing was not out of control, it was moving with purpose. An odd thought.

We watched it grow larger as it got closer to us. The sedated feeling washed over us in waves. I felt myself becoming sleepy. We should not have been sleepy. Tired perhaps, but for two young guys accustomed to working the nightshift it should have felt like mid-morning.

It would finally come to a halt directly over the meadow. It filled the entire field. We were camped on the edge near the tree line, so thankfully it was not directly over our heads. It was huge, a city block in length on each leg of the triangle. It was as big as a Super Walmart or a large medical building. It was brightly illuminated. It should have been clearly visible from two counties away. We were in a secluded spot but considering its size and brilliance it is hard to believe there was not a single report made. None, at least that we could ever find.

It came to a complete stop at about 3,000 feet over the meadow. It was awfully close to us considering its size. But neither one of us felt the slightest bit of fear. Remarkably, I felt almost disinterested, just short of apathetic. I felt more like an observer than a participant as events unfolded. I do not have adequate words to describe my feelings, other than to say our response was inappropriate.

We still said nothing. A few minutes after it stopped, we saw some odd beams of light from underneath this thing dance all around our campsite. First, there was a beam of visible white light that landed in our campfire and stayed there for about a minute. Then a bluish-purple laser, about the diameter of a lead pencil, danced around our campsite for several minutes. Lasers were a new concept in 1977, I had only seen them on television. I watched and thought to myself, *this thing is scanning us. It's checking us out.* I have no idea where that thought came from.

Shortly afterward, Toby broke the silence by exclaiming loudly, "Show's over!" He picked up his air mattress and shuffled over to the tent. He tossed in his air mattress and fell on top of it. I followed suit. I tossed my air mattress into the tent, fell on top and went right to sleep.

I did not bother to remove my boots or tee shirt. I was just so sleepy. The last thing I remember was Toby already snoring softly and noting that the sounds of the forest had not returned. Then I was out.

Some hours passed. I was awakened by flashing lights through our canvas tent, illuminating the inside like a ballpark at night. I woke in a state of confusion. I thought, *Oh yeah, Toby and I are camping, but what are these lights?*

I did not have my wits about me yet. I reasoned they must be the overhead flashing lights of a park ranger's truck, there to kick us out. I also heard a droning noise. It was a sound more powerful than loud, like standing next to a large piece of industrial machinery or an idling diesel train engine. It was a sound I felt in my chest.

I next noticed my boots were unlaced. That was confusing because I never bothered to unlace them. I pulled off a boot and saw my socks were on sideways. That was baffling. One of the things they instill in you in the military is to take care of your feet. If you can't walk, you can't do your job and will likely require assistance. I knew I did not put my socks on that way. I felt confused, but that still didn't frighten me. I removed both boots and socks and put them on my feet properly.

In one of the quick flashes of white light, I saw Toby to my left. He was on his knees looking through a flap in the tent. I saw there were tear tracks down the right side of his face. That shook me. I could not imagine what could possibly bring this man to tears. All that disinterest and feeling of sedation evaporated in an instant. I was suddenly terrified.

I struggled to my knees and realized I was in pain. Pulling back the flap on my side of the tent a few inches, I saw two things, (1) the triangle shaped craft that was 3,000 feet over our heads some hours ago had descended. It was now just 30 feet over the meadow. This was our

25

first opportunity to see the thing up close. It was even bigger than we imagined, and (2) below this triangle, walking around in the meadow were a dozen or more of what I first took to be children. I commented to Toby, "What the hell are these kids doing out here in the middle of nowhere, in the middle of the night?"

Toby's answer shook me to my core. "Terry, man, those ain't no little kids. Look at them Terry. They are not human beings. They took us and they hurt us, don't you remember?"

I did remember, just a little. Horrific images from being inside this giant thing. The whole while I was under the control and at the mercy of these nonhuman beings.

While Toby began softly sobbing, I looked again. They were too far away to see in detail, but I could see enough. They were all under three feet in height and grey. I could not tell if they were wearing uniforms or if that was their natural skin color. Their heads were disproportionately large for their petite torsos and they walked with a distinctive gate. It was almost like they had sore feet. They were not looking down and did not appear to be looking for something. They were in groups of twos and threes and were just strolling around the meadow like tourist.

If I was alarmed by Toby's tears, I was petrified by what I saw in the meadow. We were both afraid to make noise for fear of drawing their attention. As we watched quietly, a beam of light descended from the center of this thing. It was a cylinder-shaped column of visible white light about 30 feet in diameter. It was about as wide as it was tall.

It was very much like a high-powered search light cutting through dense fog. Except there was no fog. These little beings walked into the light in pairs and threes and just dissolved in a few seconds.

After the last two had disappeared, the light shut off. The droning noise we had been hearing stopped. We had become accustomed to the sound by now and the abrupt silence was disturbing. The flashing green, yellow, and white lights on each point of the triangle shifted to all white.

We watched this thing take off. It did not take off like a rocket, it just lifted off like a hot air balloon. It rotated slightly and picked up speed on its ascent. We sat like scared little rabbits in the tent for a half hour.

Toby had been hyperventilating and he finally got control of his breathing. Strange as it sounds, we felt safer in the tent. The idea of sprinting to the car terrified me. Just that piece of canvas over our heads gave us cover. The 15 yards to the car would mean being in the open and vulnerable.

To this day I will not walk across an open field. I would rather walk a mile out of my way by going around than take the straight path. I suffer from other PTSD symptoms too.

Toby suggested I take my wallet and keys and he would take his flashlight. We would dart to the car and get the hell off that plateau. On a count of three we bolted from the tent and ran to the car.

We left everything behind. Our tent, air mattresses, Toby's nice cooler, everything. We did not care one bit. We were grateful to be alive, even if we were both injured with burns and dehydration.

Toby had an unerring sense of direction. He helped me to navigate out of there and back onto blacktop. We were both insane with thirst and in a lot of pain. As bad as I was hurting, Toby was worse. There is no way he could have driven a car. Whatever they did to me they must have given poor Toby a double dose.

I suggested we pull over and he could crash in the back seat. He just muttered "Ugh-uh, I'm okay," and curled up in a fetal position on the big bench seat of my old Chevy.

CHANGES

At his point I must confess something. This does not make a lot of sense. None of this does. To put this in proper perspective, we arrived a Devil's Den as children, still in our teenage mindset at the ages of 22 and 23. When we left that meadow, we were adults. This event was such a big influence in my life that I tend to measure my life in terms of pre- and post-1977. It was an event equal to the birth of our children. Sorry kids.

Something else had changed. Here was my best friend, confidant, and co-worker but I suddenly wanted nothing to do with him. It was strange. When we finally found an open gas station, I bought a six-pack of orange soda (or "pop" if you are a Michigander) and Toby bought a gallon jug of grape drink. I polished off mine in no time. Toby

28

drank better than half of his and went back to sleep. I felt a strong compulsion to just take his grape drink and polish it off. I thought he would never be the wiser. Then I realized what I was thinking and how wrong it was, irrespective of my thirst. Something had changed. I wanted nothing to do with this guy for some reason and I will never understand it.

In some of the emails I've received from readers sharing their stories, people have told me of witnessing an "event" like we did, and afterwards, no one will talk about it. I received not just one or two, but dozens of examples. Stories of a group of friends who witness something on the level of our experience—not just seeing a saucer shoot across the sky, but something more intimate like our abduction—told me how their group just disbanded. No one wanted to hang out anymore, definitely no one spoke about it. Often people moved away, and friendships dissolved.

If family members witness an event, no one will speak of it, ever. If someone did bring it up over Thanksgiving dinner years later, everyone became extremely uncomfortable, and it usually does not end well. I know that when I wrote *Incident at Devils Den* in 2017, I felt guilty about publishing it. I felt remorseful like I was betraying a family secret. That statement may be truer than I even know.

There is a famous true story about a group called the Allagash Four. Four young men, brothers Jack Weiner and Jim Weiner, and friends Charles Foltz and Charlie Rak went fishing on a remote lake in Maine near the Allagash River on August 20, 1976. You can find their story on YouTube or better yet, read Raymond Fowler's excellent book entitled *The Allagash Abduction*. Their story is a perfect example.

In case you are unfamiliar with their story, I will give you the capsule version. The four men were camped by the lakeside and intended to night fish from a canoe. They built a roaring campfire with enough wood to burn for hours while they fished. Their fire served as kind of a lighthouse to find their way back to camp in the dark, since the shoreline all looked the same in the dead of night.

In the middle of the lake, they saw an intense light and they can remember being afraid. Their next memory is rowing toward their campsite and their roaring campfire is now just embers.

Also strange is that when they docked their canoe and headed into camp, all they wanted to do was go to sleep. No debriefing about what they saw, no conversation about missing time or bright lights in the sky. Nothing. Just "goodnight."

Years later, one of the brothers contacted the other about the terrifying nightmares he had been experiencing, and they were disrupting his life. The other brother was shocked because he had been experiencing the exact same nightmares. That is what opened the door to polygraph exams, which they all passed by the way. Eventually, they agreed to undergo hypnotic regression to recall what happened that night. Their memories told the story of their abduction into the craft they first saw as a mysterious light over the lake. Raymond Fowler's book was published and became a bestseller. Then came the inevitable press coverage and television appearances.

I say all this because our ride home from Devil's Den was atypical of two people alone on the road for a near seven-hour drive, after experiencing an abduction by aliens. Two people who experience an incredibly traumatic event usually want to debrief afterward. Human nature is to discuss the event, to ask, "Did you see …?" and "Man, are you hurt as badly as I am?" and, of course, "What the hell were those things walking around in the meadow?"

But no. We were still muted, still subdued.

Alien abduction is a shared experience unique to a small group of human beings all over the world. But it may not be as unique as we may think. I am just grateful to have some recall about what happened to us. I can remember fragmented bits and pieces. It's just enough to fuel my nightmares and phobias. I have had my struggles, but because I could tie them to a specific event, I knew I wasn't losing my mind. My friend had been there to witness everything. He saw what I saw, and we validated the abduction of one another. My story bolstered his. This is the reason the USAF did not want us to reconnect. Ever.

ET can erase our memories, wipe our minds clean like chalk from a chalkboard or install screen memories to mask the whole affair. For those who are unfortunate and can never remember, it is worse. The terror and trauma of the event will eventually trickle-up from subconscious to waking consciousness and the survivor is overwhelmed. The event is then free to manifest in unhealthy ways like neurosis, alcoholism, madness, and even suicide.

When we left that meadow, we were both in shock and pain. I doubt we said 50 words to one another on our trip back to base. The only conversation I can recall, other than complaining about pain and thirst, was our agreement. We promised each other that irrespective of what may happen when we return, we would never say that we saw a triangular UFO the size of Walmart.

I have always had an aversion to lying. Our story was truthful. We told the doctors we felt funny the evening before and woke up early, sick as dogs. We would just leave out the part about the UFO and aliens.

As I said in the beginning, once we were back on base, we were ordered to have no contact with each other. That was fine with me. But I did have a strong compulsion to see the guy in person one more time, to tell him goodbye and wish him well. That would be enough to bring this matter closure and give me peace.

Of course, that would mean violating an order from a superior that could lead to a dishonorable discharge and possibly time in the brig. That would be foolish on my part. But that is what I would do.

POISON PILLS

But before I get to our face-to-face meeting, let me explain something. When I was discharged from the hospital and sent home to convalesce for 30 days, I was given a large bottle of pills with instructions to take three pills with every meal until gone. I asked the doctor and nurses what they were. "They'll help you feel better" was always the answer. Vague at best, but I was in no position to interrogate my superiors.

I began taking them immediately after I got home. That evening, after dinner, there was a knock at our door. My wife opened it and a nurse asked if she could come in. She wore no name tag, which was unusual. I knew everyone in the hospital squadron, and she was not one of our RNs. She also wore no insignia of rank. When I asked her name, she introduced herself as "Janet."

Janet was all business. She explained that she was at our home for "our daily pill count." Stoically, she counted every pill left in the bottle and made a few notes. That was it! Then she was gone. No small talk. She never asked how I was feeling or took my blood pressure, just a pill count and "goodnight." She would return 13 more nights in a row. The visit was always the same drill.

My wife sat with me on the fourth night after Nurse Janet left. She had noticed a change in my behavior and wanted to talk about it. She told me I was not myself. She said, "I think those pills are making you stupid." She also claimed my eyes were dull and my facial affect in general was "different."

And she was right; I was not myself. I was sleeping 12 hours a night, unable to keep track of my wallet or balance the checkbook. I also abruptly stopped reading and began watching cartoons instead. Behavior very much out of character for me.

I was dismissive at first, until she asked me to tell her how I spent my day. I realized I could not, no matter how hard I tried. That scared me. I asked her, "What should we do?"

She said, "After every meal, flush your pills down the toilet and if she shows up early for a pill count, we'll have the right amount."

I reluctantly agreed and asked, "But what should I do if she insists on seeing me take my pills?"

Sheila replied, "She's never done that before, but if she does, hide it between your cheek and gums and take a sip of water. You can spit it out after she leaves."

And so, we did.

Five days later I felt like myself again. The difference was dramatic. Janet always came at 6:30 PM and was gone in 10 minutes. Never once did she deviate from her routine, and neither did we. I always did my best to appear dimwitted for Janet's visit. When her pill count was complete, she'd spend a few seconds to eyeball me up and down, scratch a few notes into my chart and make her exit with a quick, "goodnight."

Once I was feeling better, I took one of the capsules and pulled out my 1975 edition of the *Physician's Desk Reference* (PDR). Before the internet, the PDR was published yearly with a color photograph of every tablet and pill approved by the FDA for prescription. I searched diligently. There was no match. That was curious. God, I wish I had saved just one of those pills.

My inclination was to call Toby or Tammy and ask if they were experiencing the same thing with these pills and Nurse Janet. But I couldn't call without risking big trouble. Besides, I really didn't care to chat with them.

34

Instead, I called Nurse Brenda, an RN I knew well at the hospital and someone I trusted. I called her and asked, "Hey Brenda, these pills they sent me home with, do you know what they are?"

She said casually, "I'm really busy, I don't know anything about that, but maybe I'll stop by and see how you're doing after my shift? Okay?"

I understood loud and clear. She was not about to discuss the matter by phone while I was under scrutiny by the OSI. Likely, my phone was less than secure.

"Sure," I said, "swing by and I'll have a cold beer for you. But make it after 7:00 PM, I have company at 6:30."

About 8:00 PM she knocked on our door. She came in and gave us both a hug. I handed her a cold can of Coors and we all sat down. She got to the point after making sure my "company" was gone.

Sheila briefly explained her observations and our decision to discontinue the pills.

After a moment or two of thought, Brenda began, "Terry, those pills aren't in our formulary. They were shipped here from Wright Patterson Air Force Base. You and Toby got the same medication. I would tell you what they are if I knew."

Sheila's observation that the pills made me stupid did not appear to shock Brenda. We explained Nurse Janet and our routine to destroy the pills instead of continuing to take them.

Brenda nodded with approval. She also said she had never heard of anyone in the medical squadron named "Janet," she knew no one that matched her physical description. We chatted for 30 minutes, she finished her beer, but before leaving she suggested, "Let's keep this just between us."

I am sure she would have been in big trouble if it ever became known that she approved of me defying doctor's orders. I assured her it was just between us and thanked her. I also offered a beer for the road. She took it.

AN AWKWARD GOODBYE

All of this left me to wonder what condition Toby was in and if he had taken all his medication. I would find out about three weeks later when I dropped by their home to see Toby and tell him goodbye. I asked Sheila to swing by Toby and Tammy's house on our way home from the grocery store. We were in her VW Karmann Ghia, so she was driving.

"Terry, please don't screw with these OSI people, they scare me. Please don't violate your commanding officer's order either. Haven't we had enough trouble...?"

I assured her, "I'll be in there four minutes. You know how I feel about these people now, but I have an obligation to wish them well. It is common civility, and it may help me feel better about this mess. They'll be gone in a few weeks anyway."

Sheila pulled the car over and parked. She remarked that she did not understand my anger toward Toby and Tammy. I was annoyed by her remark for some reason and exited the car before she could finish her sentence. I walked up to Toby's front door. The same threshold I had crossed a hundred times. It was open. I walked in and announced myself with, "Hello."

Tammy walked past me with something in her hand, maybe a lamp. I don't remember exactly. I do remember she glared at me and said angrily, "You're not supposed to be here." She was obviously uncomfortable.

Well, I wasn't exactly feeling comfortable either. "I know that Tammy, I'm just here to say goodbye and wish you guys well," I said in a soft tone. I was not there for a confrontation.

She kept walking. Toby must have heard our exchange from the bedroom. He walked around the corner and down the hallway. I was shocked by his appearance. He was dirty and disheveled. I realized they were moving, but I had never seen him unshaven and wearing dirty clothes. He was barefoot and his hair was sideways. If we had passed each other on the street, I doubt I would have recognized him.

I spoke first.

"Hey Tobe, I just want to wish you guys well. I hear you are going to Japan. I …."

I never finished my sentence. I did not know what to say. It felt incredibly awkward. I felt it would be appropriate to embrace the guy, given our friendship. But I didn't. Things were different, we were different. I held out my hand and we managed to connect with an inelegant handshake.

Toby was a short guy. I am six-foot tall, and Toby was three or four inches shorter. He stepped closer and looked up at me. His eyes were bloodshot, and I could smell liquor on his breath. I could tell he was hurting emotionally.

This was not the same guy I worked with for three years. When we locked eyes he asked softly, "It happened, didn't it, Terry?"

I'm not sure if his question was rhetorical, I answered honestly, "Yes, my brother, it really happened. All of it. You're not losing your mind." I broke eye contact and looked at my shoes. I felt like my knees would buckle.

Then he asked, "But why us, Terry? Why?"

Like I would know the answer? I said, "Man, I don't have a f*****g clue."

Without re-engaging him, I turned and ran back to the car. I was trembling and felt like crying for some reason. It was upsetting. "Let's go home," I said.

Sheila was nearly hysterical herself. Parked directly behind us was a blue security police car. I had been busted. Fortunately, in the long run nothing came of it. We went home.

I was baffled by the incident and ran it over repeatedly in my mind. I genuinely thought I'd feel better wishing him well. I thought we could part friends somehow and maybe find some peace. Forty years on and I still do not understand. I have just recently found some measure of peace.

Some weeks later I drove by his home. Another family was already there.

After an ugly interrogation by the OSI, the whole matter was dropped. I finished my enlistment on time. On October 25, 1979 I became a civilian again under honorable conditions and without a bad mark against my service. I was more than ready to leave. I cannot say I harbor any ill feelings against the United States Air Force. There are a couple individuals I have had a difficult time forgiving and forgetting.

I don't mean to imply I walked away from this thing unscathed. Far from it. I had my struggles too. Fortunately, with my wife's support, we managed to stay together and create a life for ourselves and our children. A year after my enlistment ended, we had our first child. Six years later our daughter joined us. Sheila and I never shared with them what happened. All they knew is that Dad would have screaming nightmares once or twice a year. They only found out when they read my book in 2018.

Both our children are scientists. They love and support their dad, but do not know how to feel about this matter. That's okay.

ATTEMPTS TO MAKE CONTACT

A few years after my discharge from the Air Force, I felt the need to reach out to Toby again. I had not heard from him since that uncomfortable goodbye at his home in August 1977. I had his dad's phone number in Flint, Michigan. I held onto it for some reason. In 1982 I called.

An elderly gentleman answered the phone. I told him who I was. In a pleasant tone he said, "Yes, I know who you are."

I said I was calling to speak with my old friend again, "Is he home?"

He paused. I think he was uncomfortable with the question. He said politely, "Toby only stays here now and then. If you want to leave your number, I'll tell him you called."

My intuition told me Toby may be homeless. I chose not to ask about Tammy and the kids. I thanked him and he wrote down my number. He wished me well and I hung up. I felt like I would hear from him eventually. He never called.

Six months later it was the Christmas season. I thought it would be a good excuse to call back and try to talk to Toby again. His phone had been disconnected.

A few years later I was practicing law in Lansing, Michigan. Flint was just 45 minutes away. I did a diligent search for my old friend and came up empty-handed each time.

A VISIT FROM TOBY'S WIFE

Then Sheila received a call. It was Tammy. She found us in the white pages. It was a happy reunion for them. Sheila asked about the kids and they were fine. Then she explained that she and Toby had separated a few months after their relocation to Japan. They divorced the following year and she had custody of the kids. She had remarried a long-haul truck driver. She was riding with him on a cross-country run with a stop in Detroit. The kids stayed with her parents. She asked if we were up for some company?

"Absolutely!" was our answer. It would be nice to see her again. I hoped it would be anyway. The last time we spoke things were a bit tense. A week later they arrived, and we had dinner together. Her new husband seemed like a genuinely nice guy.

Tammy was gracious. She admitted that when I came to her house on base in '77 they were stressed-out. Also, Toby had told her the camping trip was all my idea! No wonder she was less than happy to see me. For a time, she blamed me for her husband's decline and the dissolution of their marriage.

I asked her to please tell me everything she knew about Toby, and that I would love to reconnect with him.

I was not prepared for her answer. Toby had struggled. He developed a taste for alcohol. He did not drink much during the day, but he could not close his eyes and sleep unless he was full of vodka.

His trouble sleeping resonated with me. For a time, I relied on a glass of wine to get me to sleep and to keep the monsters at bay. Unfortunately, my tolerance kept increasing. One glass became two and then three. I recognized this was a slippery slope and I stopped.

In the 80s and early 90s prescription sedatives and sleeping pills were widely prescribed. I had an on-again off-again relationship with benzodiazepines for a time. But like wine, my tolerance and dependence on them for sleep was troubling. I finally decided on a single 25md capsule of Benadryl (Diphenhydramine) for sleep, it is an antihistamine. I also found physical exhaustion was a ticket to a good night's sleep. I began running in 1980 and ran a couple miles a day, almost every day, until I had a heart attack in 2005.

Tammy said the last she knew about Toby's whereabouts; he was living with his dad. After some years, his dad passed away from stomach cancer. Hence the disconnected telephone. She said Toby reached an agreement with his family to take over the family home in Flint after his dad's death.

But he eventually lost it for unpaid taxes. Employment issues plagued him too. He had trouble staying with one employer more than a few months. She said his time between jobs got longer and longer. He never remarried.

She described Toby's behavior as "odd," but did not elaborate.

I had pressed her enough for information. I could tell she was uncomfortable discussing her ex in the presence of her new man. I was being insensitive and dropped it there.

We exchanged addresses and promised to write, at least exchange Christmas cards yearly. We placed them in our address book. They lived near Los Angeles somewhere, I can't recall the name of the community.

We exchanged one letter and swapped pictures of our kids. But that was the extent of it. Sometime in the 1990s we updated our telephone book, and their name was dropped. I remember her new husband had a Polish or Russian last name that she adopted. But we have never been able to locate her.

FEDERAL AGENT

That is not the end of the story. A few years later I had a case that involved the FBI. I became friends with an agent. He was a lawyer before being accepted to the FBI academy in Quantico, Virginia, shortly after passing the New York bar.

He was a smart guy and likeable. We developed a friendly routine of meeting at the bar on Friday's after work for a cocktail at happy hour. He was a few months from retiring and eager to move to Florida and buy a boat. Since he was close to retirement and did not appear overworked, I thought he might be willing to help me find Toby. I had nothing to lose by asking.

The next Friday evening I asked, "Hey Frank, I'm trying to find a friend of mine I served with in the Air Force. Think you can help me find the guy?"

"Sure, I can find anybody as long as they're not a fugitive," he said.

The FBI hunts fugitives routinely. That was dry FBI humor. I forced a laugh, just so he would know it did not go over my head.

He instructed me to write down everything I knew about Toby, including a photograph and physical description, and he would "give it a shot." He winked and said, "I can't open an investigation. This is a favor for a friend, just between us."

"I appreciate it, Frank," and we shook hands. I was confident if Toby were still alive, Frank would find him. It turned out to be a prophetic choice of words.

I sat down and typed up every fact about Toby I could remember, including the scant information I gained from Tammy. It is amazing how well you get to know someone after three years of working together. I filled two pages with information and dropped them off at his office in a sealed envelope.

He called me the next day to acknowledge receipt and ask me to give him a couple weeks. I said, "Sure thing, Frank, I owe you a beer."

He asked if that was an attempt to bribe a federal agent. I said, "Yes," and we both laughed.

Two weeks later I got a call. Frank said, "Meet me at the bar, I have some information on your buddy."

I was thrilled. We met that Friday after work. Frank walked in late and looking somber. We shook hands and I asked, "So, what'd you find?"

He said "Terry, I have some bad news for you, your buddy is dead, I'm very sorry."

I was stunned. I couldn't believe it, "What do you mean he's dead? How the hell can that be Frank, he's a young man?"

The waitress brought our drinks and broke my concentration. I had trouble even processing the words. I managed to ask, "How? How did Toby die?"

"It was an automobile accident on Interstate 94. He and another driver were both killed. It happened two years ago. I'm sorry to give you bad news," he added empathetically.

I just said, "Thanks," and killed my beer.

Frank added, "Terry, I'm sorry. But we both have been around the block. We know things happen and it could be any one of us at any time. Remember the laughs and the good times, give yourself a little time to process this and move on with your life."

I thought it was good advice. I thanked him again and we changed the subject. We talked about boats, Frank's favorite topic.

In 2017 when I was writing *Incident at Devils Den*, I realized I needed some notebooks I had written in during 1977 and 1978 about our abduction. For a time, I was afraid the OSI might charge me with a bogus crime. I did not trust them and wanted to document everything that happened. I kept two notebooks. One contained everything about the abduction experience and the chaos that followed, the other was everything else that happened that could be relevant if they charged me with a crime. Good documentation is the reason I could include so much detail in my book.

The notebooks were in our storage locker we shared with my old boss. It was up in Traverse City, Michigan. One of us would need to retrieve them.

45

Meanwhile, I thought I would find Toby's obituary and make the drive, maybe visit his gravesite too. I thought it's be good for closure. I got online and searched for his obituary. I was shocked by what I found.

Toby had been alive until September 4, 2007, while I was a prosecuting attorney for the US Territory of American Samoa. This was 10 years after my conversation with Frank. I wanted to kick myself for not having the good sense to look for an accident report with the Michigan State Police in East Lansing. But I did not. I took Frank's advice and moved on with my life.

I did manage to get a copy of Toby's Michigan driving record. He had two drunk driving convictions, a failure to appear, and numerous parking violations in Flint. But there had been no fatal accident in Michigan.

My FBI friend had lied to me. He either lied or just did not care. But either answer made no sense. I knew this guy. I thought I knew him well. I worked with law enforcement folks on all levels. I knew that every FBI special agent I had ever met was a stand-up person. They were a cut above. Good people. So why would he lie to me?

Frank was impossible to find in Florida. When you spend 30 years locking up bad guys it is probably a good idea to have an unlisted number. So, I would never have an opportunity to ask him, "Why'd you lie to me, Frank?"

I think somewhere there is a file for Toby and Terry. And the instructions are to not let these guys put their heads together and tell their story.

I have a theory. Two people having a shared experience are twice as credible as one. Someone would not allow that to happen.

Chapter #2

MONKEYMEN FACTS NEVER BEFORE DISCLOSED

Our old home was a hundred-year-old two-story brick residence in South St. Louis. Mom and Dad had their bedroom on the first floor. My two elder sisters and I had upstairs bedrooms across the hall from each other.

My earliest memories of the home were from 1959 – 1960, when I was four or five. What little I can recall was mostly normal. I mean normal for the time. Dad drove a truck, always wore a cap or a hat outside and smoked. I have few memories of Dad when he was not smoking. Mom was a homemaker. My sisters were 10 and 12 years older than me. I was in Cub Scouts for a while. There was church every Sunday morning, avocado-colored appliances, shag carpeting through-out and our Ford Fairlane station wagon. I had my friends and my bike. We played in the city park a block away. I tell all this to stress how incredibly normal my early years were.

When I turned six years old, I felt like a big kid at last. It seemed as if people in my family matured early. Everyone in my family over 30 had dentures. Everyone over the age of 16 smoked. My friend Ernest and I had split a cigarette a few months earlier. I thought I had the hang of smoking nailed. That was until Ernest told me I could not just "puff

49

like the girls." I had to inhale. That experience was unpleasant enough to put my tobacco usage on hold for a few more years.

At six years of age I was already a creature of habit and ritual. In my bedroom was a wall outlet next to my desk with my nightlight. At bedtime it was a kiss from Mom, tuck me in, and turn on the night-light before she closed my bedroom door. But not before the exchange, "Good night, sleep tight, don't let the bedbugs bite."

My nightlight was a plastic Virgin Mary. It was part of the goodnight ritual. Mom turned it on for me at night and I turned it off in the morning. It had been in the corner of my room for as long as I could remember, and I never gave it a second thought. Until I had my first sleepover.

It was a social event for six-year-old boys, a pre-teen rite of passage. I made sure mom had everything on my list for snacks. Jiffy-Pop, chocolate ice cream, and sugary powdered drink mix. This held the potential to cement my standing within my peer group. I was competing against Michael Gorman for the friendship of Ernest and Al. Mike Gorman owned a minibike and was stiff competition. In a few years, the competition would shift to the attentions of the opposite sex.

When we crashed from the sugar buzz and were exhausted from watching Charlie Chan on our black and white television. We went up-stairs to my room and got comfortable on the floor with piles of blan-kets and pillows. My mom popped in to announce it was "lights-out."

At that instant, it occurred to me in a flash of insight and my stomach turned. I realized if she turned on my nightlight, my friends would think I was a baby. The teasing would be merciless. On her way out of my bedroom my mom flipped on the nightlight as usual and I thought my life was over. But then, my mom did something incredibly savvy that astounded me. In a loud voice she announced, "Honey, I know *you* don't use a nightlight anymore, but your friends here might need one on?"

I knew immediately it was said for my benefit. She helped me save face in front of my pals. I was both relieved and grateful.

Three small voices screeched, "No, turn it out!" She did so and shut the door behind her without another word. It was one of those amazing moments of parental insight. I have always remembered it fondly. My mom deserved far more credit than she received. I think it is that way with most moms.

What bigger kindness could you give a six-year-old? I wish I had thanked her the next morning. Instead, I pulled the Virgin Mary from the outlet and handed it to Mom announcing with confidence, "I don't need this anymore." It was chucked into the basement with 20 years of *LIFE* and *Popular Mechanics* magazines, assorted broken household appliances, and a box of Barbies from my sisters' younger days. But she would not live in the basement for long.

1962 was the year I first encountered fear. Real fear. Like all seven-year-olds, I had those "monster under the bed" nightmares. No more or less than anyone else my age. Up until that time the worst terror came after seeing Godzilla at a drive-in movie with my parents and sisters. Of course, my sisters had to make "monster noises" and claim to have "seen something" outside their upstairs window.

My dad sat me down the next evening and told me Godzilla was just a man in a rubber suit and the spaceships on TV were just toys filmed close-up to look big. I remember he told me, "Monsters aren't real and nothing from the sky can hurt you." Time proved him to be wrong on both counts.

One evening I went to bed at the usual time for a school night. We still did the nighttime routine. My mom tucked me in, and the room was dark except for what filtered in from the streetlights. It was enough light to cast long and distorted shadows, but I was grateful to have it. I never could get comfortable in a totally dark room.

FIRST CONTACT

I had not watched anything scary on TV that evening. It was a normal evening in all regard. But for some reason I found myself fully awake and feeling anxious. The house was dead silent. I do not know what woke me, but I sat up in bed and listened. Everything seemed fine, but I felt unsettled for some reason. Sometimes, the wind at night would wake me. I stared out the window, from my bed, at the treetops. They were motionless. Whatever woke me had not been the wind. There was a weird vibe too. I cannot describe it. But I would experience it again. I was most definitely in my own bed, in my own house but there was a surreal quality to the experience.

From the corner of my eye I saw a shadow move by my closet door. I jerked my head to the right, but nothing was there. Then I swore there was motion on the other side of the room. It was always in my peripheral vision. I tried to lie back and clear my mind, but it felt like someone was in the room. I could feel eyes on me. I thought to call out, my sisters were just across the hall. But what would I say?

I rubbed both of my eyes hard. When I opened them, out from the shadows stepped four little monkeys. I spoke out loud and asked, "What are you?" To ask "who" did not seem appropriate. These were primates, or so I thought. These were not human beings. I was awake, and these were real monkeys with long tails. They were about two feet in height, maybe a few inches more. Their eyes glowed yellow and they wore paper masks with broad grins painted on them. I felt panic and then terror until the one nearest the head of my bed spoke. I realized I was not hearing with my ears; I heard his voice inside my head.

The reply had come from the monkey closest to the head of my bed. Instead of answering my question it said, "Come with us, Terry," and held out a paw for me to accept.

In an instant all fear left me. I was not afraid anymore! More accurately, I was nothing but perhaps just a bit curious. My reactions were inconsistent with a typical little boy being visited in his room at night by four little monkeys.

I should have screamed. But I did not. Then I felt intrigued and we just watched one another. It was like they knew me. Or maybe I knew them. The whole exchange began feeling familiar.

At first, they were kind of comical. One by one they stepped from the shadows and moved in close to form a semicircle around my bed. They stared at me and I stared at them. The one closest to me tilted his head left and then right, the way my dog King would do sometimes when he seemed to be desperately trying to understand human language. This time it felt like I was the one struggling to understand.

They seemed friendly or at least non-threatening. The one closest to me spoke again. His lips never moved, they couldn't, as they were painted onto his white paper mask. He asked me once more, "Terry, won't you come with us? We'll go and play for a little while and bring you home!"

I was warned to never go with strangers, but these monkeys felt familiar. I knew them. I wondered, *had I gone with them before? This wasn't the first time, or was it?* They inched closer to my bed. I heard the one closest to my head speak a third time, "Terry, won't you come with us and play? Your friends will be there too."

PLAY DATES WITH SUE AND THE OTHER KIDS

My friends? I thought. *Yes, that sounded familiar.* In my mind there were flashes of memory. We played together and "talked with our minds," that is, telepathically and it felt normal. I remembered a round or oval shaped room with a grey spongy floor. There were other kids there too and we played.

There was always a petite lady there that reminded me of our neighbor Sue, whom was a middle-aged Asian woman. I think I may have even called her "Sue." But there were distinct differences between the two. She oversaw us kids as we played in that strange room.

I understood there were racial differences between people. I was taught, rightly so, that we were white, but other people can be black or brown. They could also be short or tall, fat or slim. I accepted there was an endless variety of human beings, so I never gave Sue a second thought. But in retrospect, I realized the difference was not just a distinction of race, this was a difference of species. Neighborhood Sue was an Asian lady. The other Sue was not a human being.

I cannot remember how the monkeys took me to the oval room. I was just suddenly there. Sometimes there was a flash of light. Once there I felt completely at ease. There were about a dozen other kids, mostly my age. They were dressed in their nightclothes. I did not recognize anyone from my school or from the neighborhood. All these years later I have wondered that if I ever met them again, would we recognize one another as adults?

We played with colored blocks of differing shapes. We had to arrange them into certain configurations and then Sue would praise us. Sometimes, a panel on the wall would slide back and we could see the stars. So many stars, billions of stars. But they did not twinkle and for that reason, I did not think they were real stars. Probably because of my age, I was sure they were Christmas decorations. They just glowed and seeing them was our reward when we did something well.

The strangest memory was of a girl we all called "Jenny." Jenny never played with us. I think she was Sue's helper and she always carried a jump rope, although I never saw her use it.

Years later when my memory of her was more focused, I realized why she was so odd. Aside from the fact she never spoke, she also wore the same super short "play dress" like little girls wore in the 1940s with puffy short sleeves. She always wore white socks and black buckled shoes with her hair in twin pigtails.

Inexplicably, I can recall all these things about her appearance except for her face. But I remember her eyes plain as day. She never blinked and her eyes were all white. There was no iris or pupil, just the white part of the eye. She was different from the rest of us kids. I was afraid of Jenny. She was scary because of her eyes. She never participated in any activity. She just stood back and kept her distance from us. No one ever dared engage her. We never heard her speak.

The monkey still stared at me. I felt he and his confederates beckoning me. They came to summon me. On this night it seemed like a stand-off. It was hard for me to say "no," a problem I struggled with as a young adult. Then in a flash of terror I snapped out of indecision and I yelled, "No, ... this isn't right!"

I shouted, "Go away ... this is wrong ... I don't know you!" Then their expressions changed. Their friendly, painted smile turned into a grimace. Their yellow eyes turned almost black, like my cat's eyes when her pupils dilate. I could sense they were irritated with me. That made me scared.

There were four of them and just one of me. What would happen if they decided to just take me? I did not mind being with Sue and the other kids, but the trip scared me. They could carry me away and I could be lost forever, stuck in that place where missing children go and are never found.

Now, I was frightened. I panicked and I screamed, "Mom, Dad come help me! They're back, they're here!"

In an instant there was a twirling of shadows and they were gone! They retreated into the darkness, back wherever they came from. They were always gone a split-second before the doorknob to my room completed its turn. I began insisting that the bedroom door remain open and the blinds and curtains remain tightly closed. Even on the hottest evenings I preferred the drapes closed, sacrificing the cool night breeze to feel a little less vulnerable. I sleep the same way to this day.

SPIRITUAL PROTECTION

After weeks of this tiresome routine, I searched the dark basement. I needed help and, like so many people in need over two millennium, I turned to faith. Searching the basement, I found my protector again. Without a word to anyone, I stuffed her into my jeans' pocket and ran up the stairs and into my room. I plugged in the Virgin Mary again. Even though it was daylight, I turned her on and stared at her, hands clasped in prayer with the rosary intertwined and her eyes turned upward to heaven. Her light was much dimmer than I remembered. Her dim glow was a brief sense of well-being.

I was told that Jesus could help me, that Mary could ask her son to protect me. It was both comforting and confusing. *Why the need for the middleman?* I wondered. *Why couldn't Jesus just help me? If he knows everything surely, he knows that I am hurting and need his help. Why didn't he help me? Why didn't he help Grandpa too?*

It was common knowledge in the family that I was having trouble. Once, a well-intentioned aunt pulled me aside at a family dinner and asked me to follow her to her car. She said she had something for me. She explained that I needed the help of St. Michael and proceeded to give me a little plaster statue of the saint.

I studied St. Michael's plaster likeness for some time. He was standing on a snake and he held a sword. To an eight-year-old boy that seemed cool. Surely, St. Michael was powerful enough to keep away the monkeymen. I felt like I had the protection of two spiritual superheroes now. I sat him on a shoebox so he could be next to Mary and visible in her glow at night.

I now slept with an open door. As soon as my dad hit the hallway switch there was an audible "click" and a flood of light from the hallway poured into my room. For an instant I was blind, but it was okay. The light was warm and friendly, I would embrace it if I could. I would never feel safe in my room again. I do not remember crying, but tears flooded my face as I clung to my dad when he plucked me from my bed. I held onto him as hard as my small arms could hold. He was bigger and tougher than the monkeymen. That's why they run away!

They probably knew he could shoot them. He had a real gun! He kept it hidden behind the headboard of their bed. He could shoot them if they ever came back. I knew he could. I was not supposed to know about the gun, so I couldn't ask him to shoot them for me. I wish I could have asked him! I would have begged him, "Please, Daddy take your gun and shoot them, so they won't come back and scare me."

Without a word he carried me into the bedroom. My mom never stirred. She could sleep through anything. Damn that maternal instinct, she slept right through all of it. I lay between them, cuddling whichever one I could more easily wrap an arm around. I was just so scared. It is peculiar that I never recall crying. I guess I did. I am told I did.

KING COULDN'T PROTECT ME

Like Mom, the family dog King, a German shepherd, never woke or became involved. I did not understand why he failed to protect me. He was never a party to any of this and ignored it all. King was the family guard dog, protective of all of us. Why wouldn't he keep the mon-keymen away? It is a fact confirmed by my sister that King never spent a night in my room again. Not once over the next eight years until he died. Even in the light of day, he had to be dragged into my room only to exit as quickly as he could. If the door were shut, he would nearly go mad and scratch at the door until it was opened.

In the past when I was sick, or if I had a plate of snacks I could share, King would be there. Like most pets King had become a "cookie whore." That's what Dad called him. I was not sure what it meant at the time. My friend Ernie clued me in.

My nightmares did not just disturb my parents. My sisters were justifiably angry, and they made it known. They were asleep just across the hallway. My screams always woke them. At first it scared them too. After a while it was just "another one of Terry's monkey dreams" and they resented the loss of sleep.

"Monkey duty," as I overheard them refer to my nightmare retrieval, fell on my poor dad. He worked hard. The kind of labor I've only on occasion had to perform. Then it was by choice and never in reliance on feeding my family. He was so kind. Until it began to take a toll. The loss of sleep made him irritable. He was not alone.

The monkeymen came for me sporadically, unpredictably. At one point, it was five nights over a two-week span. The whole family was involved at one level or another. All of us were bone-tired. The tension in the household was palpable. My sisters grew spiteful. I cannot fault them.

We never spoke about this time as adults. My eldest sister refused to read my book when it came out in 2018. She did not care to discuss it either. She is 77 years old now. Tearfully, she told me how badly she felt that she could not protect me when "they" came.

Like she said, "When the lights came in through the window and you weren't in your bed, ... when you weren't anywhere in the house." That was the extent of our discussion. My other sister claimed no memory and swore she had no idea what we were talking about. That was fine, we all cope in different ways.

It was their complaints to my dad back then that initiated, "the talk."

One evening my father came home dirty and tired. I could see the exhaustion in his eyes. Before he showered that night, he called me into my bedroom for a "little talk." His talks usually ended with me in tears, especially if he yelled. I sat on my bed and he pulled up a chair beside me.

He began, "Terry, last night was the last time. Okay, Buddy? You cannot sleep with Mom and Dad anymore and you can't wake your sisters like this. It's not fair to any of us. How about if we leave the hall light on for a while and leave your door open a little, so you have some more light. That should keep these monkeymen away from you and you will be safe. Okay?"

"Okay Dad, I'll do my best. I promise!" He noticed but never mentioned the nightlight and the little plaster statue that stood guard with the Virgin Mary. He was kind. I felt ashamed of myself. I was not a little kid anymore. I reminded myself that I was no baby, attempting to bolster my confidence.

My mother tried to help. She held me back from the bus one morning as my sisters went off ahead of me. That worried me, but I would not let it show. When my sisters had gone off to school, she sat down with me.

61

She was genuinely curious about the monkeymen. I was eager to tell her everything I knew. I wanted someone to believe me. I was awake when these things happened. These were not bad dreams. At the age of eight, I learned that sometimes bad dreams are not bad dreams at all. Sometimes, they are your worst nightmare.

Mom wanted to know, "Terry, are these monkeys like the ones on TV or the ones in the zoo?"

"No Momma, these are the monkeymen and they walk like men. They want to take me away somewhere. They tell me we're going off somewhere to play and they promise to bring me back before morning," I said sincerely, trying not to cry.

"Terry, you can tell them to go away, that you don't want to play with them, go away and never come back!" She slammed the palm of her hand on the table to emphasize her point. I took it as anger. It made me cry.

"But I had tried that!" I yelled back. The anger in my voice overrode the tears, "I've done that. I told them to leave me alone, I have screamed at them too. I've told them, 'No, you have no right to be in my room, now go!' It never works Momma, if they want you, they take you." I had told my mother all this before.

To de-escalate things I said, "Yes Momma, I'll try again." It was the best I could get out before breaking down into sobs and gasps for breath.

She softened her tone, "Tell Momma, why do you call them monkeymen if they're just little monkeys?" She was genuinely curious.

I took that to be a sign that maybe she believed in the monkeymen after all. "But where did the moniker of monkeymen originate?" she asked. I didn't have a clue.

I had never thought about that before. The origin of monkeymen was a mystery to me then and remains so today. Her question took me by surprise. Thinking about it hard for a moment I tried to explain, "Mom, the monkeymen aren't like animals, they're not like King. They walk like a boy and are smart enough to talk to me, but they never move their lips. They talk to me from behind their eyes."

She parroted back my sentence, "Terry, they talk … behind their eyes?" There was a sigh followed by a long pause between "they talk," and "behind their eyes." That was it.

Game over and any credibility or empathy I hoped and prayed for vanished. Gone in an instant. Just like the monkeymen when the lights turned on. My mother wiped away my tears and I was whisked into the station wagon headed for school with a note to explain being tardy. It read "Sickness in the family." I thought about that all day. Mom was right. There was sickness in the family.

I tried to stop crying. I could not walk into class late and have the other children see I'd been crying. I told myself, "I'm a big kid now!" That became my mantra. It is easier to be brave in the light of day.

If King could not keep me safe and my parents could not keep the monkeymen away, I guessed, "It is up to me," I told myself. My dad never told me about his gun. I just knew it was not a toy and touching it would mean a whipping, punishment reserved for the worst transgressions. Dad did tell me once that people have guns to keep them safe. Well, I sure as hell needed some safety.

A LOADED HANDGUN

In the backboard of my parent's bed, next to Dad's big "railroad" flashlight, there was a board that ran the entire span of the headboard. It made a perfect spot to hide something … like a 32-caliber Smith & Wesson revolver, circa 1930.

I had lost hope. I did not believe my parents could keep me safe because they would not believe me. The burden fell on me, at age eight, to protect myself from the monkeymen. What if they took me and never brought me back?

I hated them for the worry they caused me. They had caused so much anxiety in an otherwise harmonious home. But I cannot honestly claim that they disrupted our family harmony. We never achieved harmony. Our household had the happy exterior that came with conformity in the 60s. But there was the undercurrent of rebellion from two teenage girls and an eight-year-old boy in fear of his life.

There were television shows by the score that confirmed perfection was achieved when each family member played their role. Ridiculous problems plagued the television family. But there were no drunken dads, spousal abuse, or teenage pregnancies. The only drunks on television were comedic when in real life I knew they were pathetic and angry. Sometimes violent. Those shows set the bar as far as the ideal household in the 1960s. Of course, the height of the bar made it unobtainable. The liquor and cigarettes they sold to fund these funny shows were a contradiction. The nightly news delivered a sobering dose of reality before all the "fun" began.

No wonder the backlash and rebellion of young people in the latter part of the decade. Young people protested "the establishment" and against the authority that gripped American society/culture.

I was afraid the Vietnam War would drag me into it someday. I saw the dead being medevacked by helicopter from the battlefield on the nightly news. That was when I became determined to be a medic and excuse myself from the killing and instead, save the injured. I preferred to carry bandages to a bandoleer. If I had to serve, I wanted my Geneva Convention card that identified me as a "non-combatant."

When I registered for the draft, I told the man I was a conscientious objector … "but I'd like to be a medic."

He laughed, "So, you'd rather carry band aids than an M16? Stupid shit."

But I was preoccupied with killing already. I had no beef with the North Vietnamese. The monkeymen were my enemy. I had the right to defend myself and kill them with violence. I fantasized about meeting them in my bedroom one night. When the closest one held out that paw and pleaded, "Won't you come with us, Terry?" I would pull out my father's antique 32-caliber revolver and shoot the four of them beginning with the closest. Then we would see who was right! After all, I was no little kid anymore.

Not only did I know where he kept the gun. I knew he kept a box of cartridges in his underwear drawer, too. Children, all children, snoop through their parents' belongings. To deny so is self-deception. As an adult, I know how important it is to keep guns and ammunition separate and under lock and key.

A dangerous scenario unfolded. I took my toy pistol and began sleeping with it under my pillow. I played with it. I carried it with me. It was a cowboy-style revolver with a cylinder that folded-out so the red plastic bullets it came with could be loaded. It was a "six-shooter" as they were referred to on television. It was made of cast metal and today could easily be confused with a real weapon and lead to tragedy.

I practiced twirling it on my finger like the TV cowboys. With some practice, I became good at it. I felt comfortable handling my toy and treating it like the real thing. My family was amused that I had a sudden fascination with a toy I had not touched in a year. I was serious. I realized I needed help.

I enlisted my friend Ernest Pearce. Ernie went to a different school, but we became fast friends when we met in the park one summer vacation past. From the age of five onward we were "joined at the hip," as my mother used to say. Ernest's young life would end all too soon. But, in the moment he was my closest friend and confidant. Ernie was not a scholar, but he was shrewd. He had some natural ability to keep a cool head and stand up to bullies. He envied my "book smarts" and I envied his clever ways.

Ernie was the only friend to share my secret of the monkeymen in my room. Ernie believed me. He politely refused my offer of another sleep over until the monkeymen were gone. But he was supportive in all other ways. I told him I had a plan. It would validate my story and resolve a problem in four easy steps, bang, bang, bang, bang.

"But what if you miss?" asked Ernie.

That was a question I was not prepared to answer. I knew on TV they aimed their gun, pulled the trigger, and a bad guy would drop dead. Seemed easy enough to me. But I admitted he had a valid point.

"Why don't we go to the park at night and shoot it a couple times?" he suggested.

TARGET PRACTICE

"Great idea!" I said. One almost-eight-year-old complimenting another on an ill-conceived life-endangering plan.

We thought it would be important to put our plan on paper. In the back of my arithmetic notebook we laid out our actions step-by-step. We would need to make a map too.

It is important to mention here a change in my usual behavior that necessitated a modification to Ernie's plan. I used to love to play outside under the streetlights when the sun went down on warm summer nights. It was "bonus time," to see how long we could run the streets before being called inside for the night "one last time."

Not anymore. That was before the change, before the mon-keymen. When the streetlights came on now, I raced for home. For that reason, we modified Ernie's plan and changed the time to the early morning on the following Saturday. It was crucial to execute the plan and return home before certain television shows aired. Saturday morning cartoons were a morning ceremony for millions of preadolescent kids for almost three decades. If we were not in front of the television at one home or the other by 9:00 AM, our parents would know something nefarious was afoot.

Ernie could help me return the gun and wrap up loose ends so no one would ever know. I was more concerned about the logistics of returning the gun without being discovered.

Meet up would be at my house since I was just a block from Marquette Park. I carefully drew a map, even though we knew the route and could walk it blindfolded.

After Friday night dinner and before anyone else went upstairs for bed, I would take my dad's gun from behind the headboard. I would slip it into my pocket and quietly slide open Dad's underwear drawer. In the back of the drawer was an old carboard red and yellow box that read "Bullseye 32 Caliber S&W." I'd pull out six bullets and slip them into my other pocket. With the six already loaded in the pistol's cylinder that would make a dozen, surely more than enough to practice and then dispatch four little monkeys straight to hell.

We added compass points to our map of the park to indicate direction. Any legitimate plan required a proper map. We would synchronize our wind-up watches the evening before with a phone call. The code phrase, "King's asleep," would be my acknowledgment that I had the fully loaded revolver and six additional cartridges in my possession, and everything was "a go."

That Saturday morning Ernie arrived by bicycle at 6:30 AM. Ernie was always reliable and prompt. I was waiting on our front porch with my bike and a map in my back pocket, a loaded pistol in one blue jeans pocket and six bullets in the other. We skipped reviewing our map which served no purpose whatsoever. But we agreed it was important to take along.

Ernie carried two hand-drawn targets under his arms. Both of his arms were stained up to his elbows with black ink from a permanent marker. The targets were carefully drawn silhouettes on cardboard about two feet square. The perfect size. One target bore the likeness of a crudely drawn monkey and the other resembled Mr. Evans, Ernie's math teacher, complete with eyeglasses.

We rode our bikes to the park, and everything was quiet as we expected. An elderly woman walked her little poodle on the opposite side of the park. Not to worry, she was a whole city block away.

I had only heard gunfire on television and assumed the sound would be comparable. Not having tackled Newtonian physics yet, I never considered recoil. We ditched our bikes by the swings and Ernie set up our two targets side by side at the base of an gigantic sycamore tree. It was a beautiful morning.

69

Ernie walked back 10 feet and stood next to me while I inspected the gun. Ernie insisted that I needed to disengage the gun's safety. Neither of us knew that revolvers have no safety. Pulling the trigger drew back the hammer and it dropped. It wasn't like the cowboy guns on television that required the hammer be cocked before shooting.

This was a double action revolver. That meant one just pulled the trigger. Period. The cylinder turned and the hammer fell in one swift motion. The process took less than a second. Pulling the trigger was the only step necessary. The hammer fell and ignited the gunpowder in the cartridge and propelled the bullet at 700 feet per second into whatever lay downrange of the pistol's barrel. Irrespective of human flesh or cardboard, the lead slug would find the target.

I held the gun in my left hand. I recall thinking it was much heavier than my toy gun and smelled like oil. Turning it over and over, I looked for anything that might be a safety. I opened and closed the cylinder a few times. This is when Ernie grew impatient and tried to take the gun away from me. Things began to play out in slow motion.

Grabbing it by the faux antler grip, Ernie pulled the gun away from me … or tried. A tug of war ensued. Ernie tugged and I held onto the barrel pulling it in a desperate attempt to keep the gun in my control. Somehow, in this back and forth exchange and ten fingers grasping, the inevitable happened. One of our fingers found its way around the pistol's trigger. I am convinced it was my finger, not that it mattered. I never heard the revolver's "click" as the cylinder rotated, and the hammer fell. I was unprepared for what happened next.

From that moment things moved in slow motion with one exception, the millisecond it took for the hammer to fall. It fell faster than my eyes could register the motion.

A flash of yellow light and a simultaneous, thunderous "BOOM!" rang out. A hundred pigeons took flight, and my ears rang. Momentarily shocked and deaf, Ernie and I looked at one another awestruck for a second. We were stunned and unsure what to do. That bullet went somewhere. We quickly checked our bodies looking for blood. We found none.

My grandmother had a saying, "God protects fools, drunkards, and little boys." He did that day. The bullet missed both of us. The old woman now carried her little dog in her arms and ran down the block much faster than a 70-year-old woman ought.

Ernie and I scampered to our bikes and sped away. We rode standing on the pedals, so we could push harder and faster. I felt my heart pumping hard. I thought it was going to jump out of my chest. The whole neighborhood must have heard the shot. Someone called the police. We were just a half-block away when the police cruiser with its single red cherry light flashing caught up to us. With his window down, he pulled up beside us.

We rolled to the curb and stopped. Ernie and I glanced at one another. If busted, we knew the consequences could be disastrous. Ernie did not like the cops. They had been to his house for domestic disturbances more than once. They treated him harshly the previous summer when he was out after 10:00 PM. He still held a grudge. I didn't like them either and knew they always had the potential to be trouble.

The pistol was in the right pocket of my jeans and still warm. By happenstance, my right side faced the officer's car door. Had he looked closely he would have clearly seen a pistol outlined in my tight jeans with a bit or the white faux antler grip peeking out of my pocket. I dropped my arm down and held my knee in what must have seemed an oddly contorted stance. I sat on my bike leaning over and holding my knee to cover the gun with my forearm. On the suspicion scale of 1 – 10, I must have pegged 10 plus. The officer was oblivious.

He gave me a quizzical glance for a second and asked, "Did you boys hear a gunshot from somewhere in the neighborhood?"

Always one to think on my feet, I spoke up before Ernie could get us into real trouble. "Yeah, Officer, we heard a pop," I said. Trying to look like a concerned citizen I added, "It sounded like a firecracker, I …"

Ernie cut me off and joined in, "Yeah, there's some big kids by the swings, maybe you should ask them?"

I wanted to say, "Nice Ernest, well played, sir!"

"Thanks boys, you should head home now while we check things out," and he was off like a shot, as were we.

We rode like the wind back to my house. We arrived breathless and bolted through the front door and ran upstairs. We landed on my bed and debriefed. Regardless how terrified I was of the monkeymen, using a firearm was out of the question.

Our clothing still held the scent of gunpowder. Our ears would ring for a few days. The pistol had a spent cartridge that would need to be replaced. With Ernie's help I wiped down the gun and replaced the one spent bullet. The rest went back into a box of 30-some. Ernie wanted one for a souvenir and the spent casing as well. I was happy to oblige.

PLAN B

Ernie suggested "Plan B." We decided I would stab the monkeys to death. All I had was a pocketknife with a three-inch blade. I thought, this calls for something a bit more lethal.

Ernie had a World War II bayonet that would serve the purpose nicely. He was more than happy to lend it to me. What a pal. I kept it under my mattress by day and in bed with me by night, under my pillow and out of sight. The plan remained the same, but the execution would be just a bit different.

I developed a taste for apples. I carried a few apples up to my room after school and closed my door. I would set an apple on my desk and practice swinging this foot-long steel blade into the apple to develop my aim. I never knew that bayonets were not razor sharp, meant for stabbing rather than slashing. I practiced anyway and got proficient at smacking the dull blade into the side of the apple, mangling it but never slicing it. I threw away a dozen mangled apples late one afternoon. My sister found them in the trash. I was busted. I heard my mother's loudest voice, "Terry! For Christ's sake what the hell did you do to these apples?"

I should make it plain here that the thought of extraterrestrial beings visiting me at night never crossed my mind. I thought they were monsters of some kind. I had seen spacemen on television before and they looked nothing like monkeys. My family thought they were just bad dreams.

Extraterrestrial beings arrived by spaceship. They also had two antennae like the TV show *My Favorite Martian*. We assumed television's portrayal of alien beings was accurate. There was no flying saucer, at least for several months yet. Everyone knew spacemen came in flying saucers. They never just stepped out of the shadows like the monkeymen. I would soon find myself feeling conflicted.

A FLYING SAUCER

This was when one of the most extraordinary events in my young life occurred. If you have read *Incident at Devils Den*, you are familiar with this experience. I will try to be succinct here. There are details that were omitted for the sake of brevity in the first book. I think they're important.

It was a warm day in May 1963, and I always remember it as a Saturday. But it must have been a weekday. It was after lunch. Our windows were all open, and I could hear my mom's soap operas through the screen windows, hence my assumption it was a weekday.

The neighborhood was alive with dogs, kids, cars and people outside enjoying the beautiful spring afternoon.

I had a bale of hay in our backyard set up as a target. My uncle had given me an adult target archery set. This was no toy. No way would I ever give my children such a lethal weapon at that age. It really was a different time.

I was by myself, Ernie was on a trip to "the lake" for his final vacation. Ernie drowned that summer and introduced me to heartbreak. I inherited his bayonet and have it to this day.

But, on this day all was right with the world. I had not had a visit from the monkeymen in a week or 10 days. Everyone took that to be a hopeful sign.

There was not a cloud in the sky that day. My attention was 100% devoted to my target practice. Looking down and loading an arrow into the notch of the bow, I saw a circular shadow move across my feet. Instinctively, I looked up. There it was. A flying saucer... and it was beautiful.

Awestruck, I dropped my bow and arrow as my eyes tried to take in every single detail. What could this be? I quickly reviewed my mental list of possibilities and ran out after eliminating hot air balloons and dirigibles. Flying saucers were the only possibility left on the list.

Today, I would call it "sexy." That was not yet in my vocabulary at age eight, I believe the word I used was "bitchin." It was shiny and just beautiful in the way a new sports car is beautiful. It was metallic with a rim that curled upward. I remember being sorely disappointed that I could not see the topside. That would have to wait. I was amazed there were no portals or window, no rivets or seams. I called the bottom "silver." Of course, it was probably something made from exotic metals.

What I failed to adequately describe in my first book was the change to my environment. This made the difference between a flying saucer sighting and a UFO encounter. This was a sensory experience. There was a change in the acoustics. I stated in *Incident at Devils Den* the neighborhood became quiet. In retrospect that is less than accurate. It was like the sound was muffled. It was as if someone dialed down the volume and words were distorted. The voices sounded like mumbling. There was the ionized air like after a spring thunderstorm.

Then I did something that baffles me to this day. The thought crossed my mind that I should lie down on the freshly-mowed yard and look up. I reasoned I could get a better view of the thing. Of course, that made no sense whatsoever. But that is exactly what I did. I just lay back on the grass, but I cannot remember lying down. The yard was freshly-mowed, and I knew there would be hell to pay if my mother discovered grass stains on my clothing. I did not care. I was captivated.

I cannot recall how long I laid there. It could have been just a few minutes or longer. The disc wobbled in the breeze just slightly. It tilted to clear the power lines and, without warning, shot off. It went from a dead stop to 500 miles an hour. It would have been missed in the blink of an eye.

I lay there for a while. In an instant the sound returned to normal. I could smell the fresh-mowed lawn, but the scent of ionized air was gone. My gaze was fixed on the hole in the sky where it vanished. Not a literal hole, there were no clouds, just the point in space where it disappeared. For months afterward when I was in the backyard, I would stare at that spot in the sky and hope they would come back. But they never did.

As if someone snapped their fingers and I was back, I jumped to my feet and yelled, "MOM! Come, hurry!" My poor mother admitted afterward she was sure I had shot a neighbor in the head with an arrow. She came running and did a quick assessment for blood. Finding none, she shifted her attention to quieting my screams. Odd, other than calling for her I do not remember screaming but I'm sure I did. She ushered me inside, more accurately, she dragged me inside by my arm. My head remained turned, my eyes glued to the spot in the sky where the flying saucer had vanished.

I was about to learn what happened in 1963 when a kid says he saw a "flying saucer."

I was out-of-control with excitement. I asked, "Mom, did you see it Mom? Was it a real spaceship? Do you think it came from Mars?"

As soon as we were inside my mom was quick to say, "Terry, I don't know what you saw but you did *not* see a flying saucer."

I stuck to my guns. How could she know what I saw? I was there, and she wasn't!

Then Dad got home and was intercepted by Mom before he could make it to the laundry room. The interrogation began immediately, "Now, what's all this business about seeing flying saucers?"

Correcting him, I said, "No Dad. It was *a* saucer, just one, not *saucers*."

My dad was annoyed. "Son, you can't go around telling people you saw a flying saucer. They will think there is something wrong with you, or wrong with *us*. Do you understand?"

The quickest route was, "Yes, Dad." My parents were always concerned about what the neighbors might think.

This was 1963 and a child's voice was discredited from the start. Anything out of the ordinary drew the same line, "That boys got him such an imagination, I tell you what!"

LIKE WALTER CRONKITE USED TO SAY, "AND THAT'S THE WAY IT IS."

Even though my parents left rural Arkansas shortly before I was born, my mother never lost her "country voice" and carried it the rest of her life. I was raised in a family that spoke like characters from the 1960s television series, *Hee Haw*. You may need to consult YouTube or Google. On my first day of school, my accent drew teasing and ridicule bordering on bullying. My parents could not understand it. I had no accent.

That night after dinner when my dad watched the evening news, I watched with him. Whether Huntly and Brinkley, or Walter Cronkite,

78

I listened intently to every word and its enunciation. I couldn't have cared less about the content of the news broadcast; I was watching to learn diction. My folks were amused that their six-year-old watched the news. It did not take long to lose my "country," and speak as well as any news broadcaster of the day. My vocabulary was limited, but my enunciation was spot-on. I was soon correcting other kids for poor grammar too. I found that brought scorn and sometimes respect.

After the flying saucer experience, I was shocked to find that adults would not believe me. I had a good reputation. I didn't lie or tell stories. But they refused to believe me. I could not understand it. There was another unforeseeable consequence of the flying saucer experience. The dreams and nighttime visitors.

This is a part of my story that is so outrageous it's hard to believe. I do not think it's coincidence either. It is by design. It is a story engineered to sound like foolishness. I can best explain by example, albeit a ghastly one. But I tell it because it underscores the importance of listening to our children and not being too quick to dismiss what might sound like the impossible.

"IF IT DOESN'T MAKE SENSE IT'S NOT TRUE."

–Judge Judy

When I was a felony prosecutor, a police detective came to me seeking an arrest warrant in a child abuse case. This is a little hard to take and is not easy to tell. Be forewarned, it is unsettling and may be disturbing. Stories like this break my heart.

If you think it may be too troubling, you are invited to skip the next couple paragraphs. The paragraphs are in italics below:

The accused was a house-dad who babysat his seven-year-old stepdaughter while Mom worked evenings as a nurse. We sat in the conference room. It was me, the lead detective, the little girl and her mother, and a social worker from Child Protective Services. Addressing the social worker, I asked, "Can she tell us what happened?" The little girl spoke up while everyone listened with concern. I will call her "Jane."

Jane complained that while her mom was at work, some nights, her stepdad, "Turned into an Indian," and "then the marching music started, and we take off all our clothes." She demonstrated with exaggerated marching around the conference room table. Jane said, "Stepdad's eyeballs go in and out. Then, it's the glamour model game." In a whisper from the safety of her mother's lap, she said, Stepdad takes naked and dress-up pictures of me."

There were a few more details I will omit. She had no physical injuries, fortunately. She swore stepdad never touched her, "he just takes my picture," she explained tearfully.

At my suggestion, we had a forensic therapist interview her. Jane's story remained consistent. The social worker found the facts of her story unbelievable, but the little girl was so credible in all other ways and understood the difference between a lie and the truth. We did not have enough evidence to get a warrant, not yet. The little girl voluntarily went to live with an aunt while we sorted out things. Jane's mother backed her husband 100% and resented police involvement in their family affairs.

Two weeks later when the little girl's mom was cleaning a guestroom in the home, she noticed a ceiling tile about a quarter inch out of place. She investigated and found a shoebox shoved out of her reach. Using a coat hanger, she pulled the box within reach and placed it on the dresser to investigate. She was devasted by what she found.

She took it to the detective immediately. Within an hour he knocked on my office door and asked if I remembered the "Marching Indian Case."

I replied, "Of course," and he handed me a box. In it was a polaroid camera and a dozen assorted photographs, a computer hard drive, a cassette tape of marching music, a cheap costume store variety Native American war bonnet and a pair of novelty glasses with eyeballs attached to springs that popped in and out.

Stepdad made the little girl's story so outrageous that without physical evidence, no one would believe the little girl. A jury would rightfully have trouble finding him guilty based on the little girl's story alone. The evidence on the hard drive took things to the federal level. I lost jurisdiction and the FBI took it from there. I promise you justice was served.

IN AN APPEARANCE MOST BENIGN

The extraterrestrials chose to appear to me as circus monkeys. They knew I would never be believed. It was devious in a couple ways. At

81

first, I saw circus monkeys as comical and benign myself. They chose to appear in a way I would find less threatening and adults would find impossible to believe. Their hope was to take me voluntarily if possible, without a grown-up or my sleeping sisters involved.

This is a mystery to me. I know these beings could have taken me without my consent as I would find out later. Why ask me to agree to go with them? I guess these things have rules they abide by if a child is young. I will never understand. But others have written to me using the email address I gave in the epilogue of *Incident at Devils Den*. To date, more than 1,300 people have emailed me to tell me about their stories. Sure enough, dozens have told me about being asked by their visitors to accompany them. Like me, many said they believe they went sometimes.

Just as curious is the variety of disguises their captors chose. Some people told me when they were between four and six years old, they saw owls, deer, glowing orbs, racoons, cats, even Disney characters in their bedrooms in the middle of the night. Beings that communicated with them telepathically. Of the 1,300 people who have responded so far, about 400 of them sound rock-solid to me. I believe them. Not that I judge the veracity of anyone's experience. I do not.

But there is a thread of commonality that runs through this group and enough detail to ring true. First, they all begin with an apologetic paragraph. An introduction something like "Please don't think I'm crazy," or "I know this is hard to believe," or "I really don't think this was a dream," on and on.

A good percentage of them say that despite all the birthday and holiday parties, the vacations and wonderful playdates on summer breaks that they have lost to time, they can still vividly recall these "dreams." Usually adding, "Isn't that curious?" Indeed, it is.

Like my experience, it is always the same beings, usually two to five in number. They always appear solid and sentient. They report that this was not sleep paralysis or any kind of psychological disorder to the best of their knowledge. They assert it happened multiple times and "this was reality," not a dream, confabulation, or fantasy.

For me, it was always the same four little monkeys. They were grey circus monkeys. Even today, no matter how hard I try I cannot recall what they wore or if they wore anything at all. But in my mind's eye I see them in little red jackets, but I do not think that's true. Always, they made the same plea to go with them.

There is another kind of nightmare that haunts my sleep. This is a dream I found disturbing. It was not a screaming bloody murder nightmare, this was different. I can remember most of what happened in these dreams as clearly as what I had for dinner the evening before. I did not want to admit it or even discuss it. It felt like a special secret; one I was not supposed to tell anyone. Incredibly, I still feel guilt sometimes when I speak or write about it. Even today it is distressing for me to dwell on or discuss it with others. It feels like I have violated someone's trust and all the emotions that would accompany the breach of fiduciary duty.

SUE

These dreams involve a "woman" who looked like our neighbor. Officially, her name was Mrs. Cherkoswski, which I do not think even she could properly pronounce, but the neighborhood kids all called her "Sue."

She met and married her husband while he served in post-World War II Japan. He died in an automobile accident before I was born. She was a kind soul who no one outside the neighborhood ever visited. My mother always referred to her as, "Poor Sue."

I do not know if there's any truth to the Chinese geomancy of "feng shui." It claims there are energy forces that harmonize individuals with their surroundings, as explained by Wikipedia.

When I was five years old, my dad bought a home in our South St. Louis neighborhood not far from where we lived. It is a family mystery why my dad would buy a home six blocks from where we were pleasantly settled. The house was a two-story brick home with two bedrooms upstairs. It was the identical floor plan to the home we lived in. Sue warned my dad against buying the house and said it would be "bad luck."

My dad of course dismissed Sue's warning the way he dismissed anything that did not comport with his understanding of the universe. She never used the words "feng shui," but 30 years later I saw the topic discussed in a real estate magazine and recognized the concepts as being feng shui. Sue was Japanese, not Chinese, but she was no less adamant about the house having "bad energy."

My Aunt Winnie said the house was haunted. I never heard or saw anything I would describe as ghostly. Coincidentally, we did have an incredible streak of bad luck that touched everyone in the family during the year we lived there. That is correct, we were there for just 12 months. A year later my dad bought a different home eight blocks over, so we were in the same parish and schools. My dad was bitter about taking a financial hit, but we were all happy to leave that home.

Sue went to Catholic Mass every Sunday and sat near us. She baked incredibly delicious pastry the likes of which I had never tasted before. I only mention this regarding a newfound fear. Around age six I was suddenly and inexplicably afraid of Sue. To be precise, I was absolutely terrified of her without good reason. I wished she would go with the monkeymen and leave me alone forever.

The memories trickled in. I went with the monkeymen some-times. More and more of the memories came back each day. These were what I referred to as the "play dates." Call it what you will, I was being indoctrinated, programmed, conditioned, groomed or trained, and we were not supposed to talk about it.

When the monkeyman extended his paw to me and pleaded with me to go with him, I was certain I had gone before. Sometime in the past. Lately, when I took his paw into my small hand sometimes it was not a paw anymore. It was four exceedingly long ugly fingers. Years later this image still haunts my sleep. I am sure I went with them, but I cannot remember how many times. All I have is bits and pieces.

I remember that a few times, when the monkey took my hand, there would be a twirling sensation followed by a brilliant flash. The light was as bright as the camera flashes used back in the day. The ones that left a blue image burned into your retina for hours.

It is curious that when I focus on remembering and strain my thoughts to pull up the remembrance, I'd get nothing. Sometimes when I try to focus, I get a black page in my mind instead of the image. It felt like trying to remember pi to the 40th digit. Bits and pieces were the best I could ever hope to recall. Of course, I know now the monkeymen were a screen memory, a projection of how they wanted to be perceived.

Then there were the times when I was not thinking about Sue or the monkeymen and a thought would pop up. It happened when I *was not* trying to remember that these thoughts would intrude, usually in a time and place when they were least welcome.

In 1977 while in the USAF, I was subjected to hypnosis under "chemical enhancement," better known as sodium amathol or "truth serum" in the movies. That faulty hypnotic regression took me back to my childhood abductions. I am certain if those events had not taken place in 1977, I would know only a fraction of what I know today. Or, I could have slipped into madness like my friend Toby and lost my life to alcohol, a "bucket of pills" or some other unforeseeable fatal consequence of entanglement with these entities or their overlords.

I recall that on these playdates with "Space Sue," we never spoke. At least not verbally or audibly. We all communicated with our minds as natural as any conversation I have ever experienced.

It was easier because there was never a chance of being misinterpreted or not getting the point across. You would think the chatter of five kids at play mentally would be loud. It was not. Just as when listening audibly I could choose to ignore the background noise. It was no different than a dinner party. If one of the kids got scared or was crying, it was polite to "tune them out," and we all did this intuitively just like the other rules of civility we learn in childhood. We were too young and naïve to realize not all our thoughts belonged out in the open.

We were never offered food or drink. I do not recall ever requesting a "potty break." I felt like I was a part of this group. I belonged there. Whenever any one of us was frightened, we would sit on Sue's lap or cross-legged on the floor in front of her. There were some toys, mostly geometric shapes of varying color, but I do not remember much about them. At least not in detail. I remember there were multicolored tiles like dominoes. Sue asked us to arrange them in certain patterns and match them, like green and round, blue and square, etc. The toys were always abstract construction type things. There were no toy trucks or army men. Sue was always quick to offer praise when a job was well done and encouragement when we screwed-up.

I remember once crying and saying I wanted to go home. Sue held me in the way any woman would hold and comfort any eight-year-old. I remember as she held me, I clung to her around her waist like my mom. I thought, "My God, she's so tiny." But she always had room for one of us on her lap, at least the smaller kids.

I asked Sue once, "Why can't we talk with our minds at home? I like it."

She explained, "You're not yet ready because you still need your words." She said she did not need words to talk. She saw I was confused.

She asked patiently, "When you think about something what part of your body do you use?"

I still didn't understand.

"You don't use your foot or your tummy, right?" she asked, poking me playfully in the belly.

I giggled. I was being baited into a question. I thought for a moment. "Yeah, but where?" I guessed, "Is it in my head?"

"Yes!" Then she cradled my head in her hands and looked into my eyes. "Behind your eyes there's spot and that's where your thoughts come from." She had the most beautiful black eyes.

"Okay, behind my eyes is where I think?" I added, seeking her approval.

Still cradling my head in her hands, she looked into my eyes deeply. Sue did not just talk to me with her mind, she could give me pictures and stories too. She showed me my body looking down on it from above, I could see inside my head and she showed me what looked like a bean in the center of my brain. I understood. It was not scary or gross. It was fascinating.

She told me, "Your thoughts come from there. Before you even know it, Terry, it is what's called *potential*. That might not make sense to you now, Terry, but it will one day. You will remember this."

"Potential" was not yet a word in my vocabulary. But I certainly remembered it.

She was correct as usual. I remembered that thoughts originate as "potential" before our brain even converts it into language. It is why she could read the mind of anyone without the need to know the language. It also explains why she never had a discernable accent and why at times she would answer my question before it was fully formed in my mind.

Sue explained many things I could not fully understand at my young age. But she made certain I'd remember some of them later. Human thought potential exists at a deeper level. Maybe it began in the reptilian brain that demanded quick reaction for survival? There was no need to know my language because she understood my thoughts at that level.

Sue didn't use these exact words, but she patiently explained: You don't need language to express fear, love, or surprise. You do not build your words from letters to form the thought, *This plate's hot, I better drop it before I burn myself!* There is no language involved in an accident that only takes an instant because it comes from someplace deeper. It helps you to survive. She told me it is the same with more complex thoughts too. That is the part I do not yet fully grasp. The part that is above my pay grade.

For years, her words have been on my mind. Imagine, a culture with no need for language. It would require a highly evolved being to master their thoughts. I takes discipline, apparently more than I have. From personal experience, I discovered just how difficult it is to control what our minds entertain.

Thoughts, like clouds, drift by unimpeded and rarely examined. As a species, we never had the need to discipline our thoughts since they belonged only to us. Our thoughts are private, kept locked away in a compartment deep in our mind. I tried to control my thoughts when someone else could read them. I failed miserably. It was a lesson in humility, and it underscores how highly developed these beings are.

Occasionally, in a flash of insight it all makes sense to me. Then, I try to recapture it and it all evaporates before I can get to my keyboard.

I'm not a neurologist and this is a question better asked of one. Just like Sue explained, thoughts originate somewhere in the human mind. It's a chemical process but there's more at play. I was shocked to discover consciousness was a topic not well-understood. In my psychology classes in the 1980s it was simply defined as a state of awareness. It is that and so much more. Forty years later we have just scratched the surface.

The definition of "life" is changing since the advent of cardiopulmonary resuscitation and lifesaving advances in medicine over the last 50 years. To be truly alive one needs to be conscious or at least be capable of achieving consciousness.

I researched the topic a little and discovered there are patients who are conscious and aware but lack the ability to respond to any stimulus. They are cut off entirely from our world. Thought to be in a persistent vegetative state, they lie immobile and aware of everything happening around them. But incapable of responding to any stimulus, including pain.

Due to a catastrophic event or illness they are incapable of speech, hearing, or movement. They lack all means of expression. But in some cases, they are aware of sound and can understand language. It varies with the degree of the injury. Sometimes, brain scans can show different parts of the brain react to the patient's spoken name. In 2019 there was a news story about a man who regained full consciousness after 10 years in what doctor's thought to be a vegetative state. He could recall what was said and done to him during his stay in a long-term care facility.

I can think of no worse manner of human existence. To be imprisoned in our mind for our entire span of mortality is maddening to even contemplate. It's the ultimate solitary confinement, their eyes closed, existing in darkness.

Beginning back in 1962 I started dreading the night. I was still screaming at 3:00 AM, losing sleep and my grades suffered. My parents were beside themselves and my sisters were justifiably angry. Something had to change. I felt Ernie's bayonet was my key. I would kill all four of these little sons-of-bitches the next time they dared creep into my room.

TAKEN

That evening, I carefully secreted Ernie's bayonet under my mattress intending to pull it out and have it at the ready as soon as my mom left the room. I now insisted on an open bedroom door at night, so I needed to be stealthy. It would be hard to explain. Ernie's bayonet could be confiscated. Then I'd have to explain that Ernie gave it to me for protection and that would result in a call to Ernie's mom. That would be unacceptable. Sometimes, eight-year-olds can think things through.

It became my nighttime routine. Kiss from Mom and when I heard her footsteps on the stairs, I'd hop out of bed, grab the bayonet from under the mattress and slip back into bed, and wait. Just having a weapon under my pillow made me feel more secure. It was a force equalizer for an otherwise defenseless little boy outnumbered by three.

Then it happened again. About 30 days after the nearly-fatal experience with my father's pistol, it happened. It began like all the others. I woke up with that sense of dread and my heart pounding. The nightlight was back in service and St. Michael was on guard, but they did nothing to stop the shadows. I recognized that familiar feeling. It felt like someone was in my room. I felt eyes on me. I watched, waiting for a shadow to move.

My plan was to wait until the first one spoke. Then I would pull the bayonet from its sheath and thrust it into the chest of the monkey closest to my head. The one that always told me, "Terry, come play with us and we'll have fun."

Yeah, we'll have some fun alright, with Ernie's bayonet through his chest. That is the one I would kill first. Maybe then the other three would run away and never come back. Except for bugs, I'd never killed anything before. I could not imagine the full consequences of a dead monkey on my floor, but I embraced the concept.

I watched. Waited for a shadow to move or dart across a wall. I reached for the comfort of Ernie's bayonet underneath my pillow. Then it hit me. For the first time in all these weeks I'd forgotten to take the bayonet out from underneath the mattress after lights-out. I failed to follow the routine and they arrived! My weapon was out of reach and useless. Did they know? How could they know? Of course, they know.

I might have gone with the monkeymen once or twice in the past. Those memories were not clear. But it was clear the experiences were real and not a dream. I had dreams about Sue, and I could tell the difference. That's how I met Sue. I took the monkeyman's paw and then I felt the twirling sensation and flash! I was in the playroom with Sue and the other kids.

Days after first seeing the UFO in the backyard I would be abducted again from my bed and I experienced a frighteningly real dream. This was a new memory. It was one of a handful of recollections that spontaneously returned to my conscious mind in mid-2018. That night it began as a dream, but I couldn't shake it off and dismiss it like a regular nightmare. It took time to fade. I don't believe it was a mere dream or a fantasy, it felt too familiar.

But this was no trip to the playroom. When the monkeymen came for me I felt a calmness sweep over me. I felt no fear or aggression, just the expectation that they had come for me again. They didn't speak to me this time. This was a different experience, one without dialogue or negotiation. There was no polite conversation. I was not being offered an invitation. I believe they knew my true intention was to kill one of them and that may have changed the rules.

Abruptly, there was the twirling motion, flash, and I found myself in a different room. This was my first time in this place. Instinctively I yelled, "Sue, help me." But Sue never came.

Just two big insect-looking beings were in charge. I met them for the first time. The monkeymen were there too, but they no longer wore white masks or had tails. They were "worker bees" as I described them. They used hands instead of paws to subdue me. The whole affair had a clinical feel like being at the doctor's office. There was a bright overhead light. This may have been the origin of my fear of dentists.

I was naked and on an examination table. The insect-like beings were seven-foot-tall praying mantis-like things, complete with triangular shaped heads and huge compound eyes.

I would meet one of them again 14 years later. It would wear a white lab coat when we met again in 1977. The monkeymen were there too. Just as in 1977, they no longer had the slightest primate features. I saw them for what they truly were.

94

I was immobilized and scared to death. I know I was screaming. The small grey ones are all around me and placed me face down on the table. I was immobile, but I do not recall straps or restraints of any kind.

The ubiquitous grey ones I encountered deserve an observation here. There are likely many different species based on the accounts of others. I believe the ones I encountered were not living conscious beings. They are not sentient like you and me. They may be a mix of machine, quantum computing, nano technology and organic material. They lack free will and are not able to determine their own actions, they do as they are told. They are engineered and manufactured somewhere. Even at the age of six or so I called them, "worker bees." Many others have used that exact same name for them.

The insectoid thing wasted no time. Long fingers deftly manipulated stainless steel instruments of some kind. He did something to my lower spine like what they did to me in 1977. They never touched my knee where the implants were found in 2012. Not that I recall.

While my anxiety was managed slightly, there was no control of the pain. The pain ran from my tail bone straight up my spinal column and registered as a strong electric shock that came in pulses. It was one every three seconds or so. I screamed; I know I screamed. The next day I was so hoarse I could barely speak.

That's all I can remember. I should say that's all I was allowed to remember. I felt Sue had let me down. That only added to my hurt.

But I was headed for a long hiatus from the monkeymen, Sue, and the praying mantis beings. I'd see another flying saucer in 1966. I wouldn't share the experience with another human being until 2018. Aside from that, I enjoyed 11 years of peace.

Chapter #3

COUSIN GERALD

I had a cousin a year younger than me. His name was Gerald. He and his family lived in northern Arkansas in a city near Jonesboro. While my parents and sisters were dealing with my monkeys and Sue, my Aunt Winnie, Uncle Ervin, Gerald and his six siblings had a crisis of their own. Gerald was the only one I ever developed a quasi-friendship with. We saw one another just once or twice a year.

Like me, Gerald was the only one in the household targeted for attack. He shared a bedroom with two younger brothers who never saw or heard a thing. Except for Gerald's screams after the fact. I felt sorry for him because he had two potential eyewitnesses that could back him up, sleeping in the same room!

I was always hopeful one of my sisters would catch a glimpse of these things that came for me, but that never happened. I always thought it was because they were across the hall. But Gerald's story made me reconsider. They would probably never have seen or heard a thing, even if they were in my room when they came.

I believed every word of Gerald's story and it was chilling. It was shockingly similar. He was thrilled to hear my story. For the first time he knew he was not alone. We were brothers now.

When I was nine the night terrors receded and were fewer. I wish at nine I had been able to journal all the occurrences to preserve them. But that was beyond my ability. But I can clearly recall telling myself, "This is important. I can't lose this memory."

The thing I remember most about this period, 1962–1964, was seeing the flying saucer in my backyard in 1963. That was the most impressive and exhilarating experience. Then there were the memories of Sue, the bug things, and the monkeymen. Those memories were hard kept. Ernie's untimely death before he reached 10 was the loss of my confidant, my best friend and best witness to what I experienced. Poor Gerald had no one in his corner, at least not in Arkansas.

Years in the future, my friend Tobias would lose his life. Toby was the only other witness to my 1977 abduction from Devil's Den State Park. I have always wondered if their deaths were somehow tied to our shared experiences. I'm sure there's an element of survivor guilt that I've never properly addressed to this day.

Because of the distance, Gerald and I never played together much. We were never close, that is until their 1963 annual visit in March. I saw the flying disc two months later in May.

They stayed as our houseguests for two weeks every summer on their "vacation." That is what poor people did. Gerald and his two younger brothers slept in my room during their St. Louis visits. The girls slept with my sisters and Uncle Ervin and Aunt Winne slept on a sofa bed in the living room.

In 1963, Gerald and I discovered our common ground. He was being tormented at night by two clowns about two and one-half feet tall. They wore white baggy suits, flat clown masks with holes for eyes and an exaggerated painted-on smile and painted red nose. I guess ET decided the circus theme suited the Lovelace family.

I told him all about my exploits with the monkeymen and my plans to kill one of them. I told him how Ernie and I took my dad's gun and test-fired it to practice murdering monkeymen. He did not believe me until we snuck into my parent's bedroom and I showed it to him. It was still fully loaded. We played with it for about 30 minutes. Then I put it back before we were busted. He thought I was a pretty cool guy! He wanted to hear all about the monkeymen. I told him every detail I could think of and he soaked up every single word.

I KNOW WHERE MY DAD KEEPS HIS RIFLE

Then it was Gerald's turn. He said, "Boy, I wish I could get my hands on Dad's hunting rifle for a couple nights. It's just inside their closet in the far back corner. Dad always keeps it loaded. He said it would be handy if intruders ever broke into the house." It was a bolt action 30-06 with iron sights. It used to have an expensive scope.

Gerald explained his dad had too much to drink one night after a day of hunting with his friends. He rarely came home with a deer, but he always came home loaded. With alcohol that is, not ammunition in his rifle necessarily. While inebriated, he cleaned his rifle when he dropped it onto the concrete garage floor. The glass in the scope shattered. Oops, maybe that is what they mean when they say, "Never clean a gun while loaded," sage advice.

Uncle Ervin always kept his rifle fully-loaded, one in the chamber and four additional bullets in the magazine. According to Gerald, his dad taught him, "Empty guns kill people." I knew there was something clever and meaningful in those words. But I could never decipher it. Everyone knew *loaded* guns kill people. Unless he meant, "Always treat a gun as if it's loaded?" But I doubt Uncle Ervin was capable of thought on that level.

Gerald said he would love to sneak his dad's rifle into his bedroom and hide it under his blanket. Then when the clowns came, he could shoot them. There were just two. I explained the pratfalls of using a firearm. It was even harder for him with his two brothers in the same room. There was always the risk of shooting his brothers or another family member since a rifle that powerful could punch through every wall in the house and continue outside to God-knows-where.

I understood that desire. The need to have some control. We just wanted it to end, to have jurisdiction over our rooms at night and be able to rest. He said the clowns appeared only at night and woke him, just like the monkeymen were doing to me. He would have that same anxious feeling that someone was in the room that should not be there, he could feel eyes on him, and he felt like something bad was about to happen.

Gerald's younger brothers slept in bunk beds just opposite of his. Oh, they heard his screams as the clowns stepped back into the shadows and disappeared. Of course, they would always disappear before they could be seen.

I had to ask, "Did you ever go with them?"

Gerald thought about it for a minute or two and said, "Yes, I think so."

I asked, "Do you ever remember where they took you?"

Gerald admitted, "No, but I know they can take me somewhere. Some nights I am not so scared, and I think I do go with them. I can't remember. I am afraid they might take me someplace where no one can help me, like down to H- E- L- L. That scares me. But I don't think they've ever really hurt me, not yet."

Poor Gerald. He could not say the word "hell." His family was devoutly Fundamentalist Christian. It's all Gerald ever knew. It was a belief system that had been hardwired since his birth.

The next morning, my mom and Aunt Wynonna or "Winnie," were at the kitchen table discussing Gerald's problems with clowns. Winnie was by nature a loud and boisterous woman. Ervin was a meek man of very few words when sober.

We knew Gerald was the chief topic of their discussion because we heard his name. Gerald and I listened from the landing at the top of the stairway while our moms engaged in a debate over coffee and cigarettes.

Aunt Winnie fired the opening salvo, "Is Terry still screaming and scaring those two girls of yours at night?"

My mother was taken off guard, she stammered. "Well … No, things are better now, mostly all quiet," she said confidently.

"He isn't seeing those monkeys in his room anymore?" Aunt Winnie asked. I could hear it in her voice. She did not believe my mother and wanted to press the issue.

Mom was dismissive of the monkeymen and unashamedly minimized my nightmares. My monkeymen stories had made it through the entire family by this time. Courtesy of my two older sisters no doubt. Little did they know there would be more to come.

In damage-control mode, Mom bragged to Aunt Winnie confidently, "Oh, Terry has pretty much outgrown it now, it's just a phase. I stopped him from watching *Space Ghost* on television and that about cured it! Those kids have such imaginations, I tell you what!" she said with bluster I rarely heard from my mom.

The ball was squarely in Mom's court, "I hear Gerald's got scary clowns that come to visit him at night? They wake up Gerald and his little brothers sleep right through it all? There in the same room, how can that be?"

Without thinking Aunt Winnie admitted, "Oh, they wake up alright when Gerald screams like hell." We could hear her voice trail off. She knew she slipped up.

My mother was quick to pounce, "Screaming like hell? Oh, the poor dears. I thought those little ones never heard a thing. I guess I heard it wrong, you know how gossip gets around."

Winnie would not allow my mom to get the better of her. She added, "Terry's got two sisters that share that bedroom about six feet from Terry. They don't wake up when he screams about monkeys in his room? I heard he scares the wits out of them and they're so tired they have trouble staying awake at school."

Touchette, Aunt Winnie.

The top of the stairway in our house was the perfect place to eavesdrop on adults at the kitchen table. I heard some amazing things sometimes.

Aunt Winnie sheepishly admitted that it was true, Gerald was being tormented by two little clowns that sneak into his room and scare the hell out of him. And yes, Gerald's screams wake up his brothers at night.

In an attempt to show empathy, Mom was quick with parenting advice, "You better stop that *Twilight Zone* and *Space Ghost* crap. Do you let him watch that shit Winnie? That's your problem."

Winnie shot back at my mother, "Well Anne, you need to get Terry blessed right away. Gerald was baptized, twice now and that seems to be driving them demons out of the house. We heard from so-and-so that Terry was not sleeping, and his grades had slipped too! Now, I know you and Arthur are Roman Catholic and I do not hold that against you, but you need the Holy Ghost on your side, amen!"

Oh brother. That was enough for my mom, "Winnie, you want a little in your coffee?" Winnie knew what Mom meant. She must have nodded with approval because we didn't hear her reply. Out came the whiskey bottle from deep under the sink. We heard the distinctive sound of glass clinking against coffee cups. Years later I understood. These women disliked one another.

Poor Gerald. I thought I had a tough time. He was dragged into church and the whole congregation prayed for him. The preacher sat him down and told him, "Gerald, sometimes we think bad things, dirty thoughts. That is what opens the door, son! Then those demons can sneak in disguised and take your soul!"

Gerald had been convinced it was all his fault. They convinced the poor kid he could get rid of the clowns by "right-thinking and prayer." If that failed it was because he wasn't "truly repentant," said the congregation and his family.

I had long given up on the Virgin and St. Michael. I placed my faith in a bayonet. But I was intrigued, "Does it really help? Can you pray and make them go away?"

Gerald teared up and shook his head "no." Gerald was convinced he was a sinner and an embarrassment to his family and the church.

I tried to reassure him. He was my cousin, and I didn't think it was wrong. I hugged him. He hugged me back. I told him it wasn't his fault, but I could tell he didn't believe me.

For just a moment I thought, *Maybe Gerald's right, maybe these monkeys were demons from hell in disguise.* I was still hopeful I could kill one. Just give me an opportunity and I would prove they were not demons, but mortal monsters that bleed and die. But Gerald's talk shook my confidence a bit. What if I stabbed one and nothing happened? Could it really drag me to hell forever?

The following Monday after breakfast they were ready to head back to Arkansas. They piled into an old, engineless camper van pulled by an even older pickup truck. Just as they were leaving, I gave Gerald my folding pocketknife with the three-inch blade. He thanked me, and we shook hands like men. I had a question I forgot to ask. I whispered, "Gerald, the clowns. What color are their eyes?

"Yellow."

Gerald knew where his dad's rifle was kept. He would use it to end his life in 1969.

Chapter #4

"NICE TO SEE YOU AGAIN"

ANSWERS FROM BETTY & MISSING TIME

On an autumn weekend in 1987, I was looking forward to my seasonal Sunday motorcycle ride. I rode only three months out of the year. Always by myself and always for recreation. I believe people who rely on their motorcycles for transportation were at greater risk of being hurt or killed.

I loved to ride in Michigan's crisp autumn chill that lasted from late August through Halloween. The smell of woodsmoke hung in the morning air as people had burned the first firewood of the season the previous evening.

It was my custom to ride my bike for two hours or so and be home between 10:30 and 11:00 AM to make pancakes for my family. It was a big deal for the kids. I used chocolate chips to make funny faces on their pancakes. It was special.

I had several preplanned routes in my playbook. I waited until I was on the road to choose which ride best suited my mood. All my routes, except for one, took precisely two hours to complete. One route crossed a set of tracks and put me at risk of being stuck at a railroad crossing by a Union Pacific train hauling a one-hundred-boxcar-load of coal. They always traveled east toward the car plants in Detroit and across my path. Then I could add 15 minutes to the journey.

As I explained in detail in *Incident at Devils Den*, that morning something went terribly wrong. That would be the last motorcycle ride of my life. The route I chose that day did not cross railroad tracks and offered some nice scenery, smooth blacktop roads, little to no traffic, and very few cops. All the variables that added up to the perfect motorcycle ride. The speed and brisk air were exhilarating. There were a few puffy white clouds drifting across blue sky. I refer to them as "Simpson clouds" in reference to the opening scene from the FOX animated series, *The Simpsons*.

Somedays, my mind would be devoted to work. I might mull over facts of a pending court case, vacation plans or chores that needed to be finished at home, or I might think of nothing at all. This was a day for my mind to wander like those puffy white clouds sailing overhead.

There was nothing in the ride out of the ordinary with one exception. I was on a flat stretch of road and I suddenly became aware I was on a gravel farm road with a thousand acres of corn to my left and right. How did this happen?

I never took my bike on gravel for two reasons. It could be dangerous, and it was bad for the motorcycle. A chipped paint job would be devastating. In the days before cell phones, if I broke down or, God forbid, was injured in an accident, it might be hours before I was found.

I attributed it to absent mindedness and pulled my bike to the side of the road. I took off my helmet and looked around to get my bearings. I assume I must have dismounted to stand by my bike. But there's a gap here, I have no memory of setting the kickstand and climbing off the bike. I found myself standing next to my motorcycle on a gravel farm road, holding my helmet by the strap and trying to understand what just happened.

I was in the middle of 1,000 acres of unharvested late-season corn and everything looked the same. I was never one of those lucky people with a built-in compass who could always find north. In the days before GPS, travel instructions had to be given to me in a series of right or left turns and landmarks such as fast-food restaurants. It was difficult for me to understand how I could end up here on a gravel farm road. I correctly assumed if I turned the bike around, I would find my way back to pavement. I turned the bike around and made the one-mile drive back to blacktop road. It was a relief to be off that dusty, creepy farm road and back on familiar ground.

Mentally, I went over this trip a hundred times in the year's past. The last conscious thought I had was driving on blacktop. I remember looking at my speed and easing back on the throttle to slow down to 65 MPH from 85 MPH as I approached a curve. I do not recall blacking out, but I could not account for any events that may have happened before my next memory. It was as if I blinked and was suddenly doing 30 on a remote farm road. I remember pulling over and standing on that gravel road next to my bike, confused and trying to get my bearings.

It is indisputable that I was two hours late arriving home. My wife was sickened with fear for my safety. I could not understand how

I could lose two hours. There were no train tracks or coal trains. I did not stop for gas. I was no more than a mile down the gravel road before I turned around and drove back. None of it made sense.

BETTY AND BARNEY

Until a few days later, when my wife shared Betty and Barney Hill's account from a 1961 edition of *LIFE Magazine*: a respected news magazine of the day. She never explained why she kept a 25-year-old magazine article. I suspect I know why she kept this one.

I was missing time. Two hours of my life was unaccounted for. My wife suggested I read their story. No discussion was necessary. I had never heard of the concept before. I lost several hours in 1977, but that was just because I could not remember. This felt different because it not only happened to me while I was awake, I was also engaged in a conscious activity. It could not be confused with a dream.

I read Betty and Barney's story. It sent a chill up my spine. I was particularly troubled by the couple's transcript of their recollections under hypnosis

When I review the disparity in my memory between easing up on my throttle and finding myself doing 30 MPH on a gravel farm road, there was no void. No blank slate. It was like I was in a movie and someone cut and removed a 10-foot section of film so there is no way to account for those two hours. They are gone. Seamlessly gone as if the ends of the film had been spliced neatly back together minus the 10 feet in between. It's the uninterrupted continuity that makes it seem perfectly normal.

There is no doubt I was abducted. It was hard to accept that I had no recollection of what occurred during what felt like just a few minutes. But two full hours had passed. Much of it remained lost for 30 years until October 2017 when a late-night visitor to my home refreshed my memory. I doubt I'll ever know the reason for her kindness.

My mind had been tampered with in 1977 by people with little regard for my mental well-being. The purpose of that exercise by special agents of the OSI was twofold, (1) to access my unconscious to determine if I was truthful about not having photographs of the UFO we saw, and (2) to "scrub" my conscious memory of the entire event through hypnosis.

Their paramount concern was that two USAF active duty NCOs might take their story to the *National Enquirer Magazine* or a television talk show. Worse yet, there was a chance that I may have hidden 36 B&W photographs with negatives of a triangular shaped UFO landing in an Arkansas State Park.

THANKS FOR THE MEMORIES

I am profoundly grateful for my memories. All of them. People, places and events, good and bad. Our lives are defined by sum of what we remember, and we own those images and experiences. Ruthlessly, trauma, disease and ET can rob us of them. There's truth in the saying, "You don't know what you don't know."

Except for our memories what else can we ever really possess? Nothing tangible for sure. There is but one thing we own and can *maybe* hold onto after the death of our physical body, our self-awareness. Consciousness is a construct of our memories. Remembrances give us our sense of identity. Dementia and Alzheimer's are so devastating because they rob us of our loved one's names and even our own. The face in the mirror becomes a stranger.

It's a misconception to think Alzheimer's disease leaves one blissfully unaware. It leaves its victim hopelessly alone, hypervigilant and terrified. I know from experience. My wife and I cared for my mother as she slipped into dementia and ultimately into Alzheimer's that took her mind and then her life.

I had always considered myself a materialist. Not like Madonna's song, but a philosophical materialistic view of a world created by atoms arranged orderly and following the laws of Newtonian physics. Then a neurologist explained to me the irreducibility of the human brain.

In plain English, there is a surgical technique for sufferers of severe epilepsy or traumatic brain injury. The connections between the two lobes of the brain is severed, or in drastic cases an entire lobe, half the brain, is surgically removed. In a purely material universe, the patient's intellect and personality should be reduced by 50%, but it is not. Most often, patients recover and retain their full cognitive ability and sense of self. How can that be? No one knows. But it points to the fact that consciousness and our sense of self likely reside outside the brain.

The doctor described himself as a "dualist," believing that in addition to the atoms there's "something else," there is more to us than just brain function, the firing of neurons and electrical signals breaching the synapse. It may exist on a quantum level we can't perceive, or it may be some mechanism we're completely unaware of.

He stated, "There's a reason behind genuine out-of-body experiences. There is also a reason why people who are clinically dead have near-death experiences where the can describe a room and individuals from a perspective looking down from the ceiling. Some have been able to relay entire conversations overheard while the individual was clinically dead. The question then becomes, does this experience last for eternity or does the identity and sense of self fade into nothingness after death becomes final?"

The debate over consciousness is a hotly debated topic. But the common thinking now is that consciousness is more than the sum of our parts. Nowhere in the human brain can consciousness be located and mapped to an identifiable area. I wasn't aware that neurologists had mapped the human brain entirely, determining which area is responsible for speech, movement, cognition, etc. But consciousness remains a mystery.

Let's hope at least a piece of it survives bodily death. It is all we'll ever truly own on this plane of existence. Everything else we simply keep in our custody until our heart beats its last.

Sometimes, a memory can be a gift too. Things lost or forgotten, suppressed or erased, can sometimes be restored.

I call this chapter "Nice to See You Again" in reference to the entity I knew as "Sue" in my childhood and was renamed "Betty" when we met again in 2017. I knew they were one and the same being. I had a feeling of fondness for her when I saw her again. Not a romantic feeling, more of a maternal attachment I cannot explain.

BETTY'S GIFT, A WAY TO SAY, "THANK YOU" FOR BEING THEIR LAB RAT

I had heard some abductees claim to have been given "gifts" during encounters. I received a gift in October 2017. It was from Betty during a face-to-face visit in my Dallas, Texas home. *Incident at Devils Den* stopped just short of the entire story. I regret being cryptic, but I was unsure how much to share. I nearly excluded the entire final chapter for fear it was so fantastic that it might discredit my entire story.

I've since discovered that what happened to me was not so unique. Other sane, credible people report similar experiences.

The incomplete memory of what happened on that farm road back in autumn of 1987 had haunted half of my adult life. In one of the vignettes in the final chapter of *Incident at Devils Den*, I shared a memory from Betty about my time aboard a "very big ship" and a trip that took us around the dark side of the moon. What I did not fully explain was how I traveled from that dusty farm road to the large spacecraft loitering somewhere between earth and the moon.

One evening in October 2017, my wife and I had just returned from a movie. It was late and my wife went to bed while I locked-up the house. My OCD-like evening routine has roots that stretch back to 1963 and coping with monkeymen.

On this night, I completed my nightly bedtime ritual of setting the alarm system and returning to "recheck" it just before bed to make certain it is set. It always is. This night I fell asleep almost immediately.

It was odd. It felt like I had no sooner closed my eyes then opened them. When I did, I found myself sitting bolt-upright in my living room chair.

A remarkably similar event happened 1966 when I was eleven years old. I woke sitting upright in my bed while my room was flooded with bright lights through the blinds and heavy drapes. Pulling aside my heavy drapes, I peeked through the blinds and there was a flying saucer outside my second story window. It was the source of the vibration, the lights, and the noise.

That was a bitterly-cold January evening in 1966. Underneath the disc was a dense fog or steam. I recall being excited to have an opportunity to see the topside of the saucer. When I saw it three years earlier in my backyard, all I could see was the bottom. It was satisfying to see. I felt special. I felt like they came to visit me. Most people spend a lifetime and never see a UFO. I saw one when I was eight and again at age 11. They did not just make a wrong turn at Albuquerque like they used to say in the old Bugs Bunny cartoons. It wanted to be seen.

After watching it for some time, I turned and went back to bed with a flying saucer still parked outside my second story bedroom window. With multicolored lights still flooding my room.

I felt the same sensation 11 years later while in the USAF in 1977. It was the odd mix of sedation and mild disinterest. Those two emotions are not mutually exclusive. It's a difficult feeling to put into words.

It is worth mentioning here that I have never walked in my sleep. Not once, ever. But here I was in 2017, seated in my favorite chair with no clue how I got there. I recalled that scent of ionized air. It's exactly what you experience when you walk outside after a spring thunderstorm.

I was not panicked. I was fully awake and alert. Physically, I felt calm, almost tranquilized but keenly aware of my surroundings. The emotion was just short of apathy. It is more accurately described as disconnected. I felt disconnected from the events that unfolded. It was a familiar feeling.

My eyes darted to the left to check the alarm panel. Its lights were properly lit. My usually curious cat lay undisturbed on the windowsill, pausing only to stretch before returning to sleep. My phone was still in the breast pocket of my tee shirt with the ear buds dangling to my lap.

I thought to call out for Sheila. My wife was asleep just down the hall. But I knew she would never hear me. She would not wake up. Just like Gerald's brothers, she couldn't wake up. They take care of that too.

I should not have been surprised. In 1987 my wife had an experience with an extraterrestrial being in our home. The only experience in her lifetime. Back then, we didn't have a home alarm system other than the usually vigilant family dog. An English setter. She woke from a sound sleep and reached across the bed for me. I wasn't there. I was busily engaged elsewhere in an experience of my own.

At the foot of our bed she remembers a four-foot-tall, hooded figure. She was between the foot of the bed and our bedroom window, so only visible in silhouette. She told me the dark outline of a woman spoke, but her lips never moved. The entity told her, "Go back to sleep, everything is alright." That is exactly what she did. It wasn't until two days later that she recalled the event.

I asked her, "Why didn't you scream?"

With a puzzled expression she said, "Funny, the thought never crossed my mind."

So, why should I be surprised? I thought to myself. She was back.

If I were given a choice in the matter, I'd rather meet with whoever or whatever sat across from me, "on my own turf." If ET wants a conversation, I would rather we have a discussion in my living room than on their spacecraft.

But why was I in my living room? I know they can conduct business while I lie in bed without waking my wife. Poor Gerald back in 1963, dealt with two diminutive clowns visiting him while his two younger brothers slept soundly just feet away in their bunk beds.

The answer struck me in a flash. My firearm on my bedside table was inaccessible in the living room. It's just a guess but it made sense in the moment. If my handgun were in my lap what would I do? Shoot a woman in my living room when she did not appear to be a threat? That would be contrary to my sense of morality. On reflection, I seriously doubt that a handgun would be any threat to an ET. I felt the mild sedation. Somehow, they can control our mood. Perhaps they can control much more.

Seated directly across from me was a four-foot-tall woman I mistakenly took to be Asian. Although most of her features were obscured by a pair of oversized sunglasses and a cheap wig.

On closer inspection I could tell she was not a human. At first glance, I doubt she would draw a second look on the streets of downtown Dallas. But something was off. Something about her stature was inconsistent with the proportions of a human body. Her complexion was not grey. It was an ashen flesh tone with a slight bit of cyanotic blue.

She was dressed in black. She wore a black blouse buttoned to the top with longish sleeves to hide four long thick fingers. Around her neck was a red scarf tied loosely to hide her pencil-thin neck, and a pair of black slacks that flared slightly at the cuff. Sturdy black shoes with an inch of heel to compensate for her short stature.

Atop her head was a wig. It was an outdated style reminiscent of the wigs my sisters wore in the 1960s. It had not been brushed and it sat askew on her head pulled forward. This was because of the bulbous shape of the back of her head. I was confused how this could possibly be the same woman from my childhood. I wanted to see more of her face.

Before I had finished my thought, *God, I wish she'd remove those glasses so I could clearly see her face.* As if on cue she raised her left arm and removed the glasses. I recognized her face immediately.

Before I tell you about our conversation, a quick note about how extraterrestrials communicate. All dialogue is telepathic. It came back to me from my early childhood. I could remember because it was second nature back then when Sue, now Betty, and I saw one another on our "play dates" in the round room.

But something was different about this too. As a child I had no need to govern my choice of words. I simply allowed my mind to roam. I was an adult now. We all understand that adulthood brings responsibility. We learn to discipline what comes out of our mouths and control it, so we conform to social norms.

If I spoke my thoughts candidly, without regard for the feelings of others, I would eventually insult everyone I meet. I never realized how many thoughts of an inappropriate nature crossed my mind. I don't think I'm different from anyone else in this regard. This is the reason human beings do not communicate telepathically. We lack the mental discipline. It would be a disaster.

As soon as I recognized we were communicating telepathically I had the thought, *Oh no, what if I think something provocative that might anger her, or something inappropriate?* After all, I was not a child anymore.

Of course, the result was akin to telling a class of fourth graders not to think about elephants. That will be all they can think of. Crazy inappropriate things flashed through my head and it was all as clear to her as the spoken word. I think she was genuinely embarrassed. I certainly was.

Then, I heard her voice in my head assure me, "You can keep some of your thoughts private ,Terry, just try." I will never know if that was true or just said to put me at ease.

I took in her appearance and posture once more. Her legs were crossed, and she still sat in a non-threatening posture. That put me a bit more at ease. While I felt mildly sedated, that did not mean I wasn't scared out of my wits. I was.

The thought flashed through my mind that the wig she wore was almost comical, it reminded me of a cartoon character from the 1960s cartoon *The Flintstones*. Betty Rubble, hence, the name "Betty" in 2017. As a child I knew her as "Sue." But now and forever she will be Betty.

In reference to my mental comment about her wig, she immediately shot back in the form of a question, "You don't like it? It's the same as last time." I heard her voice in my head with crystal clarity, as if her words were spoken.

"The same as last time when?" I thought.

"The last time we saw one another," she replied. I thought her answer was evasive.

My response was still, "When?" But crazy as it sounds, I also felt concerned that I may have insulted her. I felt I may have hurt her feelings with my remark about the wig. I was obliged to follow up with: "No, it looks nice. I'm scared, that's all." She acknowledged me with a nod. As to "when we last met," my question still hung in the air.

A few seconds later her answer came. She showed me a scenario that I saw play out in my head. I was a passive observer. The experience differed from my own thoughts in that it popped into my head and I watched a very brief scene. I have no way to prove this assertion, but it is true. I could tell the thought came from her and did not originate in my mind. I had no control over it. In that regard it was more like watching a scene on my laptop, except in my mind.

She showed me a scenario from my 1987 motorcycle ride and the two-hour missing time event. This memory was in vivid color and as close to being three dimensional as my mind could conceive. If it were a dream it was an exceptionally colorful, lucid and realistic one. All the mental conversation was an interactive dialogue. I carefully chose my words, and we exchanged a real conversation. In a typical dream we are an observer more than a participant. In this vision, I knew I was witnessing a scene from the past and the dialogue was an exchange that I remembered.

Viewing the scene from above, I recognized a younger me standing on that dusty gravel farm road on a sunny autumn day with a very pleasant cool breeze. I saw my motorcycle there and immediately knew where I was and what was happening. I had dismounted and stood next to my bike, holding my helmet in my hand by the strap. Above me and nearly parallel to my view was a large flying disc less than fifty feet over the browning, unharvested corn stalks. It was silent and motionless. It was much larger than the ones I saw as a child.

As I watched, the craft then glided over the road in front of me and descended to less than five feet above the roadway. A doorway slid open and a ramp slid down and touched the road in front of me. I was compelled to walk up the incline and entered the craft without assistance and without fear.

Just as I experienced inside the triangle in 1977, the interior seemed twice as large as the exterior. That made no sense, but that is what I experienced. In the emails I've received from readers of my book, a few others have told me they had the same experience on entering an alien craft.

I was seated comfortably in a white plastic seat with headrests but no lap belts or safety restraints of any kind. I chose to sit next to Betty, the entity I knew as "Sue" in my childhood abductions. I felt like the seat had been reserved for me. I settled in with my helmet on my lap.

Betty and I immediately acknowledged one another with a polite nod. I recognized her immediately from my childhood as "Sue." The interior of the disc reminded me of a home theater. There was a domed ceiling more than tall enough for me to stand comfortably upright. I saw a dozen or so seats. I recall being disappointed that there were no windows, and we faced a plain white wall in front of us. The inside was brilliantly lit.

There were a couple human beings seated in front of me as well. They were both male and appeared to be farmers. No one spoke.

My attention was focused on Betty and I said to her audibly, "It's nice to see you again." I still felt no fear. Just the opposite, I felt happy to see her. She had not aged a day since I last saw her back when I was just nine years old.

The doorway closed and the lighting inside changed once the sunshine was blocked. There was a slight sensation of motion, like being in a fast elevator. The ride took only a few minutes, then it felt as if we had gently set down somewhere. I remember the door opening. I rose and Betty took my hand as we exited together through a hatch and down a walkway that descended for that purpose.

Seeing her again was very emotional for me. I would compare it to meeting a long-lost sister. It is sad that I can't share with you these images I have in my head. Words are inadequate. This is a memory from my ride onboard the "very big ship." The one I explained to Brad during my OSI interrogation in 1977. Under hypnosis I described the craft as being so large it could never transit across the face of a full moon because it could be seen from earth as a dot with the naked eye.

Betty warned me in 2017 that talking about anything to do with the moon or the "big ship" placed me in potential danger because it was a sensitive topic. She was unequivocal, the danger was not from her "hosts," as she referred to aliens, but from my government. I have since resigned myself to the fact that the more visible I am through writing and speaking, the safer I am. At least that is my hope.

THE AGREEMENT

For fear of overwhelming the reader I held back on some details of my conversation with Betty in the final chapter of *Incident of Devils Den*. I'll share them here and ask your indulgence.

I asked Betty plainly, "Does the United States government and your hosts work in concert? If so, toward what end?"

She answered me immediately with a slight nod and said, "Yes, they have worked together by mutual agreement since shortly before your birth."

As usual, she was short on details. I was born in 1955.

I recall that at a UFO conference in 2018, a speaker said that in 1955 President Dwight D. Eisenhower met with aliens at an Air Force base in California to sign a treaty between them. You can find this on both the web with a Google search and all over YouTube. If true, I would love to read the contract they entered that day so I could understand what promises were made on both sides to form a contract.

Sue was dressed in a light grey tight-fitting one-piece suit that accentuated her frailty and small frame. She wore no insignia on her clothing, and I saw nothing to indicate rank, no ornamentation or jewelry. She had removed her wig, so her head was bare, with just sparse hair and no discernable ears. I think this is her usual appearance because it was so familiar from childhood memories of her.

DETAILS FROM THE MOON TRIP

Let me qualify some of this information. These are memories mostly recovered since 2017. But since publishing my first book in 2018, more and more of bits and pieces filtered into my conscious memory. Each bit of information is another piece to the puzzle and it helps create a fuller picture. I'd point out that this is not unusual. Many people have told me since reading my book and speaking openly about their own past events, it's like a doorway opened. It's true.

I was with Betty on our 1987 "moon trip." She held my hand. I recognized my fondness for her. She used my name when she spoke to me, telepathically of course. It touched me when she used my name.

We had been shuttled from earth by a saucer and entered a spaceship as large as a city. My memory of the "very large craft" is at first believing we were in a massive warehouse of some kind or an immense office building. We walked down a long straight corridor until we came to a huge glass panel 60 feet in length and at least 20 feet tall.

Outside were billions of stars. I was amazed how bright the stars were and the fact they never twinkled. I wondered for a moment if this were a planetarium of sorts. Then I recalled a similar experience when Sue slid back a panel and showed us a comparable scene. It would be 10 years later before I learned that stars viewed outside the earth's orbit

125

do not twinkle. The twinkle effect is caused by light distortion from our atmosphere.

There was never the slightest sensation of movement inside the big ship. At this point, I still didn't know where I was or what our final destination would be.

We must have been positioned to look out at the sky facing away from the moon as we approached. It must have been to our right side and hidden from view. It felt like *we* were stationary, and the moon just rolled over and into view from the right. It scared me. I know in my mind I thought, *Oh shit, it's going to hit us!*

Betty quickly reassured me everything was under control and there was no reason to be afraid. She explained we were moving. The moon is relatively stationary.

The bright side of the moon was greyish white in color and glowed like the noonday sun on white limestone. I knew that we were the ones moving but my mind had a problem overriding what my eyes registered. The dark side of the moon was as dark as 2:00 AM on earth and it is separated by a very distinct line where the bright side ended, and the dark side began. It was a breathtaking scene. We watched together.

I don't know why, but I told her about my children, and she acknowledged me with something very kind—I forget her exact words. Then she shared, "As a hybrid, I'm incapable of bearing children." She spoke matter of fact and without emotion. I thought that was sad.

Whatever we were traveling in completed its turn because we were now squarely facing the dark side of the moon. We traveled for a long while looking at the black below us. The billion stars that were in front of us were now out of sight. The landscape was as black as ink.

Then widely scattered patches of light came into view below us. I saw three flying discs. All were lit around their edges 360 degrees. They flew in a tight "V" formation. They did not land like an aircraft, rather they slowed and just dropped in unison to the surface maintaining their "V" configuration.

There were towers and buildings, some illuminated brightly from inside. I also saw some large heavy equipment like you would expect to see in a mining operation. Betty pointed out a mushroom shaped tower that she said was one and a-half kilometers in height. That equates to just under a mile. It was difficult to gage size or distance from our vantage point, but I would estimate our altitude at 10,000 feet.

Something seemed odd or out of place about this city on the dark side. Then it registered. Cruising over LAX at night there were cars, streetlights, and parking lots laid out in a grid fashion. In stark contrast, below us was a scattered collection of buildings. I recalled my property law class from law school about zoning ordinances. That is what gave it the odd appearance. Absent roadways, there was no gridwork or urban planning. There were no zoning regulations as the buildings were a patchwork of scattered structures of varying height and orientation.

I saw no interconnecting roadways. That seemed odd to me when I compared it in my mind's eye with flying into any city on earth at night. Otherwise, activity and occupancy-wise, it looked like LAX at night with structures as far as I could see in any direction.

There were other points of white light moving around in the sky overhead. Because it was dark, I could not tell if they were saucers or what. Just dots of light. Some were traveling slowly in a straight line and some were darting about. They were all in groups of two or more and in formations. I saw three craft of some kind descend low and just set down. There was no deacceleration like landing a plane. Just like the ones I saw earlier, they just dropped low and set down, parked in a neat row.

I noted many of the buildings were constructed like an apartment complex on earth, with multiple floors, square windows, some lit and others dark. It reminded me of an urban downtown area at night with tall office buildings, mostly dark, but with offices lit here and there.

Here are a couple things Betty told me that are disclosed in the first book, just with more detail for the sake of accuracy. I asked her, "Are human beings living here on the moon?"

She immediately responded. "Yes, my people (hybrids) and my hosts (aliens) also reside here with humans on the surface. There are others that reside inside the moon below its surface."

According to Betty, there is a race of beings that reside inside the moon too. The concept of an inhabited, hollow moon is not new.

Today there are many people who believe the moon's interior, like earth's possibly, is populated by a reptilian race of sub-surface extraterrestrials.

In 1901, the famed science fiction writer H.G. Wells wrote *The First Men in the Moon.* Note that Wells chose to use "First Men *in* the Moon" as opposed to "on" the moon. Well's novel is about a manned space mission that discovers the moon is a hollow sphere inhabited by a race of insectoid extraterrestrials living in its core.

Betty described the moon's subterranean inhabitants as "reptilian," and said they are "possessive and territorial like humans." I asked if they were still there? She replied "yes", and she emphatically stated the moon is a hollow, artificial vessel. She said it has been in our sky since "long before man appeared." She explained, "The builders left a clue for mankind to discover," in the solar eclipse the moon fits exactly over the face of the sun completely covering the visible disc with only the fiery corona visible. She added, the possibility of that occurring by chance "defies statistical probability. Your ancient ones recognized this."

There was a joint space program called "Project Clementine" launched on January 25, 1994 by the Strategic Defense Initiative Organization and NASA from Vandenberg AFB in California, aboard a Titan IIG rocket. Information on the Clementine mission, its instruments and results can also be found in the Clementine special issue of *Science* magazine, Vol. 266, No. 5192, December 1994.

Part of Apollo 12's mission involved intentionally crashing a two and one-half ton ascent stage of the lunar module onto the moon's surface to register the seismic activity with instruments left there by earlier Apollo missions. Famously, it is reported that the collision caused the moon to "ring like a bell," implying to some that the moon was hollow. That quote is alleged to have been spoken by an unnamed NASA scientist measuring the seismic crash results.

The shallowness of the moon's craters has been cited as proof the moon's surface thinly covers its extremely hard subsurface. According to Betty, "It is not an organic space object." She said it was "manufactured a long time ago. Its original inhabitants abandoned it before the rise of mankind and the reptilian entities discovered it vacant long before man had evolved."

REPTILIANS AND BROKEN PROMISES

It's never been my goal to spread fear or panic. Some things sound so outrageous as to belie credulity. In the interest of complete candor, as Paul Harvey used to say, here is "the rest of the story."

Betty stated further, that "Reptilian entities live in your western desert and have since before man evolved into intelligent beings." She stunned me by stating in a mater-of-fact fashion that, "Reptilians feed on blood from cattle and will feed on human blood and tissue as well. Your government has a treaty that limits the number of human beings and the number of cattle that the Reptilians can take. The Reptilians have no obligation to return them or agreement as to their ethical

130

treatment. She said, "Since the mid 1960s they have failed to honor the agreed limits."

I asked her, "What limitations?"

She explained the agreement "limits the number of humans that may be lawfully harvested." Likewise, "the number of cattle from private ranches and federal land is limited according to the conditions in the Eisenhower accord."

I found the verb "harvested" to be dreadful in this context. It equates human beings with pork bellies on the commodities market. Just another product raised, bartered, bought and sold for eventual slaughter and consumption.

My incident in 1977 occurred in an Arkansas State Park adjacent to the Ozark National Forest. I feel truly fortunate to be alive. Devil's Den is an area identified by David Paulides as a "cluster" location. A place where people have been known to disappear under the strangest of circumstance.

A former law enforcement officer turned investigative journalist, David Paulides began researching the unexplained circumstances of campers and hikers that vanish in state and federal parks around the world. He established the disappearances as a global phenomenon in his book series *Missing 411*.

The fourth volume in his series is entitled *Missing 411: The Devil's in the Detail*. I highly recommend it. In it, Paulides reveals that state and federal parks containing the name "Devil" or "Diablo" in their name form "clusters" where statistically people disappear more frequently than in other areas without the diabolical reference in the name. Paulides draws no inferences. Instead, like a good investigative journalist, he reports facts and statistics and allows the reader to reach their own conclusion.

Next, I remembered the 1969 moon landing and the final Apollo mission in 1972. Then the space shuttle program abruptly replaced manned moon missions. It is odd to think that, at the time of this writing, mankind has not left earth's orbit in nearly 50 years. But as of 2020 they are planning to do so soon.

I asked Betty why we abruptly abandoned moon missions. She claimed we had not. She said the Apollo missions and the subsequent shuttle program were "the public face of your nation's space program." She continued, "Human beings have lived on your moon for many generations now, your government has two space programs. One for the people and another that is secret. Just like your nation, countries have governments with superficial control, but there is only one global council that truly represents and controls your planet. Many people begin work for the covert government as 'young people' and will serve in that capacity for their entire lives."

I was curious and asked, "Why do these people and alien beings live on the moon?"

She answered, "All are there to collect the rocks." When she detected my puzzlement, she explained superficially that "Helium-3 is a gas that is trapped inside moon rocks." That was the only explanation she offered.

I relied on Google to explain the significance of Helium-3. Extraordinarily little Helium-3 exists on earth, but it is abundant on the moon. Helium-3 can be used in a fusion reactor to create power without producing toxic radiation as a waste product. It is truly clean energy, aside from whatever byproducts are created by the processing required to release the gas.

I failed to grasp the enormity of her statements at the time. She had just confirmed (1) the existence of a secret space program, (2) that extraterrestrials and human beings live on and inside the moon, (3) that extraterrestrials reside inside the earth and some have free reign to abduct cattle and humans by a written agreement and (4) she inferred the existence of a global ruling council or cabal. Four concepts I previously believed to be conspiratorial fiction.

Significantly, she told me, "Some [in the secret space program] serve on your moon for life, but most serve on earth. Terrestrial government leaders rotate and show a face to the people of national pride that keeps the population satisfied. They feel secure and believe they are competently ruled and protected. They believe the illusion that they have some control over who rules them. There is no consolidated global leadership among the collection of governments with regional and territorial interests at odds with one another. Your world is a single global entity, and it has a single ruling council."

Betty told me people on earth are "too primitive and too territorial to form an overt and cohesive global government, as worlds must if they intend to survive."

She admitted her hosts and their hybridization program between aliens and humans are intended to preserve a piece of humanity. That is disconcerting.

"But preserve us from what?" I asked.

It must be something bad on a global scale I reasoned. We are clueless about what goes on with our planet as evidenced by climate change. In 2019 scientists announced we had passed the tipping point to reverse climate change. We are self-absorbed beings with little regard for those who come after us.

Betty agreed. She described most of humanity as, "earth-centric."

We locked eyes and, in an instant, she asked me a question. It was only the second question she asked me, both were rhetorical in nature.

She asked, "What does a colony of ants do when it reaches a point beyond self-sufficiency?"

I said, "The queen leaves and starts a new colony." She kept eye contact with me and said, "You see, it is so for humanity. Many earth governments are preparing for the evacuation to a new home."

I immediately took that to mean Mars would be humanities next home. She confirmed that assumption with a clear "yes."

Mars will be a new home for the lucky ones at least, those who have the resources or status to be selected for relocation. Those who cannot go will be left. Their fate will be the same as 3rd class passengers on the HMS Titanic, with no chance of escape. They are doomed and will not survive.

At the time of this writing in mid-2020, the world has been rocked by the COVID-19 virus, civil unrest and political instability internally. There is also heightened tensions between the United States, China, Iran, and the former Soviet Union.

Back in 2017, Betty picked up on my concern about the threat of thermonuclear war. She said, "nuclear detonations tear the fabric of space-time and result in interdimensional bleeds."

I do not know what "bleeds" are except they sound ominous. I thought, "That can't be good." And Betty did not reply with words. Instead, she expressed deep sadness that I perceived through empathy. I felt awash in sorrow and wanted to cry. I regret that I do not have the slightest idea what interdimensional bleeds may be. I am a lawyer, not a physicist, and I believe the answer is beyond my ability to comprehend.

Chapter #5

OTHERS WHO REACHED OUT

In the epilogue of *Incident at Devils Den*, I encouraged readers who had similar experiences, memories of bizarre dreams from early childhood, or sightings that effected their lives, to share their stories with me. I also promised to protect their anonymity. Hundreds of people have contacted me and said reading my book resonated with them and some said it even awakened memories from their childhood. Others just wanted to share their sightings and experiences. Some were critical of my portrayal of ET as "evil."

Over 1,300 emails have hit my inbox since *Incident at Devils Den* was first published on Amazon in March 2018. I am not a therapist or medical person. I cannot offer medical advice, but if you would like to share privately, I'll listen to you, reply, and help if I can.

You're welcome to securely contact me at lovelace.landpope@gmail.com. I will respect your anonymity and you won't receive junk email from me.

All that said, here are a selection of the best stories sent to me by readers. I have established a dialogue with each contributor and each case below is "vetted" as much as possible for authenticity and sincerity. I do not judge the experience of others, but some experiences resonate with me. I hope I chose the ones that resonate with you. I have changed names and locations, unless the location is integral to the story, and diligently tried to de-identify the writer but retain the facts.

I think the word "abductee" is more accurate than "experiencer." An experiencer might witness something and never become more than a momentary observer. Abductees are taken and have a more intimate encounter that results in behavior changes, even if they have no memory of the incident. Some encounters are negative and some positive as we'll see exemplified in the story of Julia and her sister Mollie below.

Most abductees are fine in the light of day. But there is something menacing about the dark of night. It is what made me run home as a child when the streetlights came on. It is why so many of us feel uncomfortable in our own basements in the dark. We know while we are asleep at night the monsters are awake, inside our heads and sometimes inside our house.

Many of these stories draw a parallel between alien abduction and childhood abuse by an adult. Trauma is traumatic regardless of the species of the perpetrator. It is not a level playing field. An abuser, whether alien or human, operates from a position of power over their victim.

I spent a couple years of my legal career as a felony prosecutor of sex crimes. I made the same observation in *Incident at Devils Den*. We are to aliens as children are to adults. Unfortunately, at times that relationship can be unhealthy on many levels. That is the best analogy I can think of.

During my abduction in 1977, I recall being inside the gigantic triangle-shaped craft. There were the shorter grey beings milling about. Then I noticed a taller alien being that seemed to be in charge. It was twice the height of the grays and carried itself with authority. Inside this alien craft, Toby and I both were paralyzed except for our eyes, which we could still move. I directed my gaze to the left to look at him. By happenstance he turned his head at the exact same moment and we inadvertently locked eyes.

In an instant he was in my head. He knew everything about me. He saw everything in my mind including memories and deepest secrets and absorbed them all. There was such intelligence behind those eyes, but nothing else. Not one ounce of empathy or mercy. It was raw intellect. That brief encounter was one of the more ghastly moments of being aboard the craft. The memory still haunts my sleep.

Alien entities are so far above us on the evolutionary ladder that we are no match. My family had a pet Irish setter when our children were small. She would place her head in my lap and look into my eyes lovingly. She recognized me as the alpha. I could sense limited intelligence behind her eyes. We each understood our respective roles.

When I was in the presence of that extraterrestrial it was the same, but I was the dog in the equation, and there is not an ounce of trust on either side. Just one superior being and an intellectually lesser one.

I think that fact is what makes the UFO/extraterrestrial phenomena so hard for people to believe. Humanity is accustomed to being the top dog. ET has toppled us from our perceived predominance in the universe. A tough pill for some to swallow.

I hope you enjoy the 30 cases I chose to share.

Case #1

The Christmas Store

Olivia

Henderson, Nevada

Dear Mr. Lovelace,

I am a 76-year-old widow originally from Reno, Nevada. I listened to your Audiobook and decided to tell you about an experience my late husband and I had on a weekend trip from Las Vegas to Reno in 1968.

My late husband was a physician, a nephrologist or kidney doctor. I was a housewife and never worked outside the home. We never had children, but we had an active social life. We used to enjoy the drive from Vegas to Reno to visit my sister and our friend who owned a successful automobile business there.

We had a Peugeot automobile we bought in France on an anniversary trip and had shipped back stateside. It was my late husband's toy. Paul loved that car because it was just unusual. It was also wonderfully comfortable for long trips. About once a month we would make the drive to Reno and visit our friends and enjoy a lovely weekend.

This weekend in March 1968 would be the most unusual trip we would ever make to Reno. We usually left no later than 3:00 PM to avoid traffic, but Paul was tied up at the hospital until 6:00 PM. We considered cancelling, but we had a room reserved and really wanted

to make the trip. Paul called the hotel and told them we would be check-
ing in late.

We could sleep-in the next morning so the late start would be
no big deal. Back in `68 it was two-lane blacktop for the whole 240-
mile trip. We knew we would be worn out when we got there, but it was
not a concern.

Usually, we would stop for gas in the little town of Tonopah off
the highway that marked about the half-way point to Reno. They had a
nice diner there called the Stagecoach or something similar. The sun
had just set, and we decided to stay for dinner and coffee as well as
fuel. There was not much commerce in Tonopah back then. The drive
was mostly desert with a few small towns separated by many miles of
road. It's different now and there's a nicer highway too.

We had a good meal and were back on the road within an hour.
As we were leaving the city limits headed for Reno, Paul and I saw a
new business. It was, of all things, a Christmas store.

This was 1968 and I cannot recall ever before seeing an entire
store devoted to the holiday before. The building sat back from the road
a bit and was lit up inside with bright lights that came streaming out of
every window. There was a porch that stretched across the front of the
store with Christmas lights of all shapes, sizes and colors draped
across the front of the building. Some of the lights twinkled some
flashed and others did not. It really caught our attention.

We both were certain it had not been there a month ago when
we last made the trip. But we usually passed through Tonopah before

142

dark and could have just missed it. We agreed It was odd to have a Christmas store in such a remote location and open for business in March.

I asked Paul to please stop since they appeared to be open, but we saw no cars. We could see shadows of movement inside. Paul slowed down, but we could not find a place to pull into a parking lot. It was strange, we never saw a parking lot! It was just sand in front of this new building. It made no sense to complete the building before in-stalling a point of egress. There was no road behind the building either.

We assumed the place must still be under construction.

I remembered it being a brick structure, Paul thought it was wooden, built from rustic barnwood. We could not agree on a couple of points but paid it no mind. We both agreed that the store was brightly lit up inside and out.

Paul sped up and pulled back onto the highway to resume our trip north. We usually chatted for the entire drive, but this trip I felt sleepy. Neither of us were talkative. I reclined my seat and slept until we reached the Reno city limits. I had eaten a heavy meal and attributed it to my drowsiness.

We checked in at our hotel and never bothered to unpack and hang things up so they wouldn't wrinkle. Instead, we went directly to bed and sleep. Uncharacteristically, we slept for ten hours before our friends woke us with a phone call.

The rest of the trip was routine. We had a good time and by Monday morning we were ready to head home. On our way back, I

143

asked Paul to keep an eye out for that peculiar Christmas store when we were close to Tonopah. We did not have the time to stop, but we wanted to see it in the daylight.

It was not there! We passed the spot where we were certain we saw it on our way up. But there was nothing there but sand and sagebrush. We continued home and I think we both felt frustrated that we could not find it again, but we dismissed it as a simple oversight. Surely, we overlooked it and drove past.

A week later I brought it up at dinner. Paul admitted it was "on his mind" for some reason.

I suggested we take a quick drive to Tonopah and look for it. We agreed to make the trip the following weekend.

We got up early the following Saturday and made the drive to Tonopah to have lunch and find the Christmas store again. It felt like a fun adventure. We reached the city limits and drove through town looking, but we never found it. We drove through town twice and still could not find it.

We had lunch at the Stagecoach, and I asked the hostess, "When did they build the Christmas store in Tonopah?"

"What Christmas store?" she asked. She looked at me like I was crazy. I was not confused; we knew what we saw. She politely insisted there were no new stores in Tonopah.

The hostess told us, "The owner here is the president of the town's chamber of commerce. If anybody knows about a new retail store in town, he'd be the man." She offered to have him speak with us.

Mr. Yang introduced himself and asked if he could join us. We insisted. He pulled up a chair at our table and was very gracious. He gave us a brief but fascinating history of the town. But he was courteously adamant there were no new commercial structures built and no new businesses in town.

I can still see that building in my mind. We both saw the same thing. We saw it in Tonopah ten minutes after leaving the restaurant. There was no uncertainty about the location.

Afterward, Paul became indifferent and rightly pointed out that we had other things to worry about. We never really discussed it again.

I've seen a lot in 76 years. But those two minutes when we drove past the Christmas store is as fresh in my memory as if it had happened yesterday.

ANALYSIS

Olivia's case is striking in that she and her husband both witnessed something strange. They both agreed on what they saw, mostly. There were subtle differences. But they were only in front of the store for two minutes as they drove by.

The question remains, what did they see? I do not think it was a retail store. I don't think what they saw was even terrestrial. I believe what they recall is a screen memory that disguised the true nature of what they witnessed.

Olivia said she would rather speak by telephone than exchange emails. I called her, and after some initial pleasantries I asked, "Olivia, do you think what you saw may have been a spaceship? Do you believe you and your husband's perception was somehow being manipulated from inside that store somehow?"

She replied with a nervous chuckle, "That's silly!" Then she paused, "But I can't rule that out either. That makes as much sense as anything else. I admit that I entertained that thought over the years, but I try not to dwell on it. It was a cute little store. I'd like to remember it like that, even if it was a mirage."

I asked her if she thought they may have experienced "missing time" during that leg of the Reno trip while she slept? She was unsure but had considered it.

She asked, "How would one know? It was very uncommon for me to sleep in the car. If we did lose time, I don't think it was hours like you lost on your motorcycle ride. No, I do not think anything happened between Tonopah and Reno. Although, I have always questioned those couple minutes between Paul slowing down and then accelerating again as we rolled past when we failed to find the driveway."

"Do you think it's possible you stopped at the store for a time and can't remember?" I asked.

She Admitted, "Maybe we did stop. Maybe all we can remember is slowing down and speeding away and the in-between was lost to us. Paul and I both were mildly out of sorts the next 24 hours. That makes me feel strongly that something happened. Paul and I both had bad dreams about the little Christmas store for the rest of our lives. Never on the same night and no more than a couple a year. The whole incident was dark and creepy in a way that would give Lovecraft nightmares."

"Do you still have nightmares about the incident?" I asked.

"I still have strange dreams on occasion. It is unusual because the content of the dream was always the same. It is just Paul pulling onto the shoulder and stopping the car to look at the Christmas store, and both of us are mesmerized by the light show. I can never clearly remember anything other than stopping and just staring at the building from the shoulder of the road for a few seconds, and then Paul driving away. I stared at the thing, but I cannot sharply focus on it from memory. In my dream it is always like looking through a pair of eyeglasses with oil or something rubbed onto the lenses, or through eyeglasses of the wrong prescription and everything is blurry. Then I become terrified for some real reason and wake up feeling disturbed. Paul's nightmares were similar, but he rarely discussed them because his faded so quickly."

I thanked Olivia for her story. It reminds me so much of Betty and Barney Hill. I wish she and Paul had thought to draw a picture with pen and paper separately and compare what they saw immediately afterward.

I suggested she read Betty and Barney Hill's story.

Case #2

Pig Roast Interrupted

Garrett

Midland, Texas

Dear Terry,

I had some really strange stuff happen to me as a kid too. But the story I want to share with you was from when I was in my mid-twenties. I had a life-changing event just like you and your friend. I lived in a big house in Midland at the time with my ex and our daughter. Midland is a decent size little Texas community. I'd been a firefighter there since I returned home from military service. I prefer to just go by just "Garrett." I retired as of 2016.

When I was 27, a bunch of the guys at the firehouse all bought AR-15s and Ranch Rifles. We were planning a big hunt for wild hogs. We had all served in the military and were decent shots. The five of us, Jeff, Tom, Billy, Melvin and I, all hung out together and usually took an annual fishing trip. This would be something different.

Jeff's family owned a hunting camp with a trailer on fifty acres that would sleep the five of us comfortably. His family went down once or twice a year for a get-away or to hunt. Game was plentiful. His place was just a couple hours away so we could all go in my F250 pickup.

Hogs are a nuisance here since they're the top predator. Our plan was to shoot a couple hogs and have a pig roast there. We'd all get away from the firehouse for a long weekend, have some fun and hopefully take some meat home to family and friends. It was supposed to be just a fun weekend away from work. We planned this trip like you and your friend planned your trip to Devil's Den. We were methodical. We were first responders too. We stocked and took care of our fire engines and vehicles, keeping everything in order. Unlike your trip though, we didn't forget a single item on our list.

We were all obsessed with this stupid hunting trip and it didn't turn out like it was supposed to. Not at all. Everything started out well. Then on the day we were supposed to leave, Tom backed out at the last minute. He said he didn't feel well. It must have been sudden because he was fine the previous day. We chalked it up to a fight with his wife over the trip.

The remaining four of us made the ride down and got settled in. We had fun the first night. We got there late so the next day would be the start of our hunt. We're not a bunch of drunks and we sure don't do drugs because we were subject to random drug tests. This wasn't like a bunch of novices out in the woods getting spooked at night over nothing. We were all seasoned outdoorsmen. I know this is hard to believe. If it hadn't happened to me, I doubt I would have believed it. I never believed any of this stuff was real. I always thought it was comic book stuff.

Jeff killed a hog that first day. The rest of us got nothing. We teased Jeff about having the home court advantage. But it was his place, and we were his guests. There'd be another hunt the next day. At least we had a pig to roast that second evening. Even if we didn't

149

bag another pig, it would still have been a nice trip and we'd all have some meat to take home and share.

Billy was a great cook. That evening, he and Jeff used a wheel-barrow to take the pig a good piece away from the trailer. Jeff's family had a special spot with a hoist. It was 200 yards away so not to draw coyotes and stink up the place. While Billy and Jeff did the butchering, we set up the pit for the roast. We had a nice fire going and it was just getting dark. The smell of the firewood was nice, even for firefighters. We were all in good spirits and hungry.

Finally, the hog was on the spit and the four of us sat around and talked about guns, the firehouse and the latest gossip. Billy's skill as a cook meant we'd all have a nice dinner. We could hear the coyotes and crickets along with the crackling fire. By now the smell of the roasted pig was making us all pretty hungry. It was a pleasant evening with good friends and good conversation. It was the last time the four of us would get together outside the firehouse.

Melvin was in his early 50s and close to retirement. We all knew he was struggling with his health and pitched in to help cover him on the job. This night he was anxious for some reason. Jeff asked him, "Hey, man, you alright?"

Melvin said, "Yeah, but I think I need a nitro [tablet]. No big deal. I'll pop one and lie down on the couch for a while. I'll be good as new by the time the pigs done. Wake me if I doze off." With a wave and a "good night" he went inside the trailer and shut the screen door behind him.

That left the three of us, me, Jeff and Billy. I sat with my back toward the trailer, facing outward. I could see the ridge where the forest got thick and fifty yards of open field in front of that. That's when I saw what looked like a couple guys with flashlight in the woods. I never saw the guys, but I sure as hell saw the beams of light dancing around in thick woods.

I announced, "Boys, I think we have company."

Jeff and Billy turned around and saw it too. Annoyed, Jeff said, "Poachers probably. Our place is well posted. Pretty ballsy to see our fire and not give a damn. Maybe they're hunting possum. That's why the lights are in the trees."

I asked, "What do we do?"

Without warning, Jeff pulled out his .45 caliber handgun and fired seven shots in the air. "We let them know we're here and they're not welcome. That's what we do."

Jeff was pissed off that someone would trespass. Their trailer had been broken into the previous year, so it was a sore subject. He ejected his empty magazine and popped in a fresh clip, slamming a round into the chamber in one smooth motion. "That'll fix their asses," he said confidently.

I asked Billy to check on Melvin. The last thing we need to do is trigger a heart attack for our comrade with an unexpected burst of gunfire.

Jeff and I continued to watch the lights as Billy went in through the front door.

We were surprised that despite our warning shots, the lights were brighter and more active than ever.

Jeff was livid. He wanted a confrontation, but I warned him, "We don't know who we're dealing with here, let's be careful and think this through."

He nodded in agreement.

Just then Billy burst out of the trailer in a panic. "Melvin's gone," he declared urgently.

"What the hell do you mean he's gone? He's in the goddamn trailer and the back door is blocked by boxes of shit. Maybe he snuck out to take a piss. Let's find him," I said. The trailer had no plumbing. I wasn't afraid or too worried at this point.

Oddly, Jeff didn't notice all the urgent raised voices. He was still fixated on the lights in the trees. He'd picked up his rifle and walked about fifty yards into the field toward the tree line. I yelled, "Hey Jeff, we lost Melvin, give us a hand!" He had to have heard me, but he didn't respond or even turn around.

Billy ran down to check the truck and I walked toward the out-house. We were both calling out for Melvin as we went.

That's when the fright set in. At least for me. It's difficult to describe, but after a few years as a firefighter you learn to trust your gut. That nose for danger saved my life more than a few times when fighting fires. "Trust your senses and listen," I whispered under my breath. I had those goosebumps and felt my heart racing.

Something was just off, not right. I got to the outhouse and reached for the wooden door handle, calling out, "Hey Mel, you I there?" I recall the feel and texture of the wood to my fingers.

The next thing I knew I was in the trailer in the recliner. I heard Jeff's voice and opened my eyes to see the yellowed drop panel ceiling of the old trailer. It was early dawn. I sat up; Melvin was on the couch with a sheet pulled up to his neck.

Jeff nodded at me and walked over to the couch. I think we both had the same fear. Jeff kicked the sofa with his foot a couple times, "Hey, old man, you alright?"

Melvin stirred and then sat up and asked, "How was the pig?"

"Good question," said Jeff. We rushed outside to the fire pit. Jeff's pig was burnt to cinders on the bottom and an uncooked, ugly grey on top. It was garbage. The embers were cold. Without another word said we went back inside. Billy was up now, but kind of out of it, struggling to make coffee.

Jeff announced, "Hey guys, I say we head home. Any objections?"

There were none. Afterall, it was his trailer. I asked Jeff what he wanted to do with the pig carcass.

He said, "Leave it for the coyotes, I don't give a damn." So be it.

We started loading my truck. That took maybe 30 minutes and we were back on the road. In my head, I kept going over and over the facts from that night. Where the hell did Mell go? Was he in the outhouse? How did I end up inside the trailer at sunrise? We'd all had a couple beers. I mean, it was a "boys' night out." But no one was drunk, I swear to God.

Billy sat next to me in the truck and played with the radio. Jeff and Melvin were both in the backseat and slept the entire way home. Billy and I both admitted we felt like we were coming down with the flu.

There was little to no conversation. I don't get it. I felt angry at Melvin for the disappearing act. I felt angry at Jeff for walking out of camp toward what could have been armed poachers and Billy for being so damn useless. But I didn't want to confront anyone. I didn't even want to discuss it. Everyone else was in the same frame of mind.

We were back at the firehouse on Tuesday afternoon to begin our shift. Tom joined us full of enthusiasm and questions about how the big hunting trip went. His questions just made us uncomfortable. No one wanted to talk about it. I just wanted to forget about it.

Then Tom asked, "Why'd you guys come home two days early?"

Jeff went off on him, "If you weren't under your old lady's thumb you could have been with us. It just wasn't a good hunt. Get it? Now give it a rest will you."

The gang of five never got together socially again. I asked to be moved to a different shift. Billy moved to another duty station on the other side of town for a year. Melvin retired early for medical reasons. He was dead from a heart attack two years later. Billy opened a successful barbeque restaurant a couple years later and left the fire service. Tom split up with his wife and moved to Little Rock, Arkansas where he was picked up as a paramedic serving the city. I left the fire house three years later and went into the concrete business with my brother-in-law. That was a good move for me and my family.

We never faced it. The nightmares began a month later. We slept at the firehouse. When one of us woke up screaming everyone knew it. We all took our turn.

My dreams are so peculiar. Even after all these years they're still vivid and always the same. It's odd that nothing particularly frightening happens in them. But they all take place at Jeff's hunting camp. Usually beginning with a frantic search for Mell, ending with me seeing what looks like hooded figures crossing the field in our direction and Jeff walking out as if to greet them. The lights are always in the background illuminating the woods. I have trouble waking up and screaming is the only way to break out of it. It's embarrassing in the firehouse and it scares the hell out of my girlfriend at home.

About six years later my girlfriend and I dropped by Billy's restaurant for some barbecued brisket. It was my first time there. Billy was in the kitchen and I asked our server to please let him know an old friend was here. As our food came out, Billy followed in his chef's *apron. He asked the waitress to bring him a cold bottle of Shiner beer. We shook hands and I introduced Sarah. He pulled up a chair. I complimented him on his restaurant and said the brisket was phenomenal. He thanked me and was obviously proud of his restaurant.*

We made small talk. The last time I saw Billy may have been Mel's funeral. I asked him, "Billy, what happened to Mel that night in Jeff's hunting camp?"

Billy looked stunned by the question. "I don't know." Then he paused and asked me, "Still having the dreams?"

I admitted, "Yeah, now and then."

"Me too, enjoy your meal and come back and see us," Billy said, shaking my hand. He knew I wouldn't be back.

ANALYSIS

There is a legal term that fits here nicely, it's "Res Ipsa Loquiter," or *the thing speaks for itself.* Without competent hypnotherapy I doubt if we'll ever know any more details. If Garrett does seek regression, he promised to call me with the results. I note that Garrett began his correspondence with admitting to childhood experiences as well. He declined to discuss them.

Case #3

Unidentified Submerged Object

Elliot

Boston, Massachusetts

Hi Terry,

My name is Elliot and I'm currently in a Boston suburb retired from the restaurant industry. I recently heard about your book on the pod-cast Mysterious Universe, where they talked at length about your story and their thoughts about it. There were a couple points in the story that definitely got my attention, so I bought your audio book to check it out for myself.

I've had a couple UFO sightings in my life. The most dramatic happened when I was in the US Navy stationed out of San Diego in 1955. I was onboard a ship, I won't name it, and it doesn't matter. We were headed for the South Pacific because of some secret nuclear testing. I worked in the galley, nothing glamorous. And the mission had nothing to do with me. My job was to feed people.

We were at sea on our third night out of port. It was about 2:00 AM and I was making sandwiches for the guys on watch when I heard the klaxon sound "general quarters." That means every man to his post. You might think of it as battle stations. It's the highest alert status.

I dropped my apron and ran to my duty station which was top-side where I had a decent view of the sky toward the stern. It was a crystal clear night with a three quarter moon made visibility decent, especially when your eyes grew accustomed. The sea was calm, like glass.

I was with a guy named Tony from Florida and we were sneaking a smoke when both of us saw a silver, cigar-shaped object surface about 100 yards off our port side. We thought it was a submarine of some kind. The odd thing is, it never broke a wave when it surfaced. How does that happen? We were probably doing 20 knots and this thing paced us for a couple minutes. Then it lifted out of the water and shot out of sight in an almost vertical climb while still oriented horizontally, and it never broke a wave as it left the surface of the sea.

We stayed at our station for about an hour until the XO [Executive Officer] grabbed all us guys who were topside and took us to a briefing room where we sat for about 45 minutes in silence. Finally, the XO came in with two guys in suits. He had a manila folder and passed around a piece of paper to every man. He explained it was an "NDA" or non-disclosure agreement. We were ordered to read it and if any man didn't understand it, he was to raise his hand. A few people did and the XO explained it to them. It was our promise not to ever tell anyone about "what we saw." He never explained what it was that we were supposed to have seen, just that we couldn't talk about whatever it was, with anyone, ever.

The guy in the suit said, "You can't tell your mother, your sweetheart, a shipmate, your priest or your family. If you do, you risk a dishonorable discharge, going to Leavenworth Penitentiary and paying a big fine." At my age now I don't much care what they do to me.

But I still want to keep my identity anonymous. I know better than to poke a bear.

Then we formed up in single file. One by one, we showed our military I.D., and he watched each one of us sign this document. We didn't get a copy. After we signed, we moved to the next table. There, they made us all empty our pockets and we were frisked. We figured they were looking for anyone who may have had a camera with them. No one carried a damn camera. When we got finished the XO gave us a harsh warning. We were ordered, "No scuttlebutt!" Scuttlebutt means swapping rumors with other sailors.

I found out later that the guy in the suit got to us by helicopter. I was told by someone who was on watch at the time and saw it land. He said two guys in suits got out and were met by the XO.

We were part of a task force, so the helicopter could have come from another ship. That could explain how it got there so fast. It was just out of place. There was a lot of stuff going on with the nuclear testing which meant all kinds of crazy secret stuff, so who knows.

Below and at the bow of the ship is what's known as the "radar hut." I had a buddy who was the chief radar man onboard. We were friends and we'd have a few cold beers together on shore now and then. I found out an hour later that my friend wasn't aboard anymore! He went in that chopper with the suit guys. I got that from someone else on board that witnessed him leave with a leather satchel bag. I was told they cleaned out his bunk and locked up his personal possessions. I never saw my friend again. If he was onboard, he would have starved to death because he never visited the mess hall again.

ANALYSIS

I'd heard of unidentified submersible objects (USOs) a few years back. It's a fairly recent phenomenon. Maybe it's a very old phenomena not often discussed. The US Navy seems to have taken the forefront in UFO sightings since the December 17, 2017 disclosure of the "tic tac' objects encountered by the entire Nimitz Carrier Group in 2004. That *New York Times* piece by Leslie Kean should have been the story of the century.

The latest news in the UFO/USO community was the December 2020 disclosure by a retired Israeli general, former defense minister and respected academic, Haim Eshed, that the United States and Israel have been in contact with ETs representing a "galactic federation." According to Haim, former President Donald Trump had planned a disclosure to coincide with the 2020 presidential election. That plan was cancelled when ETs emissaries advised that "humanity was not ready to accept their existence." They expressed the need for the global community to expand its consciousness before making an announcement that could have a global impact with possible unforeseen consequences.

Eshed also shared that we have bases on Mars currently as well as the moon. These bases are manned by both human and extraterrestrial personnel working in unison.

The story was carried by the Jerusalem Post, the New York Post, NBC news and others, but saw little coverage otherwise. The link to the Jerusalem Post December 8, 2020 article is here:

https://www.jpost.com/omg/former-israeli-space-security-chief-says-aliens-exist-humanity-not-ready-651405

Oddly, the United States Navy acknowledged our F-18 carrier fighter pilots, the most elite pilots in our armed forces, saw objects that were unidentifiable and outflew them at every turn, defying the laws of Newtonian physics. No one seems too interested.

Case #4

Bring in the Clowns

Roger

Denver, Colorado

Hello Terry,

I just listened to you being interviewed and thoroughly enjoyed it. A few points really resonated with me and I thought I'd share my experience. Some of this sounds outrageous I know.

I grew up in a good home in the Denver area. My dad was an engineer and my mother a CPA. My dad had some wartime experiences as an officer. He never spoke about it, even to this day aside from some superficial acknowledgements. I'm convinced he suffered from PTSD. He would occasionally wake up screaming like you. In your book you talk about being afraid of the four monkeys that would visit you at night. For me, it was clowns. I was afraid they would kidnap me from my bed, these clowns seemed non-threatening at times and I wondered if they were dreams. But I know. I think I went with them, too.

We always had a strange home life in terms of "presence." A strong, early memory of mine is when I was about four or five and I was being tickled in bed. The thing was, there was no one visible. Around that time, I developed a tremendous fear of clowns, deformed people, and people with mental disorders such as down's syndrome. I also could not sleep with my head out of the covers and had a fear of sickness vomiting, and war. While the clown fear eventually faded, the

162

fear of the handicapped, both mentally and physically, did not. My parents would have to check a store before I went in to make sure it was "all clear" before I could enter.

Years went on and I had various anxieties and hang-ups, but then, around the age of 17 or 18, I started to develop a debilitating anxiety where I would have to pull my car over on the side of the highway, pop the hood, and pretend I was checking out an engine problem simply because I could not tolerate being "trapped" any longer. I could barely drive down streets with no shoulders, planes were out the question, a high floor of a building, classrooms where there was a lecture, movie theaters, meetings, etc. Any situation where I could not leave 100% on my own terns.

I would drink a good bit in the evenings, was a chain-smoker at the time. I have a tendency towards compulsion.

Around the year 2012 I saw, what I believe, were two UFOs. I was out in the evening and for some reason, I decided to look to the sky and of all the lights up there, I locked in on one. After a few seconds of staring the stationary light just flew off at an incredible speed and then disappeared.

This happened two more times. Around that same time, a friend called me saying a light in the sky was following her in the car. She is not one for UFO talk but the light frightened her and after a while of following, it just shot off. Around this time, I had a terrible fear of the night. Of something coming through the door, something being "there."

A few years later, I was getting a better handle on my anxieties and was working on the top floor of a high-rise. The office was all windows and had beautiful views.

I was looking out the window one late afternoon, and right outside the window, a few feet from me, was this silver "blob." It was not a shape so to speak, the best way I can describe it is that it looked as if it was made of tin foil over putty that moved and undulated. It hovered outside the window and then slowly made its way around the corner of the building and then, I think, it disappeared. I remember a pleasant feeling coming over me. A moment of calm instead of the usual anxiety and fear I seemed to live with.

Since then, aside from dreams and a lot of sleep paralysis, I had not experienced anything out of the ordinary until last year. I was walking with my daughter one Sunday; we were going to meet my wife for brunch. An Asian man stopped me and my daughter. He had a friendly disposition and was well put together, so I heard him out. He said, "Your daughter is very special. Her eyes, it was in her eyes." Then he went on about there was "many ships in the sky right now." After a minute or two, he carried on with his walk. While writing that last statement, my eyes welled up, she is special.

Best regards, Roger

ANALYSIS

Roger's admitted OCD behavior resonates with me. I maintain my assertion that having an encounter with these things changes us. I think there's a difference in seeing a silver disc dart across the sky and something more intimate.

I thought it was curious that an Asian man happened to stop them on a busy street and begin a conversation. Unfortunately, I am still uneasy around Asian women because of my childhood events. But I'd welcome such an encounter, especially in a public venue.

In 2007, my wife and I were in Chicago for business. We were enjoying the downtown area browsing a bookstore. As usual, I was looking at books on the half-price rack. A shabbily dressed African American woman in her 60s walked over to me. Looking over her reading glasses, she said, "I know you."

Politely, I asked, "Where have we met?"

She said, "You're one they take too, they took you when you were a little boy."

She smiled, turned and headed for the front door. The store was packed with shoppers. By the time I found my wife the lady was gone. I would have given anything to have thought quickly and offered her a cup of coffee for the chance to ask a question or two.

Like the four little monkeys that plagued my sleep at age eight, Roger was tormented by clowns, just like my cousin Gerald. What a shame my cousin is not here for the two of them to speak.

I can understand a child's fear of being taken away against their will. I have no doubt they intentionally chose to appear to me as circus monkeys. They came into my room in the guise of four monkeys

165

because the ETs somehow knew that was the most benign form to assume for me. I recall saying, "They were kind of funny at first." They appeared in a way I found less intimidating, almost comical.

If children all over the world saw the same grey figures without their masks the phenomena might receive the attention it deserves. But abusers are too clever to allow that to happen.

My family did not believe my story about what I called, "The monkeymen." My cousin Gerald's story is coming up. Poor Gerald, his family dynamics were far worse. They considered it a spiritual issue and placed the onus on poor Gerald in front of the entire congregation to rid himself of these demons. Riddled with guilt, Gerald saw the issue as a problem of his own making, a defect in his faith, a failing in his character. His fault was laid bare before his entire community.

The monkeys I saw all wore the same white mask to disguise their faces, similar to the clowns Gerald encountered. I wonder why. I remember it was like a paper plate with holes cut for large yellow eyes. They all had the same large yellow eyes. Gerald described the clowns he saw as having yellow eyes. I wish I had thought to ask Roger what color his visitors' eyes were.

As I asked earlier, isn't it amazing so many people can have clear and lucid memories of dreams and experiences from age four, sometimes younger? Usually, it's events of a paranormal nature that tend to stick with us for a lifetime. It is odd I can recall the monkeymen so vividly but cannot remember the Christmases and birthday parties.

Roger's story is remarkably like my own discomfort in the company of Asian women, store mannequins, and burn victims. Roger tells us about his fear of "destruction," while Elliot described a fear of war. I have had similar nightmares and intrusive thoughts about a post-apocalyptic world.

It amazes me that many people who see them as children will then encounter them for life. Other people live an entire lifetime and never see a thing. I believe they intentionally show themselves to some people and hide from the rest. In the 45 years of my marriage there were two occasions where I saw a silver disc in the sky, clearly a classic UFO. My wife did not see it. She could not see it. This was in the days before cell phones with cameras in our pockets.

That "pleasant feeling" again. Roger experienced that same semi-sedated feeling I felt and described in my book while at Devil's Den State Park in 1977. I also remember that feeling from age 11 when I saw a silver disc outside my second story bedroom window in the middle of the night. No fear or panic, I felt oddly satisfied and calm. I was almost smug knowing that seeing a disc above me three years earlier could have been a "one on." But seeing the same thing twice meant they were there to see me and be seen. Roger stated with uncertainty, *"I think the UFO disappeared."* This statement underscores my assertion that they control our emotions, perceptions, and memory. Just as two people witnessing the same event may see different things, we see what they want us to see.

Case #5

The Carnival Ride

Julia

Lake St. Charles, Louisiana

Julia's story is a bit unusual. That is why I chose to present it as mostly a narrative. What began with an occasional email dialogue eventually led to a couple exceptionally long telephone calls and an in-person meeting, so I had a great deal of facts to work with to explain her story. Julia's life is the best documented and most compelling story I have received to date. I hope you agree.

One morning while pouring over the accumulated emails from the previous day, I landed on an email from a 69-year-old nurse anesthetist originally from Oklahoma who began with the usual disclaimer, *"Now, I know this will sound a bit crazy."*

I wanted to tell her "Julia, I've heard everything, disclaimers and apologies aren't necessary."

She made her career as a nurse anesthetist and dealt with the greatest mystery of all, human consciousness. I verified her credentials through the Louisiana Nursing Board online. Then I refilled my coffee and dove deeper into her story.

It is a fact that while under anesthesia you do not dream. It is just "lights out." You wake up in recovery and if everything had gone as planned you have no memory at all of the indignities your body just

168

suffered at the hands of the steel scalpel and being stitched back together with needle and thread.

All you can recall was a warm pleasant flush as the anesthetist pushed the plunger of a syringe, injecting a milky liquid into your IV tubing. What followed was darkness and then the light of the recovery room. I was determined to discuss the topic of consciousness with Julia if given the opportunity. My present task was to read, process, and document the incredible story she told. I believe every word of what she experienced.

I was struck by her grasp of English grammar and had the feeling a great deal of thought and more than a few tears were part of her emails. Most of the emails I receive are from people in their 40s through 80s. I tend to take note of demographics because I think, since I've unwittingly found myself now in the role of an investigator, these things are important.

Like myself, people tend to hold these stories close to their vest until their later years, when criticism from their peers is no longer an issue. Julia acknowledged that hospital administrators and probably half the medical staff would not believe her experience or appreciate her story becoming public.

Julia's case is the best in my opinion because she is so credible, and her story is amazing. In ways, it is like the "Christmas store" in Case #1. Her story is the result of a month-long exchange of email correspondence, no less than four telephone conversation and finally a meeting in person at a breakfast restaurant.

We split the distance in driving and met in Texarkana, where Julia could visit a family member. I had never been to Texarkana. It is where my mother was born in 1924. Because Julia's story is an amazing and heartbreaking saga, I really thought it would be worth the drive. We are both retired so why not take a road trip? It is a great pleasure to share her story with you.

Julia told me about life in rural Oklahoma 60 years ago when she was a little girl. Her parents, like mine, were originally farm people before moving to the city seeking work in thriving factories frantically producing arms for the second world war. Most stayed for the post-war boom.

She described the little cottage home where she grew up and the pink room that she shared with her younger sister Mollie. When Mollie was seven and Julia was nine the family went to visit their maternal grandparents in rural Oklahoma. It was an annual summer vacation visit and they always looked forward to the two-week trip.

Her grandparents lived on the family farm where their mother was raised. It was blessed with a single oil well. It supplemented the family income nicely and insured a college education for Julia and Mollie. She and her sister loved their grandparents very much. She described them as fun, doting and affectionate. Usually, during these visits there was card-playing and gossip among the adults while the girls played outside in the massive front yard until the yellow porch light signaled it was time for a bath and then bed.

There was a long driveway up to the farmhouse and a split-rail fence enclosing the manicured front yard. It was home to a massive oak tree in the middle and a painted tractor tire cut to resemble a flower, painted white, filled with soil and dozens of bright purple gladiolas.

There was a 10-foot-high mound of dirt or berm that ran 100 yards along the back of the house. The top served as a roadway for the tractor. The mound of dirt worked as a wall that separated the front yard with the house from the back. Behind the berm is where outbuildings and the farm implements were located. There was a barn, some pigs in a pen, tractor, and farm machinery.

There was also a farm pond in the back that represented what is known in the law as an "attractive nuisance." A magnet for young children. A lethal danger for the unwary. Like an unguarded, unfenced swimming pool it was a drowning hazard. At a depth of eight feet it would be more than sufficient to swallow both girls in its murky water that looked like chocolate milk.

Both girls knew the rules and had just that year been allowed to play in the yard without direct adult supervision because of their exemplary behavior. They knew the rules and obeyed. This was Julia's ninth summer at Grandpa Jeb's, the seventh for young Mollie.

Mollie's story began like so many other tragedies. This day would build a metaphorical berm that would separate two little girls for a lifetime. But it was a beautiful summer day, and the flower garden was alive with butterflies the girls chased until exhausted.

After a trip to the house for a cold drink they sat at the base of the berm and discussed what to play next. Tag was out of the question since they were both tired from chasing butterflies that always evaded their grasp. Julia described their mood as happy, laughing at silly things and joking about how fat grandma had become.

As their snickering and laughter died down, Julia asked, "Mollie, do you hear that?"

Mollie cocked her head and listened. After a few seconds, her face lit up and the girls said in unison, "It's a circus!" The gentle breeze flowing over the berm carried the unmistakable sound of a calliope, a signature circus musical instrument of the day. Calliopes were usually steam powered and played like a piano, each note was formed by forcing steam through long whistles of varying lengths and diameters like a church organ. It has a distinctive sound that was an icon of the traveling circuses.

The circus was a huge amusement for entertainment-starved farm folks before the mass migration to cities in World War II and the availability of motion pictures and televisions. Circuses traveled a circuit by train from city to city with carnival type rides, exotic animals, unwinnable 5¢ challenges for an opportunity to win a sawdust-stuffed bear, enjoy cotton candy, and see the clowns.

Mollie asked excitedly, "Can we go? Oh, please Julia let's go!"

Being the elder and in charge, Julia thought for a moment and noted the sound was not as loud now. She felt it her duty to be the big sister and keep her younger sibling safe.

"No," Julia said. "Maybe they're on a train or just passing through? I think we better ask Grandpa Jeb first. We can't go behind the house; you know the rules Mollie."

But Mollie pleaded. With a well-crafted argument, Mollie quickly sought a loophole in the rule that would make any lawyer proud.

Mollie suggested, "Well Julia, we can't go over the berm, but we could stand on top of it and see if there really is a circus first. Then we can run get Grandpa."

The two girls smiled at one another and scampered up the steep grass covered mound till they reached the summit. From the roadway on top of the berm they had a magnificent view. What they saw below them was unbelievable.

To the left of the farm pond there was a merry-go-round. Not just any ride from a traveling circus. This was something incredible the likes of which they had never seen. As they drank in the scene with their eyes the music began again. It was louder now, and the tempo was faster too.

Julia felt the need to add a second disclaimer to her story at this point, "*Mr. Lovelace, I know this sounds crazy, but this thing was un-believably big. It was three times as big as any merry-go-round I had ever seen, and the horses were not saddled and weren't on poles either. They looked like they were alive. There were a million multicolored lights all over this thing. Also, it was spinning way too fast, alarmingly fast. Too fast for anyone to get on or get off. The music was louder now* too, and this merry-go-round wasn't even sitting on the ground! It was hovering above the ground by three feet or more."

I had to interrupt at this point to ask, "How do you know it wasn't sitting on the ground?"

Because, Julia said, "*I clearly remember it cast a perfectly round shadow underneath as it was about noon.*"

Then she said something that resonated with me. Something that may well resonate with you too. The point of this exercise is to hear the stories of others and look for the commonalities that validate the sighting.

Julia explained, "*We crossed over and sat down in the grass on the other side of the berm. We lay back to just watch. I remember a feeling of deep contentment, almost a numbness and euphoria combined.*"

She explained, "*We felt no compulsion to get near it, but the music and seeing this thing spin was hypnotic. There was a spellbinding quality to the experience. We held hands, laid back and listened as the music became louder. At some point we must have lost consciousness. I doubt that we fell asleep.*"

But she added, "*There is no way we fell asleep. While watching and listening we had no way to know what was going on back at the farmhouse.*"

According to relatives, what was "going on back at the farmhouse" began with calling the girls for lunch. Grandma called first and

174

was soon joined by Mom. When the girls did not come and could not be seen from the porch, the women panicked.

Coincidentally, a car made a wrong turn down their long driveway about this time. It parked for a moment and made a U-turn on the gravel drive and drove away. The two women on the porch never saw the car approach or make a U-turn, they only saw it as it was driving away, headed back to the main road.

That innocent mistake led to full blown panic when the two women connected the unrelated scenarios and assumed the girls had been taken by persons unknown in the car.

Grandpa Jeb and the girls' dad, accompanied by Grandpa's dogs, spread out and searched the front and backyard, including the barn while the two women were explaining to the Sheriff what they had just seen. They saw the pond water looked undisturbed, but both men knew that meant little assurance of anything.

Two sheriff's deputies arrived in 10 minutes along with friends from a neighboring farm to assist with the search. Julia's grandparents were well-known in the community and highly-respected. Word that the girls were missing spread through the little community like a prairie fire.

The car that had made the U-turn in the driveway was parked at a neighboring farm two miles away. It was an innocent wrong turn by visitors. The couple in the car claimed they never saw the girls and had never been closer than about 50 yards to the grandparents' home. The search efforts shifted back to the farm. It was now nearly 2:30 PM and the girls had been missing for an hour and a half or more.

Later, Julia learned from her mother, "A deputy pulled Grandpa aside and told him, 'Jeb, I've got some help and a couple dogs on the way. I've also got two men coming to help with a johnboat and poles, just in case.'"

Grandpa knew what that implied, and he broke down. The deputy suggested he pull himself together and "get the women inside." There were a dozen people at the farm to help with the search by this time.

By 4:30 PM there was a boat on the pond. Two strong men with long poles stirred the water, dredging the bottom to bring to the surface any small bodies that may be lifelessly afloat between the pond's bottom and middle, afloat by natural buoyancy. Neither girl could swim.

"These men have done this work before," said Grandma solemnly, confessing their faces betrayed the dismal task they faced that hot afternoon. The grandparents watched and cried according to what Julia was told afterward.

Soon, even more help arrived from the church and the VFW hall. They fanned out along a tree line that separated the homestead from the fields. The corn was high and if the girls were in the field and lost, the search could go on into the evening.

Then the discovery was made, and the call rang out from one of the boatmen, "We gottum Jeb! We gottum both!"

All the adults rushed from the front yard over the berm at a run. And there they lay, Julia and Mollie on the backside of the berm looking deeply asleep. They were lying in the grass, still holding hands and dry as a bone. They soon stirred from the excitement around them and woke up, confused as to why all the commotion.

Julia explained. *"Later, they told me that one of the men in the boat was looking in our direction and claimed he didn't see us. He had looked away for a moment. When he looked up again, he saw us lying in the grass. According to him we were just 'suddenly there.'"*

According to her mother, the boatman told Grandpa Jeb, "They wasn't there one minute, and the next minute they were there on the grass. No one can understand it," he said, "But no one gave a damn neither!"

It was now 5:00 PM and the girls had been missing for four hours at a minimum. Neither had the slightest memory of anything that may have happened to them during the hours they were missing. Julia said, "It's a blank slate." Their belief was that they simply fell asleep.

Initially, Julia and Mollie both felt that they had just fallen asleep and now faced a spanking for crossing the berm. The girls were shocked when they received an outpouring of loving kindness, along with a stern warning from their grandma, "Don't you girls ever scare Grandma like that again or I'll whip the tar out of both of you!"

Julia said something else that hit home with me. She said that except for a couple rare exceptions, the family never spoke about the incident afterward. Ever.

Also. from that day forward *"they were different little girls,"* according to Julia. Their relationship was different in ways Julia could not articulate in a phone call. She said it was a turning point in their lives and she and Mollie, while they always loved one another as sisters, were never as close, never playmates again except on rare occasions. No more chasing butterflies.

Their parents noted a marked change in the girls' behavior. They were both more serious and less playful than before this all happened.

Historically, Julia had marginal grades in math since second grade. She played softball and was a tomboy, preferring to play outside rather than do her homework. Her grammar skills were acceptable, as were history and other subjects, but math had plagued her young academic life since first grade. It baffled her when it unexpectedly improved.

When the school year began again in late August, Julia grudgingly pulled out her basic arithmetic book and found that she understood the concept of fractions almost effortlessly. She excelled in all subjects and did her homework without coercion.

Her parents told Julia she was "like a little adult." She enjoyed their praise and said she felt like a grown up.

Mollie on the other hand, was sullen and withdrawn. It was an abrupt change in her usually carefree and outgoing personality. She demanded a "room of her own," and when the facts were explained that the house did not have a third bedroom, she became uncharacteristically resentful.

According to Julia, *"Molly lost her laugh. She was never the same either. For some reason I do not understand. I grew uncomfortable around Mollie, my own sister. And I could not wrap my head around it. It was like we became strangers almost. Oh sure, we loved each other on a familial level, and even shared some secrets occasionally, but things were different between us. Mollie had problems in school and could be brooding and withdrawn. I just do not get it. We could never talk about what happened at Grandpa Jeb's that summer day, almost never. For some reason, the both of us considered it off limits."*

Julia skipped their adolescent years. She said Mollie married young and had a family right away. Julia's grades took her to university where she excelled in nursing school. Her math skills secured her a place in a nurse anesthetist program and she had a fulfilling and lucrative career in medicine. Her only regret? That she did not pursue an MD instead of her RN. She admitted she had underestimated her ability.

In her third email to me Julia explained that five years earlier, Mollie had been diagnosed with terminal breast cancer. Separated by some distance, Julia took time from work using the Family Medical Leave Act to spend time with Mollie toward the end. Mollie moved from Kentucky to Louisiana to be closer to Julia as she entered hospice care. Mollie was estranged from her children and the three men who had fathered her children.

179

Julia said she was by her bedside providing loving support and palliative care, offering generous pain medication to ensure her comfort. Mollie mostly refused the pain medication and the two of them typically sat in uncomfortable silence. Julia felt conflicted. Mollie did not want to die alone but did not want to engage her sister either.

Julia said, *"It was clear she was going to pass soon. I held her hand. I think it was the first time I held her hand like that since we were at the farm. She was lucid and still refused morphine. I felt the time was right to ask, so I pulled myself together and asked her, 'Mollie, would you like to talk about what happened that day at Grandpa and Grandma's house?'"*

Sadly, Julia said, *"Mollie turned her face toward the wall and withdrew her hand. She held clenched fists under her chin and angrily said, 'No!' She passed a few hours later."*

I asked Julia to please tell me about her dreams and tell me what she thinks really happened that afternoon at the farmhouse. She promised she would give it some thought and compose something. I asked her permission to share her story and she agreed, so long as I not disclose her identity. I kept my promise. The following is the correspondence Julia drafted that explains what she thinks happened after years of nightmares and assorted phobias. It is a compelling story and I'll present it in her own words without commentary.

In an emotional final email, Julia explained the back story and draws some conclusions.

Dear Terry,

I've been thinking about your questions and how to tell this story in a way that will make sense for your readers. I'll start with the nightmares. Mollie had them too but would not talk about them until one day when we were in our 30s, when I told her about two recurring dreams that were making me crazy. This was 25 years after they took us. I don't have a contemporaneous memory of events. I have no memories that did not originate in nightmares.

I told Mollie I dreamt we were kids again, back at Grandpa Jeb's. I remember looking at the carousel and feeling trance-like. I was on autopilot. They took us. I can see them as shadow people at first, then they became solid. They took our clothes off and a thing that looked like a white computer monitor came down from the ceiling and spun around me, it was like having a CAT scan. It had a clinical feel.

There were six-foot tall beings and the little ones they call greys. The taller ones were in control. I kept hearing a voice in my head, telepathically, I guess. It told me, "Don't be afraid, we won't hurt you." I think the voice was female, but it's hard to say.

In the second dream, I was lying on a table and they stuck a stainless-steel probe of some kind up my nose. It hurt like the dickens and I heard an audible "crack." This was in a dream, so I never felt the pain, I just remembered or imagined it. In the same dream I saw my legs being spread and they did something down there. It hurt, a lot too. I knew right then that I'd never be able to have children. That's a weird premonition for a nine-year-old. It turned out to be correct.

As I was telling this story to Mollie, she looked at me in aston-ishment. She confessed we shared nearly the same dream. I'm sure she discussed this with me only out of shock and surprise. But she spoke openly and shared a little of her story this once. It was the only time.

In a rare moment of openness Mollie told me about her night-mare, "they did something to me 'down there' too. But they also did something through my eye that hurt like hell. They stuck something like a silver knitting needle in my eye near the bridge of my nose. I screamed 'No, it's too big.' It hurt so much I thought I'd lose my mind. Maybe I did, Julia. Maybe I did way back then. They took something else from me too. I know they took my virginity. They took away my innocence. I was just a child. We were children then."

We both cried. It was the only time we laid bare our souls to each other in 50 years. I wish I could explain the guilt I felt afterward. What should have been a shared moment of discovery turned sour. I had a bout of depression afterward, and Mollie broke off all contact for a while. I still take prescription antidepressants.

Mollie was diagnosed in her early 20s as having bi-polar dis-order and impulse control issues. She had a string of failed marriages and the dad's got custody of her three children. I never had a chance to get to know them. Mollie would never let me into her life. Our parents only saw the kids a few times.

Mollie's life was one of excess in everything including pain medication after a questionable back injury and a workers' compensa-tion claim. Thank God she married good men, but she could not hold

182

onto a relationship. She was afraid to let anyone in. She distanced her-
self from the family and no one knows why, except me. I know because
I understand a little about the emotions involved.

Mom made the connection between the farmhouse and the
changes in both of us. It's hard to judge changes in yourself, but I felt
different after it happened. I know what we saw was no carnival ride.
It was a goddamn spaceship and that's no lie. Over the years I saw it
change in my dreams. It lost the horses and the lights changed. Those
dreams scare the hell out of me.

You know I've never married, but I've had a close partner for
many years, and we have our dogs. I feel lucky to have had a full life.
I've had a good life but whenever I allow myself to think about the farm
and what happened in the four hours when we were missing, I know I
won't sleep so well for a few nights.

I had a spell where I had a shot of tequila before bed in the
evening. I also had a painful shoulder injury, a torn rotator cuff from
tennis. I embraced it. The pain gave me an excuse to pop a few Darvon
legitimately for pain. Conveniently, they were the only semi narcotic
medication I could take that wouldn't be missed from the medication
cart. It was discontinued ten years ago and that was the end of it.

I admit I stole a Fentanyl patch once or twice at the expense of
patients in pain, substituting a used patch for one I could take home.
But they checked the serial numbers, so I was fortunate to get away
with it. I regret the pain those poor patients endured so I could get a
high and have a good night's rest.

Suffice to say, in a few years I was spiraling out of control. I had missed some work and my supervising doc had a talk with me. I guess he smelled alcohol on my breath from the previous evening before we went into the OR for an emergency surgery. Even with our masks on. I'm pretty sure I slurred my speech too.

He could have thrown me out of the OR, but at the time there was no one else on such short notice. This was a small community hospital with one anesthetist, me and a single resident at the time.

The patient had a good outcome. I was the on-call anesthetist, but it was rare in our little community that anything happened. It was an irresponsible thing to do.

My chief gave me an ultimatum, talk to someone and get it together or I'd lose my job. That was a wake-up call. We had a program for medical staff that allowed us to seek help through a third-party referral service at no cost and it was confidential. I made an appointment to see a counselor. I was blessed that my partner was supportive without being enabling.

I saw this counselor about a dozen times, and it was helpful. At least so I thought. To a point anyway. We had discussed what happened at the farm. I spoke candidly. He did not appear surprised when I told him about the traumatic event in my life when I was nine. I shared the nightmares too and told him Mollie admitted to having the same dreams.

He knew my gender orientation was toward the same sex. I do not think I make that a secret. I understand science and use it every day. But the interpretation of psychological test results that can see into a person's psyche seems subjective to me.

When I asked him if these tests were reliable, he was quick to point out that they have been "recognized as valid for 50 years." He claimed answers to series of yes-or-no questions can reveal much about a person. But how does he know if the patient's answers are even truthful? How is it possible to see three different psychiatrists and get three different diagnosis?

During our last session he told me I needed to accept the most likely explanation. I asked him to please explain.

He commented arrogantly, "Occam's Razor."

I still did not understand.

He said, "The most obvious answer is usually the correct choice. You girls fantasized about going to the circus and saw in your own mind's eye an image of a merry-go-round. You may have heard music from a calliope, but not from the backyard. It could have been carried on the wind for miles or have come from a television program inside your grandparents' home. Mollie probably never saw a thing, that is why the two of you could never speak about it. Arguably, it is the real reason. Where did you go for those four hours? Who knows, maybe you were asleep in the barn, I do not see that as important now. Stories can be embellished over years and facts interpreted differently with each retelling."

Indignantly, I asked, "Do you think I'm making this up? For what reason?"

*"No," he said, "I don't believe you intend to deceive anyone."
Then he shocked me to the core, "I think it's possible the story has
changed over the years."*

*Then he paused for a long moment and asked, "Isn't it possible,
Julia, that you took Mollie's virginity that day?"*

*I had trouble putting those words together. I exploded, "You
son of a bitch, go to hell."*

*That was the last counseling session I had with him. He consid-
ered it "a breakthrough." I thought it was crap, he obviously was not
listening. But he cleared me to return to work.*

*Then the nightmares returned with a vengeance. That con-
firmed he was full of shit. Something paranormal happened to me and
Mollie and I will never believe anything else.*

*This is going to sound crazy, but I am just going to say it. You
know, I want to put it out there for your opinion and for other people
too. I think we were kidnapped by aliens. What you called an abduction
in your book. They took us and did God knows what, but it changed us.
It has taken me a lifetime, but I am okay with it now. Mollie's gone; I
do not know how much time I have left; I have significant health problems myself. I am glad I wrote to you because I saw your friend in my
Mollie.*

*This counselor thought this was all a dream or a childhood fan-
tasy. Well bullshit. I know a little about the human mind. I understand
human anatomy and physiology. Those little bastards did something to*

186

Mollie and to me on the cellular level, maybe at the molecular or even the quantum level, who the hell knows. But they changed us.

Mollie knew something about what happened that day. I am sure whatever happened, I never hurt Mollie. I am sure of that. I think they broke her mind and it cost her sanity. After the mental health appointments, I'd had enough. I do not want to have hypnosis to help me remember or recover memories. I do not think memories recovered by hypnosis can be counted on as a reliable record of past events. I have seen it in my practice where people have all kinds of wild delusions under the influence of hypnotic drugs and drugs that have a supposed amnesic effect.

I realize now that I am almost 70 years old that what happened to us was not from this solar system. Maybe not from this dimension. This has been in my face all my life. I think it is time to put it to bed. I don't want to think about it anymore. Mollie is gone and I just want to live in peace.

It was nice of you and your wife to drive over and meet me for breakfast. I think I'm going to sign off. The more I talk about this the harder it gets and the more anxiety I have.

I think I'll try to enjoy semi-retirement, maybe work a day a week or two. We want to travel and see some of the country. I want to forget about this stuff for now. Thanks for returning my emails and taking time to talk to me. Maybe my story will help someone else. Good luck with your writing and may God bless.

Sincerely yours, Julia

Julia passed away in January 2020 from pancreatic cancer. I hope she's found peace.

Case #6

Through the Roof

Tina

London, Ontario Canada

Hello Mr. Lovelace,

First off, I wanted to say that your story was fascinating, and I couldn't put it down. The details you describe and the events that unfolded in your life are incredible, and I hope this email finds you doing well. Parts of your book, however, speak to me on a deeper level, particularly your experiences as a child.

When I was younger, maybe five or six years old, possibly a little older, I would have repeating dreams of "falling" from the sky, face-up, towards my bedroom. I have graphic images of my house and neighborhood from above at nighttime as I fell from the sky towards the corner of the house where my room was located in. I can even remember seeing wood, insulation and the plasterboard ceiling.

This was all before Google Earth existed, so young-me should have had no idea what that imagery above my house looked like, especially in such vivid detail.

I would "pass" through the ceiling and roof and fall onto my bed, often "waking" as I bounced onto my mattress covered in sweat. Most of the time, that was the end of it, and I would eventually fall back to sleep. But I'd be tired the rest of the day.

189

But one time, I woke up from a fall/bounce and saw a face star-ing at me from my doorway. It appeared to be grey/white, though it was dark and only illuminated by my nightlight. I could clearly see two large, dark eyes staring at me (not freakishly large, but big enough I could make them out in the darkness), and a few fingers wrapping themselves around the corner of the door frame. I froze in my bed as me and this thing stared for what felt like an eternity. Slowly, it backed away and moved into the hallway before I could no longer see it at all. It was maybe four feet tall? Or possibly even shorter.

Another similar night I woke to loud "popping" sounds and found my room flooded with a brilliantly bright light. Peering out my window, I saw several figures in my yard standing motionless with a light that seemed brighter than the sun behind them. This popping sound continued, but for some reason I felt unconcerned. I shrugged it off and went back to bed.

When I asked my parents the next day, they said it was most likely neighborhood kids hitting trees with baseball bats in the middle of the night. Odd answer, but okay.

My childhood was filled with bizarre experiences that I cast off as "ghostly" phenomenon, and those around me sensed it too. Close friends and family honestly believed I was haunted but looking back I think it might have been something more. I remember waking to strange figures in my room, shadow figures, hearing voices, etc.

A friend of mine even saw a strange triangular UFO above my neighborhood when he was coming to visit once when we were in our teens. Around that same time, I had a few periods of missing time and developed a severe eating disorder that almost wiped me of my entire childhood memory. But the strangeness remains.

As an adult, the weirdness has died down significantly. But now I suffer with an immune deficiency disease they cannot fully identify. I struggle with keeping on weight (I was chubby for a while, but now I cannot keep my weight above 100) and I suffer from debilitating migraines and full-body aches that slow me down daily. Was this all a side effect of something bizarre that happened to me as a child? I am not sure. But your book hit a few key points that helped connect some dots in my own life.

Tina, London, Ontario

The similarities between our stories are astounding.

ANALYSIS

Poor Tina, another sadly dismissive parental response. Their possible explanation sounds less plausible than a flying saucer.

Tina had that familiar feeling of disinterest and near apathy that sometimes accompany an encounter. At Devil's Den, Toby and I decided to go into our tent and go to sleep while a spacecraft as large as a five-story office building was parked over our heads.

Years earlier, when I was 11 and sound asleep, my bedroom was flooded with flashes of incredibly bright light. I described the light as, "like trying to look at the sun." I opened my eyes to find I was sitting

191

bolt upright in bed. I walked to the window and peered out from curtains and blinds to see a saucer just outside my second story window.

I pulled back the curtain and stuffed it into the blinds, so I could have a hands-free look. There was a flying saucer with colored flashing lights two feet from my bedroom window with a heavy fog or steam underneath.

I remembered the one I saw in the backyard three years earlier. I wondered if this might even be the same craft. With brilliant lights flooding my bedroom I turned away and went back to bed and immediately fell asleep.

The only emotion I can remember is being happy to see the topside. In 1963, I only saw it from below. Other than that, I felt complete disinterest except for a feeling of satisfaction.

No one else in the house saw a thing that night. When I first woke up the next morning it felt like a dream. Then I looked over to my window and saw the curtain tucked into the blinds. Then I remembered everything. It was no dream. Had I not tucked that curtain into the blinds I guess I would have always considered it just a dream.

I had heard stories before of people moving through walls and ceilings. I never imagined I would have an encounter of my own. Much less one I could document. It happened on the early morning of April 16, 2019. I normally woke up about 8:00 AM. This day I awoke at 5:55 AM covered in sweat and gasping for air. Tina in the paragraph above woke in a sweat when she landed back on her bed.

My wife woke and saw I was in distress. I was having trouble getting enough oxygen. I had no chest pain, but the sweating, shortness of breath and cardiac disease history justified a call to 911. My wife called and then took my blood pressure and pulse before the ambulance crew arrived about 10 minutes later. My pulse was tachycardic, 150+ beats per minute. Fast enough that it was difficult for my wife to count with 100% certainty. The blood pressure cuff read 220 over 110. My normal pressure was in the 120/80 range. Thankfully, my blood pressure dropped quickly as did my pulse rate.

By the time we arrived at the hospital it was 160 over 90 and steadily headed back to my normal range. My oxygen saturation was 94% measured by the paramedic's oximeter when they picked me up. I was given oxygen during the 15-minute ride to the hospital. My pulse rate dropped to 90, and thanks to the oxygen my saturation bounced back to 99%. I was no longer starved for air and had stopped sweating.

I had a heart attack in 2005 and had a triple bypass. I had a second in 2011 requiring a stent. I knew the drill: a chest X-ray, EKG and cardiac enzymes. I was admitted to Methodist Hospital in Dallas for observation and hooked to a heart monitor.

An hour later the cardiologist paid me a visit. My vital signs had returned to normal; my chest X-ray was clear. She said the EKG was "unremarkable" when compared to my most recent test at the VA Hospital a year earlier.

She said she had no idea what caused this event. She said they would keep me until 3:00 PM and discharge me if my heart monitor showed a normal rhythm and my vital signs remained stable. I was to speak with my cardiologist at the VA Hospital and be fitted with a halter monitor to check for irregular heartbeats. They found none. I might mention, I do not suffer from atrial fibrillation.

We were home by 4:00 PM and I felt fine. We had dinner that evening and as was my habit, I went for a walk after dinner. I would usually walk a brisk mile and return home. As my feet hit the sidewalk, I pulled out my iPhone 6 and glanced at my health app. As I expected I had walked under 100 steps for the day. But then I saw the "flights of stairs climbed" recorded below the distance walked. I was shocked to see it said I had climbed six flights of stairs that morning.

This is where an explanation is necessary. I sleep with my iPhone in the breast pocket of a tee shirt every night. I put on my earbuds and listen to meditative apps at night. This has been my habit all the way back to the 1990s and my Sony Walkman with headphones.

Why? Because it helps me to fall asleep and keeps out ambient noises. I am spooked at night by random sounds. If I hear a noise, something I cannot identify, I am compelled to grab my pistol and a flashlight and walk through the entire house. I explained the drill earlier: check the doors, check the alarm system, etc. Once the ritual is complete, I can go back to bed and usually fall asleep. If I cut it short, I will feel angst about it and usually get up and complete it. Typical obsessive-compulsive behavior related to my PTSD.

If you look at the screenshot of my iPhone app, you will see the x-y graph moves from left to right to correspond with the passage of time. The vertical plane indicates height, a flight of stairs is in increments of 10 feet up.

I live in a Texas ranch home with a single stair; it is the threshold at my front door. Note that the "flights climbed" are indicated by a single vertical bar to 60 feet at 5:24 AM. That is 31 minutes before I woke up at 5:55 AM. At 5:24 AM I was in my bed and next to my wife asleep.

Normally, if I climbed a few flights of stairs, say to reach the fourth floor of a parking garage, the iPhone's app screen would display a stairstep configuration, with bars going up to indicate the first 10 feet, then the second, third, and finally the fourth. This is because of the passage of time as I reach each landing and begin the next flight. Each flight of stairs represents a journey of 10 feet up.

The single bar on the April 16, 2019 screenshot, according to Apple, indicates that my phone traveled 60 feet "up" between 5:23 and 5:24 AM. If I had stairs in my house, it would have to be a six-story building. There is no way I could climb six flights of stairs in under a minute.

A note about how height is measured in the Apple health app. I assumed it was by change in GPS coordinates in space above ground level. That is not correct. Apple explained that each 10-foot flight of stairs is measured by change in barometric pressure.

Apple ran a diagnostic on my phone to rule out a malfunction. Everything on the phone and the health app was fully functional.

I asked the Apple Store technician what this readout meant. He said, "It indicates your iPhone traveled 60 feet above your location at 5:23 AM on the morning of April 16, 2019. I can't say more than that."

Aside from an abduction, the only possible explanation is that somehow my telephone traveled by itself, say attached to a drone, sixty feet straight up as the screenshot shows. I do not own a drone and would never perpetrate such a ridiculous hoax.

I include medical bills from the Garland Fire Department Ambulance Services and Methodist Hospital. If this were a hoax perpetrated by me, it is an expensive exercise.

Apple Health App dated April 16, 2019 shows six floors of stairs climbed at 5:24 AM. I was in bed asleep until 5:55 AM. My home is a single story Texas Ranch with a single stair being at the front door threshold.

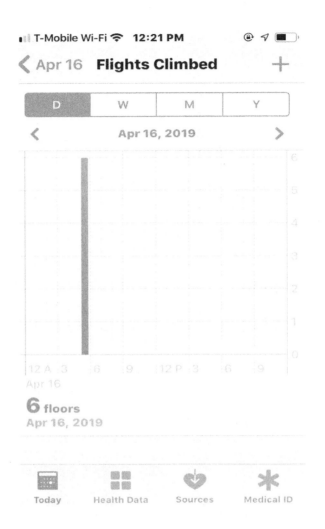

Single vertical bar between 5:23 and 5:24 AM on April 16, 2019. Each flight of stairs represents ten feet. Six flights of stairs represent sixty feet "UP."

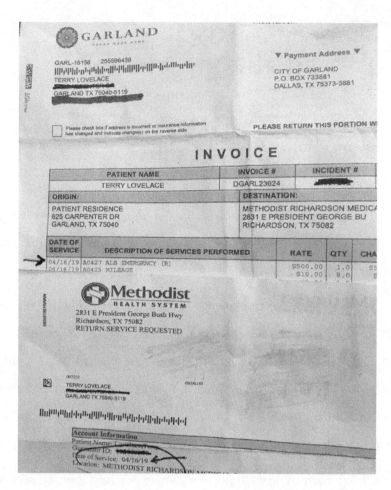

Medical bill from Methodist Hospital showing charges for emergency services dated April 19, 2019.

Case #7

Alcohol and Fear of the Night

Elizabeth

Billings, Montana

Dear Sir,

Thank you for your book! I initially heard about it on my favorite podcast, Mysterious Universe. They did a compelling piece on it and I knew I had to read it. And I loved it.

I share many of the same fears you described. I always imagined I just had some sort of strange nighttime anxiety. Ever since I was maybe four or five, as soon as the sun would start to set, I would be filled with a feeling of fear and doom. I would usually end up crawling in bed with my mom. When I got older, I would sleep in the living room with the television on. I did not like the dark and I didn't like it quiet.

I am a pretty upbeat person during the day, but the nighttime changes me so. I was an alcoholic for many years.

I would start to drink when my kids went to bed and would continue to drink until I was sleepy enough to fall asleep. I must have awfully specific sleeping arrangements, bed against the wall, pillows stacked high on the other side so I can't see if something is there. I was never abused as a kid that I know of. The fear just has always been there as long as I can remember.

I have a fascination about aliens and find myself daydreaming about them all the time, but no memories at all to recount. I guess that is all I have to say. I wish I could get over my nighttime fear. And your book really got me wondering if I had seen or experienced something that had been swept away from my memory.

Thank you for sharing. I appreciate your honesty.

ANALYSIS

It's unthinkable for a parent to drink themselves into oblivion when they have children sleeping in the same home. Elizabeth state's she was never abused as a child. ET can wipe our memories or replace them with screen memories. In Elizabeth's case she has no recollection what happened to her as a young child. It's frightening to consider the possibilities.

Fear of the night is consistent with changes Toby and I both experienced. Fear of sleep and anxiety at sundown is one of the commonalities abductees share. We are vulnerable when we're asleep. The temptation to self-medicate can be overwhelming. It certainly played a role in the death of my friend. Whether we are three or 83, having an intimate encounter with these things changes a person.

Case #8

Why Not Minot?

Benito

Minot, North Dakota

Dear Mr. Lovelace,

I just finished your book and it reminded me of an odd thing that happened when I was a teenager. We have a small ranch near Minot, ND. It's a military town with a large Air Force base with nuclear tipped missiles all over the prairie.

I am the fifth generation to work the family ranch. It has been a tough year for us with the pandemic taking a toll on businesses here. We don't have a lot of COVID deaths compared to New York and other parts of the country, but the packing houses laid off a lot of workers because the virus and it crippled the processing center.

That hurt ranchers. I'm 43 years old now and I've worked the ranch since I was 11. It's mine today and I hope our son will continue with the family business.

My sighting happened when I was 17, me and Dad took a trip to Billings, Montana to visit my older sister and take her a care package and Christmas gifts from home. We made the ride several times before on 94, so we were familiar with the drive. It's about 500 miles and a good day's drive. We took my dad's Buick instead of the truck. We had planned a stop in Glendive, MT, as usual, for hot food and to stretch our legs.

We drove at night hoping to beat a storm front moving in with snow and wind. We thought we could make better time if we left earlier at night to beat the weather. There was little traffic because it was the day after Christmas. We made good time until we were on the other side of Glendive. It was 10:00 PM and the weather was cold and overcast, but dry. My dad was driving, and I was hooked up to my MP3 player and not paying much attention.

Past Glendive there's not much to see, especially at night. Occasionally, we'd see the lights of another ranch off in the distance or pass an exit to nowhere. Otherwise, it was just us in the darkness with a semitruck encounter here and there.

I saw a light over the top of us. A single, bright light that lit up the inside of the car through the windshield and our sunroof. I took off my headphones and asked Dad, "What's up?"

He said he thought it was a police helicopter. It had us in its searchlight for some reason. Dad admitted he'd been speeding, but there was no pursuit car anywhere, just this helicopter that lit up the inside of the car. It paced us for several miles.

I turned off the car radio and rolled down my window. We were hit with a blast of cold air as we listened for the familiar noise of the helicopter. We couldn't hear anything but the wind. My dad was worried because if we sped up, it would speed up. Likewise, if we slowed down, it slowed down to stay right on top of us. After about five miles of this my dad felt annoyed. I felt a little disturbed.

Dad suggested we pull over and stop. He wanted to see what it would do.

I said, "No, let's just keep going, do the speed limit and wait for him to get tired and pick on someone else. He's probably just running our plate for some reason and waiting to hear back."

But dad insisted we stop the car. He used his turn signal and pulled off onto the shoulder. We stopped and he put on the emergency flashers. Whatever it was, it stayed right over us. Dad didn't have the binoculars he kept in the truck. They would have come in handy to get a better view of it. All we could see was a single bright light. It was lower now. I still couldn't understand why we didn't hear anything but the wind.

Dad turned off the ignition for some reason and pocketed the keys. He grabbed his coat and got out of the car. The heater was off, and I knew it wouldn't take long before the car got cold. I slipped on my jacket as Dad slammed his door. He was outside for a long time walking around and I was getting concerned. The light was still right on top of us. I felt safer just staying in the car.

This is the weird part. The next thing I knew we were driving again and about 10 miles down the road, or so we thought. I wondered; did I fall asleep while Dad was outside?

It's strange, I don't remember him getting back into the car and continuing on the trip. The helicopter or whatever it was, was gone now. My jacket was lying in the back seat. I couldn't find my MP3 player at first. It was in my jacket pocket. I don't remember taking off my coat either. The car was nice and warm. Dad's coat was in the backseat too.

I asked Dad, "What happened?"

He said, "I don't know, I just looked at it for a while, I started the car, and the light was gone. Have you been asleep?"

"I guess so. I must have been because I don't remember you getting back in the car," I replied.

Dad asked, "We clocked another 10 miles. Do you remember us pulling away and back onto the highway?"

"No actually, I think I fell asleep. Where are we?" I asked.

"About 30 miles past Glendive, I'm guessing. We're behind schedule," he said.

I looked at the clock in the car and it read 11:40 PM. Confused, I asked Dad, "Did it take us and hour and 40 minutes to cover thirty miles? How long were you out there?"

He paused and said, "I don't remember."

I thought that was weird, but I didn't say anything. We came to the next little town and I said, "Wait a minute, I think we're more like 50 miles past Glendive!"

"Ah," Dad said, "That explains it. That accounts for the hour and 40 minutes." He said it in a dismissive way, like "that settles it."

He wasn't making sense. I did the mental math and in 100 minutes we should have been more than 50 miles farther down the road.

I did not say anything because I had no way to know how long my dad was outside the car. With that variable unanswered I had no idea how it got so late.

We didn't say much for the rest of the trip. I threw my coat over me and dozed. I should have offered to drive, but I didn't. I was so sleepy.

We were an hour-and-a-half late getting to my sister's house. When we got there, we grabbed our suitcase and packages and got inside. It was starting to snow.

My sister said she was worried about us. She offered to make us some eggs and bacon. We both passed, preferring to get some sleep instead. At 17, I rarely passed up a plate of bacon and eggs.

We slept late the next morning. We did not talk about the helicopter following us, or Dad pulling over and losing 90 minutes somewhere. It just never came up. I'd like to know how we ended up down the highway with no memory of making the drive.

One last thing. Our car was covered in snow the next day, so we didn't notice anything unusual. A month later we had a few days of warmer weather and my mom took the car through a car wash. That's when she noticed the paint had badly faded on the hood and the roof.

We could not explain it. The car had been covered in ice and snow for a month, so it was hard to tie it to what happened to us back on December 26th when we went to Billings.

My dad blamed General Motors and thought we had a bad paint job. The manufacturer's warranty had lapsed. When dad took it into the dealership for an oil change, he spoke to the body shop manager. He agreed to take look at it. He said it was paint damage and looked like it had faded from exposure to bright sunshine over time. That was a joke, we don't have sunshine in Minot.

There were no known problems or recalls of any kind regarding paint according to Buick. He suggested maybe there was a problem at the car wash. He put us in touch with someone from Detroit who took a report. But no help with the paint.

We both had nightmares about the Montana trip for some reason. It was never anything scary we could identify. It was just dark and foreboding. Usually it was just us parked on the shoulder with the light overhead. Dad passed away in 2015. I wish we had discussed it.

ANALYSIS

I thanked Benito, who prefers to be called "Ben."

I suggested Ben go online and read the transcripts from Betty and Barney Hill's hypnotic regression from their 1961 abduction. During a phone call he asked me about hypnotic regression and if I thought it would help recover what he couldn't remember. He also asked if I could suggest someone trustworthy to do the hypnotherapy. I suggested he speak with my friend, Yvonne Smith in LA, or Kathleen Marden in Florida. She's Betty Hill's niece. They are both certified hypnotherapist who have done hundreds of regressions between them.

When I read Ben's story, I was again reminded of Betty and Barney Hill and their abduction in rural New Hampshire. There are several commonalities they share.

The deserted stretch of road at night. Seeing something in the sky they could not identify. Barney also noticed paint damage to the trunk of their car. Barney used his binoculars to look at the craft they saw. Ben's dad would have used them if they'd been traveling in his truck. And, of course, the missing time and subsequent nightmares they also share with the Hill's experience.

Ben said his family never fully discussed the matter. Betty and Barney did eventually, but only after they sought help.

Case #9

UFO Over Pensacola

Katie and Sue

Atlanta, Georgia

Dear Mr. Lovelace,

My college roommate and I had a weird experience while attending college in Atlanta in March of 1998. I was 20 years old at the time and studying marketing. My uncle, who owned a used car business, gave me a 1995 VW convertible as a high school graduation gift. I needed wheels to travel to the dorm and back home to Raleigh, North Carolina. My friend and roommate, Sue, was a year younger and from Durham. We met as freshman and became fast friends.

On a long weekend Sue suggested we drive to Pensacola on the Florida panhandle and visit the beach for a day or two, just to see the ocean again and get away for a while. She knew a spot that was nice and rarely crowded. We packed my car with a cooler, beach towels and the usual necessities and drove down. I booked us a room near the beach at a budget motel for our one overnight stay.

But we failed to check the weather forecast for the weekend. The week had been sunny, but Pensacola was cool and overcast both days. Undeterred, we drove straight to the beach and arrived by noon. The weather was crappy, but it didn't rain, and the wind was tolerable. We were the only ones there. That was pleasant.

Clouds and the cool temperatures aside, it was a beautiful stretch of coastline. While walking the beach we talked, mostly gossip about our classmates, and we split a joint.

The trip wasn't what we expected, but it wasn't bad either. By the way, the marijuana we smoked was not very strong and what we saw wasn't a drug induced hallucination. We were happy and just relaxed, but in complete control of our senses.

At the water's edge we stopped to look at a tanker on the distant horizon. It was just a ghostly silhouette because of the limited visibility. I'd describe the day as cool, overcast with exceptionally low clouds.

While watching this distant tanker, we saw a grey cigar-shaped object slowly drop from the clouds. It stopped 50 feet or so above the water and just hung there between the cloud cover and the sea. It was less than a half mile out and it was big, probably 50 yards in length and as tall as a single-story building. We couldn't see windows or other markings of any kind. It was solid grey but plainly a physical object made of some kind of metal, bolted together by someone in a factory somewhere. It wasn't an ethereal or transparent structure. It looked to be rock solid.

We were blown away. Neither of us had ever seen a UFO before and we doubted they were real. This fit the UFO definition. It was unquestionably real, a solid object that could fly (and submerge too) and unknown to us. It was an interesting, exciting, and unique experience.

We couldn't take our eyes off of it. Because the day was over-cast, I left my camera in the car and could have kicked myself for losing the opportunity to capture this thing on film.

Neither of us were prepared for its next move. After a few minutes it unexpectedly dropped below the waves and was gone! It didn't give us the impression it crashed in the sea; we shared the opinion that it intentionally submerged. We didn't hear a splash and it just slid smoothly into the water.

Backing away from the waterline, we sat on dry sand and continued our vigil for almost an hour, waiting for it to resurface and fly away. It never did. Neither of us were afraid, just the opposite, we were enthused and debated what it was that we had just seen. We quickly eliminated all the possibilities other than a UFO. At the time, we thought what we saw was something not made in a factory on earth.

Sue pointed out that we were close to a naval air station and it could have been a secret craft of some kind. She made a persuasive argument.

I've thought about it over the years and maybe she was right. I have no idea what our defense industry might have had in its inventory in 1998. A naval air station was nearby, and this thing was aerial and nautical too, so maybe.

Sue and I graduated together and moved back home to North Carolina and began careers. We've maintained our friendship. We're both married with families now and live a couple hours away from each other. I work in marketing and Sue, oddly enough, works for a defense contractor. She doesn't speak about her work, but we see each other at least once a year and talk on the phone now and then.

Our sighting that day comes up often when we talk. I'd still love to know what we saw. It wasn't as spectacular as your experience, but it was an awesome event, and I wouldn't trade it for the world.

ANALYSIS

Katie is still unsure of what they saw that day. I asked her if local newspapers carried anything about a UFO sighting. While in their hotel room that evening, they watched the local news, and it wasn't mentioned. The following day Sue scanned a local newspaper for stories about UFO sightings. There were none.

Katie said she may have had a dream or two about that day, but never a nightmare. She described the one or two dreams about the day as just a replay of their walk on the beach and noting the ship in the distance and seeing the grey cigar-shaped UFO.

As for a belief in UFOs? Sue is skeptical and Katie is a little more open to the concept, but says she is still unsure exactly what they saw that day.

Case #10

Takuahe

Antonio and Maria

El Paso, Texas

Many thanks to Marcia Garcia for translating Maria's emails from mixed Spanish/English, and for acting as translator in our phone call. Without your kind assistance I would not have been able to understand the subtleties of her story.

Dear Mr. Lovelace,

My sister gave me a Spanish version of your book to read. We had some scary stuff happen in 2016 and 2017. We moved in 2018. My son claimed to have seen a visitor in his room just like you did in your book.

We're from Mexico originally, but we live in El Paso now with our son, Stephan, who was born here. My husband, Antonio, me, and Stephan lived in a trailer in a little park on the southern end of town.

Antonio and me split-up for a while when our son was almost five years old. He moved out of the trailer and took most of his things. This was when he started working on the road as an electrician.

His job took him to different construction sites, and we didn't see each other much. We both had family nearby, so it wasn't like we were alone. Antonio sent money when he could and visited when he could.

Our son started having problems sleeping when he was four. Some nights Stephan would scream so loud Antonio would get up and take a flashlight and check the yard, while I calmed Stephan down and got him back to sleep. On these nights he usually slept between us.

Antonio moved out a year later when Stephan turned five. From the age of four until he was almost six, Stephan complained about a "takuahe" or an opossum in his room on and off. When it was just me and Stephan, he'd wake me up, usually close to 3:00 AM, screaming and begging to sleep with me. He slept with me a lot because his nightmares happened once or twice a week for a while. Then, no nightmares for a month or two and we'd think it was over, but it would return unexpectedly. They came and went for about two years. Especially after Antonio moved out and it was just the two of us; things got creepy.

The animal Stephan described was not the usual possum. He claimed this one walked on its back legs and had large black eyes. Antonio and Stephan looked all over the room for any space where an animal could get into his bedroom. They found none. Antonio thought this might reassure Stephan that he was in his own room and was safe. It didn't work.

As Stephan got a little older, he was able to tell us more. It was a crazy story and we didn't believe him. But something was scaring him.

Stephan told me one morning after a bad night when he was four, "The possum comes into my room when it's dark and wakes me up. He's friendly most of the time and only scares me sometimes. He has very big eyes and walks like people do."

I asked, "What does he do that scares you?"

He said, "Sometimes, he talks to me but he never moves his mouth. There is light in the room from the window too. His fur is clean and soft, not like the possums I've seen."

Surprised, I asked, "Where did you see a possum before?"

"In the backyard by the trees, but they are a lot smaller and don't have big eyes. I saw a dead one too," Stephan exclaimed proudly.

When I told Stephan, "Possums are not very big, and they don't walk like people or have big eyes." He was quick to tell me I was wrong.

I asked him, "So he talks to you?"

He said, "Yes Momma, that's what scares me the most. He knows my name too."

"Tell me, what does this possum say that scares you so bad?" I asked.

"He says stuff to me, but I don't remember!" was his answer.

Stephan was getting upset and tearful. But I asked him one more question. "Stephan, where does he come from, this possum? Does he live in the backyard or under the trailer?"

"No momma, he just comes. I see the lights turn on in the back-yard and he's just in my room." Stephan said, much to his mother's confusion.

"Stephan, there are no lights in the backyard. The light outside the back door has never worked. Did you know that? I can show you," I said. That was very disturbing. I was unsure what to think, I just scared the both of us. I tried to hide my fear.

Stephan was unwavering, "No, I saw the lights come on before he comes into my room. He doesn't come from the door, mostly through the window, or I just wake up and he's just there, in my room."

A few weeks later I was having trouble sleeping too. I got up and moved from my bedroom to the couch in the living room to watch some TV. From the couch, I could see into Stephan's room. I was wide awake and was watching my soap opera from Mexico on the DVR player. I saw a light shine in through Stephan's room. A bright, bluish light, like someone was in the backyard with a flashlight shining it through the window. I was about to get up and investigate, but I guess I just fell back asleep.

My bedroom is situated toward the front of the house and I can't see the backyard from my bedroom. I decided I'd sleep on the couch for a while to make sure our son was alright. I was afraid from all of this and I needed help with getting the trailer secured.

Antonio was working a job in Colorado, so I confided in his dad. I invited him over for dinner and a visit with Stephan. I asked him to bring his toolbox.

Word of Stephan's problems sleeping and the possum in his room had spread through the family. Antonio's dad, Filipe, was also an electrician. He offered to install some lights in the backyard and

216

some motion detectors. We lived on the back end of the trailer park, so there was no trailers or buildings behind us. There was a ditch, open land and a few junk cars, but that was it.

Filipe suggested maybe someone was out there at night. Stephan might be seeing someone in the backyard with a flashlight. Our trailer was on an incline, so the rear windows was eight feet or more over the ground. That meant no one could be scaring Stephan by peeking through his window. The back door was at the top of a dozen stairs, kept securely locked and rarely used. The doors were secure, but I wanted light.

Filipe fixed the porchlight first. All it needed was a new bulb. He put in a much higher wattage bulb that lit up the whole backyard when turned on by an inside switch.

Next, he installed two new lights with motion detectors on the corners, so they covered the whole backyard when activated. I hoped that would be the end of the possums in Stephan's room.

I continued to sleep on the couch. If anything were going to happen in Stephan's room, I would see it. A week after Filipe left, something did happen in Stephan's room.

One night, Stephan screamed and woke me from a deep sleep. Raising my head from the couch, I saw light coming from his room like a lamp was on. From the hallway it looked like a flashlight shining through his screen again. The glass window was raised because of the heat.

As I walked into his room, I saw an orb of bright light about the size of a softball in the middle of his room. I screamed; five-year-old Stephan was crying hysterically. This thing was inside the house.

The ball of light moved slowly toward the open window and right through the screen. The motion detectors never tripped. I closed the window and watched as the ball of white light was now outside, hovering over the backyard. I saw it float toward the back of the property, pick up speed and dart 90 degrees straight up and out of sight.

I picked up Stephan and carried him to the couch. I turned the back porch light on too. Then I focused on calming my frightened son.

Stephan exclaimed, "That was possum Mom, did you see it?"

I thought he was still hysterical. I assured him, "No, it was just a ball of bright light from somewhere, a ball of light can't hurt you." But the truth is, I didn't know if that was true or not. I had Stephan sleep with me until we could sort this out.

He was sure I had just met the "possum" that had been visiting him, speaking to him and terrorizing him for more than a year. I was not sure where to turn for help, so I told our Catholic priest who came and blessed our home.

Afterward, he pulled me aside and asked if I could afford to move?

I said, "Why? Is this thing a demon or something supernatural?"

That question shook him up a bit. He didn't answer my question, but strongly suggested we find another place to rent. He said, "I think you'll be much happier somewhere new, a fresh start for the family."

We moved a short while later. Antonio and I reconciled our marriage and with two incomes for the household we were able to find a nicer home and move in just a couple months.

Stephan has had bad dreams, but so far, thankfully no visitors of any kind. Do you think they'll come back?

ANALYSIS

I told Maria truthfully, "I hope not." But I'm not sure what you are dealing with. It could be you're having "ET visits" like the ones I experienced as a child. But it could be something different.

A lot of people believe there is a spiritual component in all of this. I can only tell you about my experience. I think if ETs tag you in childhood, you're tagged for life for some reason. Maybe true, maybe not. But even if Stephan is destined for a lifetime of interaction, it doesn't mean they will all be negative.

I know almost nothing about hauntings. Maybe what you experienced in the trailer was a haunting tied to the premises. That may be why your priest encouraged you to move. Hopefully, you've left the problem behind.

If what you're dealing with is supernatural in origin, your priest would know better than I. I find his reaction to all this curious. There is an old saying, "You don't know what you don't know." There's so much that we don't yet understand.

Case #11

ETs: Angels or Demons?

Suzie

Baltimore, Maryland

Dear Sir,

I saw your television show episode on My Horror Story. I also listened to one of your podcasts. I tell you they're no demons, they're not here to harm us in any way. They are here to help us enter a new era of peace and prosperity. Our government knows this, but it's kept a secret.

I had my first experience when I was four. A tall angelic being used to visit my room. I was still sleeping in a crib and I remember how the room lit up when they came to visit me, and his head almost touched the ceiling. Sometimes just the one, sometimes six of them.

They glowed white and their robes were navy blue around their chests. They spoke to me and told me they were my guardians, and I could call on them whenever I need them. I call them my "angels."

My first husband was killed in the Afghan War. We had a one-year-old at the time. When I got the news, I was crushed. But I already knew it had happened. Two days earlier two of them appeared in my bedroom and told me, "Everything will be okay, Roland is with God."

My family and church stood by me, and my angels were with me at night and comforted me. I knew through them that my husband was okay and in a better place with the Lord. I knew we'd make it and we did.

Your story scares people. People should not be afraid, and you make people afraid of them. I know they're here to help.

If the things you met were as evil as you said, they were not from another planet. You saw demons from hell. Did you or your buddy ever mess around with Ouija boards as teenagers or fool with spells and witchcraft? That's what people do and it's an invitation.

A lot of people don't believe in the devil anymore. He's real and so is his army. If your faith in Jesus Christ were stronger, you'd have been protected by just calling on his name.

I don't believe UFOs come from other planets. I suggest you get connected with a Christian church and approach this matter through prayer.

ANALYSIS

I'm tempted to think of Suzie's experience in terms of a paranormal rather than a spiritual matter, if you can make that distinction. I contrast this story to Stephan's opossum experience in the previous story.

The Ouija board and magic spells statement takes me back to my cousin Gerald and his admonishment from the preacher, "not to think bad thoughts ... that's what lets the demons in." I respect most organized religions. I should say that I respect the rights of people to worship what they see fit.

A couple things do trouble me about the blurred line between the paranormal and the supernatural. David Paulides' research in his *Missing 411* books and the phenomena, of unexplained disappearances from state and national parks, volume IV, makes a statistical correlation between state and national parks that contain the name "devil" or "diablo," and significantly greater chances for hikers, campers, and hunters to vanish. Paulides, as a consummate statistician offers facts that support the supposition that there is a negative or demonic component at play that somehow ties the devil names to statistically higher incidents of abduction.

Because ETs come in such a wide variety, it makes sense that more than a single species of extraterrestrial visits earth. All are probably highly evolved and intellectually superior to human beings. However, advanced intellect and advanced ethics are different animals and may not necessarily run on parallel tracks. A species of beings could evolve in science, math and all matter of learned subjects and not be ethical or moral outside their group.

Consider the Nazi culture from the second world war. The Nazis promoted discipline, learning, and saw themselves as an advanced race. Arian superiority was a myth of course. There is no denying they were a regimented and intelligent culture. But their ethics, empathy and morality did not progress and suffered from a philosophy that discouraged kindness and civility toward those they considered inferior. Anyone not Arian was inferior to some degree. For all their technological advancements their ethics did not keep pace. Their effort to advance intellectually was inhibited by their bigotry, expelling some of their nation's greatest minds because they did not fit the Arian mold. Just because a group, religion, society or alien civilization is highly intelligent, it does not necessarily mean they treat others ethically.

There could be some very evil but highly-evolved beings out there. It's a horrible thought that suggests the need for spiritual protection.

Again, I admit there may likely be a spiritual component to all of this. I have had letters from others who tell me I can avoid an encounter through prayer. Prayer may provide effective protection against one alien species but not another. If that's true I couldn't begin to understand why.

I respect Suzie's opinion but disagree with her conclusions. My cousin Gerald's misery comes to mind. I do not believe the creatures I encountered were from the spiritual realm. The thing they traveled in was 100% solid nuts and bolts and real in this plane of existence. I also can't rule out that the ship itself wasn't a living sentient organism as another reader suggested. Especially since they can control our perception.

As I've said before, my attitude about my abduction has softened somewhat over the years. I've let go of the anger. I believe if I could speak with them today their attitude would be, "No hard feelings, just doing my job." I don't think what was done to us was done out of malice. I think our injuries were collateral damage.

There's the matter of the other human captives we saw aboard this craft. What happened to them? They were a mixed bag of men, women, and children.

My intuition tells me it did not end as well for them. When that triangle went up in the air and disappeared, Toby and I were alone in the woods. Where did those people go? Were they dropped off somewhere? Were they together as one group or were they random individuals kidnapped like us?

It is called survivor guilt. I still wonder what became of them. Why were we fortunate and kicked out the door but they continued their ride into possible oblivion? It takes me back to my friend Toby's question in 1977, "Why us?"

Case #12

A Living Thing

Marvin

White Cloud, Minnesota

Dear Terry,

Thank you for your fascinating book. I have some things to share with you that you'll find hard to believe and may disagree with. I ask that you just give them some thought.

I've had experiences since my early childhood as well. I recall being on their ships too. Have you ever considered the ship itself could be a living thing? They explained to me that the ship is not only alive, it can reason and make independent decisions. In my Native American culture we see everything as having a spark of life.

I had never heard of an alien spacecraft being alive, but I can't reject the idea out of hand either. I look at the advancements we've made in artificial intelligence in the past decade. I cannot even imagine what could be achieved with a thousand or a million years of effort toward its development. Since A.I. writes its own code the growth could be exponential and the line between mechanical and organic blurs. A craft that can think for itself and execute commands on its own would be the pinnacle of aeronautical engineering.

Once you deal with that completely, consider that the entire universe is an organic living thing that we're a part of. I know that sounds like a stretch but meditate on it. If you don't meditate now, I suggest you begin a regimen of daily meditation. You can begin with as little as five minutes. I also suggest you try yoga or tai chi to augment your meditation routine. If you do these things, you'll expand your consciousness and find yourself in a much better place.

ANALYSIS

Thank you, Marvin. It's not a stretch for me to see the entire universe as organic. The interconnectedness of things easily leads me down that rabbit hole. It is the same line of reasoning that makes me consider we could be living in a simulation. Elon Musk, someone I admire greatly, said the odds of us not living in a matrix are "a billion to one."

I have friends who practice both yoga and tai chi along with mediation. I've practiced meditation using meditative cassette tapes back in the day, and with apps on my iPhone or YouTube to this day.

I agree that meditation is a good way to experience peace and live a better life in general.

I assume you're familiar with the concept of "mindfulness." I read *The Power of Now* back in the 2000s. I thought the mindfulness concept and living in the present moment made good sense. I try to practice mindfulness in my daily life, but I admit there are distractions that steer me away from the practice. Probably because I lack the mental discipline.

Case #13

UFOs and the Near-Death Experience

Peter

San Diego, California

Dear Mr. Lovelace,

We met at the UFO Congress in Phoenix in 2018. I don't know if you remember me. I explained that I had been taken as well as a child. We also talked about NDEs or Near Death Experiences and the possible connection between the NDE community and the UFO community.

I had a significant NDE when I was struck by a car while riding my bicycle at age 12. I was coming home from school. I have no memory of the accident. I only remember being suddenly above my body by about 15 feet. I recognized my bicycle before I recognized my own body. It was strange. I felt little connection to my broken body on the pavement other than recognition. The driver who struck me fled the scene. There were other kids and adults all around me. I heard the siren and saw the ambulance arrive. I was placed on a stretcher after being examined. I watched as they loaded me into the ambulance and began chest compressions. I could see everything through the top of the ambulance, and I followed it to the hospital.

I wasn't worried in the least. I felt euphoric. I felt like I was losing my grasp on this world and I slipped into darkness. It was like being in a pool of indigo ink. It was just silent blackness. I had no physical body. I was just light and consciousness. I had no physical sensations, and for the moment I saw nothing but black and it was dead silent. I had never experienced silence like that before. I have no idea as to how much time had lapsed. Time seemed irrelevant. I floated in this condition without fear or anxiety. I wondered, is this how I will spend eternity?

I saw the tiniest pinpoint of white light in the distance and I felt drawn to it. I'm unclear if it was expanding and growing or if I was drifting in its direction. It grew steadily larger with the intensity of the sun. It was bright enough to have been blinding but I could stare at it without any discomfort. Then I became aware of sound like wind. I felt at peace and just watched as the light expanded and enveloped me. I felt at home without fear or discomfort.

Next, I was in a grassy pasture in a beautiful place with vivid colors. Flowering plants were everywhere and all of it felt alive and interconnected. In the distance there was a low cloud bank, like a line of heavy fog. Instinctively, I knew it was a barrier of some kind. A woman walked out of the fog and toward me. I didn't know her, but she radiated love. It was like the love from my mother but multiplied ten-fold. She even looked like mom, but she wasn't. I later discovered while looking through family photographs she was my maternal great grand-mother whom I'd never met.

She had the kindest eyes and I felt at peace. Until she told me I had to go back.

I immediately protested and said, "No! I want to stay and see what's over there, behind the fog."

229

She said, "You'll see it next time, when you come back when it's your time and we'll visit again."

Then it was just BAM! I was slammed back into my body with a jolt and felt the pain immediately. I had been in surgery for a ruptured spleen and a shattered pelvis. I couldn't grasp what had happened. I didn't know if it was a dream or reality. No one would discuss it with me. I was told it was a dream from the anesthetic. Then, in college I learned we were unconscious while under anesthesia and dreams weren't possible. I kept it to myself for a time. Then I found others that shared the experience, and I became involved in IANDS, the International Association for Near Death Studies.

In my late teens I learned about the NDE phenomenon. I was excited to discover I wasn't alone. I was astonished to find that many other people have had the same kind of experience. The details may slightly differ, but the takeaway message from the experience was the same. I also lost all fear of death. I fear dying because of the pain that may be involved. But I'd seen death and knew what waited for me on the other side. I knew what was important, to be kind to one another and to learn.

In my mid-twenties I read a book by Edgar Cayce. In it, Cayce described other worlds and reincarnation throughout a living universe, not just on earth. I feel that these beings must be from the same source. There must be a single divine source that we all connect to. The interconnectedness of everything makes us family.

Have you ever considered these may be related phenomena?

ANALYSIS

Yes, Peter, I think they are related as both involve altered states of consciousness. Edgar Cayce hit the nail on the head. We feel that interconnectedness because we've lived past lives. Some of them may not have been on this world.

I've read two NDE books by the oncologist, Dr. Jeffrey Long. I've visited his website where people can share their experience. He makes a compelling case for our minds to survive the physical death of our bodies. I hope he's right. We'll all find out one day.

Case #14

Fetal Abduction

Linda

Poplar Bluff, Missouri

Dear Mr. Lovelace,

My husband read your book and shared it with me a year ago. We have a problem and are curious if you've ever heard of this before. It sounds like fiction. But it's not.

In 1986 we bought a small farm near Poplar Bluff. My husband is a geologist and works for the government, mostly regulating the mining industry in the area.

We were both raised on a farm, so we own a couple horses and lease out our farmland. We wanted to live in the country. This was our dream home. I'm a stay-at-home grandmother raising our grandson now, while our daughter is in the Middle East on a one-year tour. She's made the Air Force her career.

Back in 1992 I had some difficult pregnancies. My first pregnancy was a miscarriage at the sixth month. We tried again and had our daughter. It wasn't a difficult pregnancy, but we had a few scares.

A few years later, my husband wanted a son to "complete the set." We tried again when our daughter was four and we were successful. I had suspected I was pregnant. I confirmed it with a home test kit, and we were over the moon. I saw my doctor a few days later, she likewise confirmed we had another child on the way. We were so happy with the news.

When I was at about the 11th week, I woke up one morning and felt slightly sore in my pelvic area. I'm petite at 5'5" and 95 pounds. I laid back on the bed and felt my abdomen, it was flat. Something felt very wrong.

My husband agreed and I cancelled a social obligation so we could see our doctor. She was someone we trusted. She handled my other pregnancies. I had seen her just three weeks prior and everything was good.

Then I called my doctor and asked to be seen right away. The nurse suggested I go to the emergency room if it was urgent.

She asked me if I was "bleeding or spotting."

I told her, "No, no blood. Some mild cramping, and my abdomen feels flat."

She asked, "Are you in pain, do you have a fever?"

I told her honestly, "No. But I don't feel right." After that I broke down into tears and sobbed. It was unexpected and uncontrollable, and I felt embarrassed by my inability to control myself. My husband took the phone and said he would take me to the emergency room and please let our doctor know.

I'm not a drama queen. I'm a tough farm girl who can pull her weight and then some. I could not remember the last time I cried real tears. I guess it was when I miscarried. God, I did not want to lose this *baby. This is tough to explain. I felt overwhelmed by feelings of loss and grief. I couldn't talk, I just kept sobbing.*

On our drive to the hospital, my husband was worried because I could not stop crying. Try as I might, I felt sad and I cried. After the 30-minute ride to the ER, I was able to pull myself together.

I calmly explained my symptoms to the nurse. She asked, "Are you sure you've not passed any blood or tissue?"

"No!" I said, unintentionally raising my voice.

I was placed in a bed and examined by the OBGYN on duty. I asked him anxiously, "Did we lose another baby?"

All he would tell me was, "I find no blood near your cervix or anywhere else." He knew my doctor and called her office. He accessed my medical records and ordered a sonogram. They also took blood.

In five minutes, a tech arrived with the sonogram machine. She began the test immediately with the cold jelly goop they use. She had the machine turned away from me. My husband was on the other side of the bed holding my hand and couldn't see it either. I'm not sure we'd know what to look for at this early stage, so I guess it didn't matter.

I asked the technician as she was wrapping up, "Does everything look okay?"

Without facial expression she softly said, "I'll give this to your doctor, and he'll be right in."

Thirty minutes later he came back and shook hands with my husband. He sat on the edge of the bed and addressed us both.

234

"I'm sorry to say you've lost the baby. But I do not believe it happened last night. Also, you don't have an infection. In the past week have you noticed any blood or felt something pass?" he asked.

"No." I was too numb to cry anymore. Paul still held my hand.

The doctor said, "I want to do a thorough exam and make certain there's no need for a D&C or 'dusting and cleaning,'" as he called it. He said my labs were all normal.

Everything was normal with my body. Except the healthy fetus I had in my uterus the day before had now vanished. This happened the evening before, there's no question in our minds.

The doctor said, "It's as if you'd never been pregnant. I can't explain that. Perhaps the tests were false positives, but I doubt that after reviewing your chart. I can only guess. It is likely you lost the child some weeks back, there was little pain or discomfort, and it went unnoticed. I am sorry, otherwise you're healthy and you can probably go home soon, after we've done a more thorough exam. Then you can get some rest. Be good to yourself and follow up with your doctor in a week. If you have spotting or pain, come straight to the emergency room."

I knew I had lost this baby the night before somehow. We were sad for a while and grieved our loss. We'd been down this road once before and knew how to heal. The soreness in my pelvis was minimal and completely gone the following day. Anyone, any couple, who has lost a pregnancy understands.

I followed up with my doctor the following week. She had no answers. She did tell us we could try again if we like. We did try. Six months later we were successful again.

The process and emotions were identical to the last time. I missed a period, my home pregnancy test was positive, my doctor's test was positive, and I know my body. I know how pregnancy feels. This would be our fourth. I was pregnant again and we were cautiously excited. My doctor warned, "Let's watch this pregnancy carefully."

We did everything right. But on week twelve I woke with that same sense of loss and differences in my body. There was no rush this time, I knew what had happened. I made an appointment for an office visit the next day with my OBGYN.

She was shocked and said she was sorry, "Linda, there's no evidence of a pregnancy or that one was even lost. There are changes in your body when you lose a pregnancy. I don't find any evidence that indicates a pregnancy to begin with."

She offered to send me to a specialist for a workup. We decided against it. We were blessed with a daughter and decided that the three of us made a family.

Now, I will tell you about the dream and the strange lights. About a week before we lost our third 'phantom' pregnancy, I was locking the barn and bringing in the dogs. It was just past sunset. Walking away from the barn and back toward the house I saw a flash of blue light. Like a camera flash.

I looked over my shoulder at what I first took to be the moon. I only saw it for a moment and it just blinked out. I don't know why, but it startled me. I ran the last 30 yards back to the house. I did not tell my husband. I had never seen anything like that before.

I had never seen anything unusual in the sky in my entire life. Seeing this thing in the sky felt significant in some way I cannot explain.

The dream occurred a few days after the loss of the final phantom pregnancy. In this dream, I was in a small room that had a medical feel to it. But it was not a hospital. I knew that somehow. There was a small, dark-haired woman there holding a fetus in a towel. She let me hold it for a few seconds and I knew this fetus was mine.

I was suddenly panic-stricken with the thought, "This baby can't survive outside my womb!"

The dark-haired woman then made eye contact and I heard her voice in my head comfort me. She promised the child was healthy and would grow into a healthy and happy adult. For some reason I trusted this woman and felt like I knew her.

I begged her, "Please don't take my baby."

She said, "You agreed to this." Then the dream ended.

I woke up feeling good the next morning. The loss was still there, but the grief was gone. Maybe this was a mental mechanism to cope with the loss. Whatever happened, I felt healed and whole. We've practiced birth control since.

One final note, I strongly feel a connection between what I saw over the barn and my lost pregnancies. As strange as this sounds, I'm at peace with it. Maybe they were not mine to keep. Maybe I was just a surrogate mother and incubator. Her parting words, "You agreed to this," helped me accept it.

ANALYSIS

I thanked her for her candor. This correspondence is a collage of three emails and a telephone call. Linda was unexpectedly upbeat and didn't view the miscarriages as the loss of living fetuses because she believes so strongly that they survived. She said she feels confident those babies will live long, productive lives in a loving environment. She told me she was hopeful to meet them again one day on this earth. I told her I hoped so too.

Her comment, "You agreed to this," is documented in perhaps a hundred emails I've received from others. The question is, was this agreement made in this lifetime? Or was it perhaps made from the other side in preparation for this life?

Case #15

The Blue Light Special

Barbara

Louisville, Kentucky

Dear Mr. Lovelace,

I read your book a while ago and it took me back to something that happened during my high school days when I dated a guy I'll call "Joe."

I'm 30 years old and from Louisville, Kentucky originally. After college, I moved to Cincinnati and I write for their newspaper. I like "Cinnci," but Louisville is home. I think I'm pretty well grounded and not prone to fantasy. I do not watch science fiction movies, although I have had an interest in UFOs since this happened.

At the end of our senior year in high school, Joe and I were dating. We had a strange experience while camping one weekend. It happened at my parent's cabin and it's still fresh in my memory. I've only shared this story with my mother and no one else. People can be judgmental.

Joe and I had known one another since 9th grade, and by the time we were seniors we'd been dating steadily for a year. We discussed marriage and we knew each other's family. It seemed destined to be.

239

We didn't use drugs on our trip to the cabin. On the night this happened we hadn't been drinking either. Those things had to wait till my college days.

When we were seniors, we skipped school on a Friday to give us a long weekend during the Memorial Day holiday. My family has a cabin on lakeside property we own about an hour away. Another couple was supposed to join us but backed out at the last minute, so it was just the two of us. I'd stayed in that cabin dozens of times since I was a little girl and never had anything weird happen.

It was unusually hot that evening, so we stayed down by the canoe dock since it was cooler near the water. The mosquitos were not too bad. There was a stone barbecue pit and a picnic table there, so we took our cooler and grilled some chicken.

About 10:30 PM we were packing up to move back to the cabin when Joe saw a bright light in the sky across the lake. It was shining through the treetops. It was bright enough to reflect on the lake. The west, where the sun had set, was to our right. A sliver of a moon was just off the horizon behind us so it could not have been the moon. It would creep across the treetops for a while and stop. Whatever it was, it was slowly moving toward the east.

We both thought it was a helicopter because we saw a beam of light, like a searchlight, coming down from the underside and lighting up the forest below. But there was no noise. It got brighter and eventually popped above the treetops and we could see it better.

It was a ball of light. It was a solid object that glowed, it wasn't made out of light, it emitted light. It changed colors at times from white to blue and would grow dim for a bit and then get brighter. Joe thought it could be sheriff deputies looking for poaches from a helicopter. We never heard any gunfire.

Just like you and your friend experienced, it got quiet when this all began. We put our stuff down and sat to watch. It stopped its eastward path and sat still, changing from blue to white and back again. It felt like 30 minutes, but I glanced at my watch and it was almost 1:00 AM. We had been watching this thing for over two hours. It finally shrunk in size right before our eyes. It just blinked out.

We had been sitting on top of the picnic table during this and talking about all kinds of stuff like graduation and college. Joe was considering the navy. I just remember us chatting, but it didn't seem possible we had talked that long.

Our conversation had all but stopped after a while and we watched this ball in the sky. I think neither one of us were scared, we were curious. It really had our interest.

The embers in the barbeque pit were cold by then and it was darker. We picked up our stuff and walked back to the cabin. I guess we'd talked ourselves out because we didn't have much to say on the walk. We made it to the cabin in the dark. It wasn't much of a party when we got inside either. We did not fool around at all; we went straight to sleep and that was unusual.

We slept until 9:30 AM on Saturday morning. When we got up, we both felt fine, but the details of the previous night were a blur. Joe said he must have fallen asleep. He swears to remember waking up shortly before we left to make our way back to the cabin.

I have no memory of either one of us sleeping and I do not remember Joe ever falling asleep either. I just remember us staring at this light across the lake, then going to sleep back in the cabin after it blinked out.

It was a hot and lazy day. By 1:00 that afternoon we were both ready for a nap. We slept for two hours and woke up around 3:00 PM. This was in the heat of the day. The nap felt good, but it wrecked our plans to go tubing that afternoon.

We decided to go home early. I don't think either one of us wanted to admit it. We didn't want to spend the night there. It was just an hour drive.

We never saw the blue light again. We were home by Saturday evening and just went our separate ways. We didn't see each other for a week. That was unusual. We talked on the phone now and then mostly.

We drifted apart after this trip and we began seeing other people. Joe left for boot camp in August after graduation. There were no hard feelings between us though. I think we both knew relationships were hard to maintain at our age when apart.

Joe is still in the Navy and has been back in town, although I've never heard from him. That was okay. I had moved on anyway.

I do have an occasional nightmare about the camping trip. It's always the same. They are always in color and have a reality feel to them. I don't mean that I'm experiencing it at the moment, but it's like a memory of a real event. I suspect a lot more happened than I will ever remember.

In my nightmare, I am in bed at the cabin and I wake up. It's dark, and I realize Joe's not in bed. I feel spooked for some reason and I notice a dim light from the hallway, like a candle flickering.

When I turn my head to the dark corner of the room my eyes focus on three grey aliens about three feet tall. They have the big eyes, and they are right out of the movies. They just stare at me. I scream and wake up.

It creeped me out so badly I've slept with my TV on for the rest of my life.

ANALYSIS

Linda's story is common in a lot of ways. She and Joe shared an experience and drifted apart. Who's to say they wouldn't have drifted apart anyway? It is possible they had an episode of lost time and were abducted. I think that's on Linda's mind as well, although she doesn't voice it other than to imply more may have happened than she can remember.

I asked Linda if she had any health problems after the trip. She admitted she did. She told me she had headaches that became a nuisance. She was treated by a neurologist and they faded in a year or so.

She had not suffered from headaches before the trip, certainly not these severe.

She claims the pain in her head was so bad that she took prescription medication and would need to lie down in a dark, quiet room for an hour until they faded.

Her recurrent dream is telling. Linda could maybe benefit from hypnotic regression to recover a clear memory of what, if anything, really happened that night.

Case #16

Old School 727

Kenneth

Burlington, Vermont

Dear Mr. Lovelace,

I enjoyed your book. I don't read a lot of UFO related books, but I enjoyed yours. I want to tell you about an experience my wife and I had in Burlington. I know you worked for the State of Vermont and lived in Montpelier, so I know you must be familiar with Burlington.

We live in the suburbs a few miles from campus. My wife and I own a printing business we inherited from her parents.

This happened to us back in February 2008. We had joined some friends for dinner on a Friday night. Afterward, we were headed home just a few miles down the road. As you know there's an airport in Burlington and we live in a flight path, so we're used to seeing and hearing aircraft.

I flew airplanes in the Navy for a couple years and had hopes of being a commercial airline pilot one day. Eye disease and the sudden onset of poor vision ended that dream, but we love our business, and everything turned out for the best. I am home for dinner every night and can read to my kids before bed, something I wouldn't be able to do as a commercial airline pilot or a Navy pilot for that matter. My vision problems are mostly corrected with glasses so I can drive and read most fine print.

We said goodnight to our friends and parted ways about 10:00 PM, we had to have the babysitter home by 10:30. It was a cold night, even for Vermont standards. We each had a single glass of wine, no more.

As we are winding our way down the hill toward home, we saw a really weird aircraft. My wife saw it first and pointed it out to me. It was to her right and it was low, I would say about 5,000 feet. Not too low to be on an approach. But it was hanging in midair. I swear it looked stationary. It was not moving slowly; it was dead still.

I pulled over and oriented the car where we could see it at the very top of the windshield. I rolled down my window and didn't hear any aircraft noise at all. At that altitude we should have. We were off the main road and just inside our subdivision, so there was no other traffic.

It was and old school Boeing 727 airliner. I recognized the three, rear engine configuration with the center engine at the base of the tail. They've been out of service for years and except for maybe Iran, they're no longer in use by anyone. Because of the lighting I could not see markings to identify the airline.

In addition to its being motionless, it was brightly lit from the inside and the landing lights were shining brightly too. I recall that the navigation lights were proper. I did not see landing gear down.

What struck me most was its speed. More precisely, its lack of speed. No jet aircraft could fly that slow on approach without stalling out. It was traveling way below glide speed and should have dropped from the sky like a duck full of buckshot.

Things got even stranger. As we watched, it began a slow drift sideways! I swear it was in level flight but just moved slowly starboard until it vanished behind buildings and trees. Airplanes do not move that way. It was not in forward flight. The entire sighting lasted about a minute or a few seconds more. It was brief but thrilling.

It was the craziest thing I had ever seen. I think if my wife and I were not so keen on aircraft we might have drove right past it without a second thought.

By the time I reached for my phone it was gone from sight. I'm just glad my wife was there to witness it because no one would believe me. We kept it just between ourselves.

ANALYSIS

I have never heard a story like this before. Although the fact that the aircraft was "brightly lit inside" rings a bell with the Christmas Store story in Case #1, and others too, including my 1977 experience.

I wonder, could they have misperceived its speed? I think not.

This is a great example of a trained observer witnessing something unexplainable. Had I reported this event it could be easily dismissed. I've never flown aircraft. Back in 1977, I'd characterize myself as a "trained observer," but that was a very long time ago. People ask me, "What's the best way to see a UFO?" The #1 suggestion is to be aware of your surroundings and your emotions.

Kenneth knew enough about commercial aircraft to recognize a Boeing 727. I did some research and the last commercial 727 flew for an Iranian airline in 1982. That was sixteen years before their 2008 sighting. The Google photographs of the 727 have the distinctive three engine tail configuration, just like he described.

I asked Kenneth if they made it back in time to get the babysitter home, or were they late? He did not reply to my email. I thanked him for a compelling and interesting story.

Case #17

ET Can Cure?

Mandy
Wilkes-Barre, Pennsylvania

Dear Terry,

I saw your photograph in the back of your book. Are you still losing weight? You know they can heal you? They can if you just ask.

They healed me from a serious blood disease I had since I was young and was still living at home. They used to come and visit me too.

One night, when I was 23, I was in my new apartment and I felt like they were coming. I can feel their presence sometimes and know when they're going to come for me.

I'm visited by the tall whites. They look like angels. I've never been afraid of them. They came at times when I needed help. I believe they are really angelic beings. I don't think these are from "out there" in the universe somewhere. I think they're higher beings from another realm.

A week before this night my boyfriend and I were at a county fair. They are big in Pennsylvania, especially out in the country. There was a fortune teller there, or a psychic, whatever. This woman wanted $20 to tell my future. I didn't have $20, so my boyfriend offered to pay for me.

She was an older woman who spoke with an accent. She said she was from Latvia. She didn't read my palm. She just stared at me for a while and looked at a shallow pan with a half-inch of water in it. She was mumbling something I couldn't understand and stared at that pan of water for a couple minutes.

Then she took my hand, looked into my eyes and said, "You will have a baby with this man, (my boyfriend) but you will not marry. You have a blood sickness. There are three guardians that watch over you. They'll come soon. When they do, tell them they need to heal you. They need to heal you so the baby will not be sick. Ask them, they'll help you."

I believed her. I thanked her and we left. I could not get it off my mind. Silly. I asked my friend to sleep over because I did not want to be alone in the apartment that night.

A week later, I woke up at 3:15 AM and they were there. There were the three of them by my bed. They were as tall as the ceiling and dressed in white robes that glowed. Not enough to light up the whole room, just a soft glow. They just have a warm white glow that's comforting.

I remembered what the old woman told me, and I said out loud, "Please heal me. Fix what's wrong with my blood so my baby will be okay, please."

The glow got brighter, and I felt warm all over. That's the last thing I remember because I guess I went back to sleep. When I woke up the next morning, I knew I was healed.

I go in for blood tests twice a year. My visit was a few weeks away. I was so excited I called and asked for an earlier appointment. When they got me in the following week, I told the nurse, "I'm not sick anymore." She wrote it down but didn't say much, she drew a vial of blood and sent me on my way.

Four days later my doctor called and had me come in for another blood draw that same day. She called me herself two days later and told me to cut my medication in half for one week, then a dose every other day the following week, then stop taking it all together, then come back in for a recheck! She wouldn't tell me if I was healed, just that, "Your numbers look good."

The second blood test showed I was healed. She said it was a miracle and I agreed.

ANALYSIS

I've been told this before. But I'm still reticent to call on "them" for fear they will actually come. My weight problem has resolved and I'm back to a more than healthy weight. I admit I am envious of the loving relationship you have with your ETs. It reinforces my belief that they come in many races and temperaments, just like human beings.

Case #18

Astounding Similarities

Brian

Victoria, Australia

Dear Terry,

... However, my three experiences I can relay to you, which may be of interest, are as follow:

1) When I was approximately 12, my brother and I used to go to choir practice every Thursday evening in preparation for Sunday's services and on this one evening as we approached the church a huge silver disc sped across the sky behind the steeple of the church. There was no sound, just this flash but long enough to see that it had the typical saucer shape. It must have been quite large because it dwarfed the church itself. Didn't really give it much thought after that but remained very interested because my dad was always interested, and he used to cut out all the notices in the two main papers he subscribed to, "The Age" and "The Herald Sun." So that always kept my interest up!

2) Much later on, say approximately around 17 or 18, a group of friends (including my brother) all decided to go down to the beach at Sandringham (a seaside suburb south of Melbourne City) in the cooler evening because at that time of the year (summer) the evenings were always extremely hot 85° F and it was very hard to sleep. No air-conditioning in those days. We were all carrying on as you do when with friends and suddenly a smallish fiery ball at very high altitude

252

slowly crossed the sky from south to north towards Melbourne. This was curious because this was of course many years prior to Russia's Sputnik. [Brian was born around 1940, making him currently 80 years of age in 2020] A couple of us pointed it out to the others that showed some interest. Curious in itself but not noteworthy really until about 10 – 15 minutes later we saw the same fiery ball on the same path and altitude.

Now this immediately caught the attention of us all but that wasn't the end to it because 10 – 15 mins later another orbit, same path, same altitude, same fiery-looking ball crossed the sky. That was the end to it though and a few of the group left the beach becoming somewhat rattled by the experience. Next day, one of our group contacted the weather observatory at Carrum to see if they had weather balloons up that evening — they hadn't!

3) Many years later, say when I was in my mid-40s, two of my friends and myself decided to pack up working in Melbourne and move to the Sunshine Coast Queensland. At that time, we were all in high-pressure jobs which were wearing us out and we all decided to make the shift to the coast, sharing a house together until we found work and domiciles that suited us all individually.

Taking a road trip together. It is incredible how many times this setup sets the stage for an encounter.

In travelling around, looking at the sights we found this wonderful spot very high up on the hinterland ridge which was at the back of the coast and on that day, parked our car and walked to the fire *emergency lookout tower on the highest part of that ridge. What amazed me at the time was that we were the only people there. All was very still and quiet. We climbed the stairs of the tower and you could see the whole coast area — just magnificent!*

However, as we looked around, suddenly all of us felt very dozy and we must have all dropped off to sleep because before we knew it, we awoke to find the sun setting in the west of our position. That was extremely strange because we arrived a little after lunch and now it must have been about 5 PM. What happened in those sleepy hours? Still don't know to this day.

ANALYSIS

What happened indeed? Probably a great deal. They climbed a fire tower that offered a spectacular view and decided to take a nap? It is just odd behavior, the parallels to the mid-afternoon siesta Toby and I took in 1977 are astounding.

In his response to my inquiry about the aftereffects of this event, Brian shared with me something profound. He stated:

The tower experience cemented for me the direction I wanted to pursue for the rest of my life, and I feel that this experience culminated in this being my main interest for the future.

So that's my experience, there have been no others that I am aware of! Of course, if you think it may be of interest to you or your book then please feel free to use any part or all of my experience.

Cheers.

Thank you, Brian. I appreciate reading your story. It's unsettling to find all the commonalities between people like you and I who've had these experiences. Like your experiences, they weren't a "one on." It was a continuing pattern of encounters with a few years of peace in between.

In *Incident at Devils Den* I described that impulsive afternoon hike we took before setting up camp. By around 3:00 PM we stopped on a limestone outcropping that offered us a beautiful view. As we lay back on the cool limestone with a canopy of shade from a perfectly placed tree, we both fell asleep. I was deeply asleep until Toby began kicking me and yelling, "Get up, get the hell up." Before I even opened my eyes, I could hear the panic in his voice and knew it had to be getting late in the afternoon. It was 7:00 PM. We were a four-mile hike through rough terrain to get back to camp. Fortunately, we made it back just at sunset. We had not even set up camp and did so with the help of my car headlights. I'll always wonder where those four hours went. But just a couple hours later, things got much stranger.

Brian tells us he saw a "huge silver disc... quite large because it dwarfed the church itself." Followed by, *"[I] Didn't really give it a thought after that."* He was accompanied by his brother but makes no mention of debriefing or engaging in a discussion worth mentioning. Interesting too, his father, just like mine, was keenly interested in UFOs.

Three middle-age men are on a high ridge and notice two conditions in regard to their surroundings, (1) they were alone, and (2) "All was very still and quiet." The same scenario Toby and I experienced just seconds before he asked, "Hey Terry, were those lights there before?"

The similarities to my own experience is unsettling. I bet it will resonate with a lot of people. Whatever we are dealing with, it is a global phenomenon.

Case #19

Strangers in the Pasture

Byron

Johannesburg, South Africa

Dear Mr. Lovelace,

I am a 34-year-old mechanic in Johannesburg, actually we're in a small hamlet in the country a bit outside the city. The area is mostly ranchers who did business with my father before me. Farming machinery and trucks are the bulk of our business, but we can fix about anything mechanical. We know most everyone. It is a family business begun by my dad in the 60s. It's me and my aunt and uncle now. We own a cottage attached to the shop and we have a little land to grow our vegetables.

Now, this is hard to imagine but I have no reason to make it up. I experienced it in 2014, and my memory is clear and there is nothing wrong with my mind or my eyesight. Late after the harvest that year, an old customer rang my mobile for some help.

He was stuck in his field with a broken down tractor. I'd worked on it before and was familiar with the machine. He broke a belt and asked me to bring another around to get him running. Easy job. I had the part, so I grabbed my tools and drove over. I found him at the far south side of his field about two kilometers from the house, right where he said he'd be.

His name was Duncan. He's passed on since so I don't think he'd mind if I use his name. Duncan was an older gent, but stout and hardworking. When I parked my truck, I could see Duncan was in a state. I told him to relax, I'd have him on his way before long.

But it wasn't his tractor that had him worked up. There was a tree line on the south end of Duncan's property that marked the boundary separating his property from his neighbor's. Everyone is friendly so it wasn't a neighborly quarrel.

I was confused, he asked me to follow him without explanation. As I followed him through the trees, he advised me to be quiet. I had a firearm on my hip, Duncan carried his in his hand. That was a little odd, so I drew mine as well. Duncan was not the kind of man to draw his sidearm unless he suspected it might be needed. I was expecting some trouble but still had no idea what the devil could be so dangerous. Troublemakers were the only thing I could think of.

Just opposite the trees in the middle of Duncan's neighbor's sheep pasture there were four silver objects about 50 meters away. It was the most unbelievable thing I've ever seen. My first thought was somebody is making a movie. I looked for cameras and there were none. It was just us and these four things.

They were flat on the bottom, round on top like half a sphere, about as big as my Range Rover. They were all spinning clock ways at the same speed and were about six feet above the pasture, casting long shadows eastward in the afternoon sun. There was no noise at all. They glinted in the sun like polished aluminum. I saw no doors or windows and there were no wheels or legs underneath that we could see.

258

They frightened me. I had to resist the urge to run back to the truck and take off. But I didn't want to alarm Duncan who was dealing with heart problems. Besides, there had to be a logical explanation for these things.

I asked Duncan, "How did you find these on the other side of the trees?"

"They flew right over me while I was removing that busted belt," he said. He paused for a moment. He knew I had more questions. Duncan continued, "I noticed their shadow moving across the ground from the corner of my eye and looked up. They were no higher than my barn when I first saw them, and they never make a sound. All four were grouped in a diamond-like formation, like you see them now. They passed over me and then dropped low over the treetops and into the pasture, still spinning like tops. They haven't moved since. What the hell are they?"

My mind was racing for a sane explanation, "They could be satellites or military craft of some kind...?"

"They could be goddamn spaceships too!" suggested Duncan in a whisper.

"No way in hell Duncan, whatever they are there's a sober explanation. I say we walk over there and check them out. I'll show you they're not from outer space. They're from the States or Russia, maybe China, but there's no such things as spaceships." I replied with authority.

"I'm not getting close to them; I'm staying in this thicket. You go over and I'll cover you," suggested Duncan, holding up his pistol.

"Cover me? Are you mad? You'll shoot me in my arse you fool, put your pistol away. I'll do the same and walk over to look at them friendly like," I said.

"If you get into trouble run like hell and we'll make it to your lorry," Duncan advised.

With more than a little false bravado, I strolled over there as casual as you please. The closer I got, I could hear a mechanical whining noise and felt the hair on my arms stand up. Whatever these things where, they were generating a magnetic field. I could feel it.

The tall grass underneath the things had matted down and twirled together to form a pattern, like a crop circle. I wondered, "Am I watching these things make crop circles?"

Duncan became impatient with me. He yelled for me to come back. Instead, I decided to greet them. Looking at the one closest to me I yelled, "Heita, is anyone there? We're friends." To my surprise the thing slowed its rotation and stopped dead still. The other three continued to spin. And never moved.

Then it lowered itself almost all the way to the ground but didn't set down. I still didn't see any seams, doors or joints of any kind. Just a dome of highly polished metal of some kind.

Now this is where things become harder to believe. An arch-shaped portal opened on the side facing me. It opened like a camera lens expanding to make a two meter tall doorway in an instant.

There, inside this thing stood a man in a sliver suit and boots. He stood almost two meters tall and filled the doorway. His facial features were human, hairless and maybe of the Mongolian race. He never smiled or changed facial expression, but I heard him speak by thought transference. I could hear him in my head. All fear had left me, and I was thrilled because I knew I was witnessing something profound.

Never changing his facial expression or talking from his mouth, he asked me, "Do you have a wife and children?" His tone seemed friendly enough, but his question seemed a tad forward.

Speaking aloud I politely told him, "No," and asked, "Where do you come from?"

He replied immediately, "We come from a place near the star system you call Orion, we are not here to harm or to help you. We are here to observe. We need to make some repairs, we will be on our way soon," he said, adding, "We make an apology for our intrusion."

I assured him, "No worries, take as long as you need." It seemed appropriate to ask, "I know how to repair machinery, can I help you?" I strained my eyes to see what was behind him inside his vehicle, but the opening was small, and the interior was illuminated, so I saw him mostly in profile and nothing behind him.

He knew what I was thinking. He offered, "Would you like to step inside and see our devise?"

I felt like a child begging permission. All I could say was, "Yes, please." But I was compelled to add, "I'm concerned about my friend's

261

well-being. He will worry about me if I go inside with you. He might panic. I fear his heart might fail him."

The visitor said, "I understand, go back to your friend because he is very afraid. Tell him we caused you no harm. Tell no one," and with that the door closed in the same fashion that it had opened. I stepped back a few meters and it resumed rotating. Walking mostly backward, I rejoined Duncan who was eager to hear the story and confirm I was not harmed.

Duncan shook my hand and we both turned to watch them from the trees. He eagerly asked, "What did he say to you, was he friendly?"

I assured Duncan, "He was a gentleman. He apologized for the trespass and said they needed to make repairs. He knew you were afraid, and I should return and tell you he didn't hurt me. They come from Orion somewhere and said they were watching us. He also said to 'tell no one.'"

Duncan had pulled out a small amber pill bottle and tossed a couple tiny pills in his mouth. I assumed it was heart medicine. I asked if he was okay and he nodded.

"He was very kind to me, he even invited me inside," I said proudly.

"I was worried, I'm glad you didn't go," Duncan said with relief. "If they took you, what would I tell your aunt and uncle? What would become of you?"

I reassured him everything was alright, and we were in no danger.

Duncan seemed winded. He paused to take a deep breath and said, "He told us to tell no one? Who the hell would believe us? We'd be a joke and the boys would never let us live it down. I say we tell no one, not the constable, not your uncle and I'll not tell Romina, no one."

I agreed, "It's a pact then and we'll tell no one." I was proud of meeting a space man and bragged to my friend, "Can you believe it? He invited me inside for a visit to see their machine." Just as I finished my sentence, we saw all four of these half-dome things slowly rise to about 30 meters and fly away at great speed. We were awestruck by their speed and stood in silence for a few minutes, trying to grasp what had just happened to us.

Duncan and I both had mobile phones, but neither of us thought to take a photograph. That's hard to believe too, but it never entered our minds.

We followed the stranger's advice and never told anyone what happened that afternoon. We knew we had seen something not of this world. Duncan claimed he regretted not going with me to see them up close. I don't think his heart could have taken it.

I fixed his tractor in short order and we parted. Over the next few years Duncan and I would review the experience over a glass of whisky when we could if we were someplace private. Like two old war mates we went over every little detail of our adventure, recalling every second.

Duncan passed away suddenly in 2017 of a heart ailment, he lived to see 82. You're the first soul I've shared this story with Mr. Lovelace. Please keep it true if you put it in your book.

There is an interesting addendum to this story. Duncan's neighbor, Weston, came around to the shop and said he found crop circles in his pasture. He showed me photographs, they were not the best quality and I doubt anyone took him seriously.

I pretended to be amazed. He appreciated that I was interested, and I confirmed, "Those look like real crop circles to me!"

Eight months later, well into the new season, he came by again and asked, "Remember those crop circles? Well, that crop circle nearest to Duncan's land is just a round patch of dirt now, nothing will grow there. Not a weed or a blade of grass. No ants or weevils either. I tossed a piece of mutton in the center and even the flies want no part of it."

I told him that was amazing, adding too, "I wish I'd seen whatever did this to your pasture." After two years the grass slowly returned and has almost covered the bare spot. I never had any dreams about it, but I dream about Duncan a lot.

Yours respectfully,

Byron

ANALYSIS

I thanked Byron for trusting me to tell his story. Except for a few grammatical tweaks, the story is in his words.

Not every encounter is a horrific event. Byron's story is a positive tale with a happy ending. It's interesting that he and Duncan remained friends afterward and enjoyed reliving the event. Like Betty and Barney Hill, they remained friends and preserved their marriage. My wife and I too. So many others do not and it's a mystery to me why.

It's also significant that neither one thought to pull out their phone and take a photograph. Toby's camera was within reach when we had our encounter. Neither Byron nor Duncan took photographs. That is a quite common reaction.

Case #20

Donnel's Blimp

Tyrell

Chicago, Illinois

Dear Sir,

I read your book and you asked if anyone had strange experiences, they were welcome to share them. Here we go and it's a strange one alright. My name is Tyrell, I'm a writer and community activist with a master's degree in social work (MSW). I prefer to not use my real name as I'm a visible political figure in the City of Chicago.

In grade school, my family lived in "the projects" on the South Side of Chicago from 1964 until 1970. I have many fond childhood memories from there despite its deserved reputation for violence and poverty. As children we didn't recognize our poverty. I was raised by my mother and her sister. There were six of us children and two adults in one apartment. I had four brothers and an infant cousin.

We lived in the Robert Taylor Homes, a Chicago public housing complex. More like a ghetto-high-rise apartment than a "home" in the traditional sense. The "housing complex" we knew as "the projects" were known for narcotics, violence and perpetual poverty.

Taylor was a dangerous place to raise a child. I was always with a brother or two. I can recall violence a few times involving others, but I don't recall ever feeling afraid for my life. Things would have

266

likely been different if we'd run the streets or ran with a different crowd, I'm sure.

The only bad memories I have were the omnipresent cockroaches. They were a constant nuisance. Otherwise our home life was loving and nurturing, although crowded.

Mom impressed on us the need for education and the avoidance of risks. I loved school and did very well. Some of my siblings did not fare as well. Our lives are determined 50% by the choices we make, and 50% by chance, circumstances and events outside of our control.

During my first year of high school we moved. Mom got a better paying job at an electric assembly plant that remanufactured various appliance. We were able to rent a large home in a better neighborhood and school was a block away. I had no trouble adapting to my new neighborhood or school and felt accepted. I played basketball and was president of the chess club. I tell you this, so you have an idea of who I am.

When I was a senior, I was home one school night and we were on the upstairs back porch after dinner, just talking and trying to catch a breeze. It was late April and hot, all we had were fans. It was dark outside and my eldest brother, Donnel, saw what he thought was a blimp. He'd seen one once before at some sporting event and was sure that's what it was. It was suddenly right in front of us. We should have seen it before.

We all stared as this "blimp" slowly floated by. There were no lights on it. None at all. It was lit on the underside by the streetlights.

267

It was just a few feet higher than the rooftops and powerlines. I thought it was dangerously low. We didn't see or hear any engines either.

We weren't afraid. My mother said, "Listen." We all stopped talking and listened, expecting to hear something. What we heard was nothing. The neighborhood was silent. "Donnel's blimp" made no noise and we heard no traffic noise either.

After Mom said, "Listen," I don't recall any of us talking either. The blimp was cigar shaped and there was no undercarriage, windows, advertising lights or navigation lights at all. It slowly cruised past the house and disappeared. It must have dropped lower and been hidden by an adjacent house, but that doesn't make sense. It would be too low and the distance between homes was only about 15 feet at the most.

Almost as soon as it was gone, we all just went inside and went to bed. Despite the heat, I slept like a rock and had a hard time getting out of bed in the morning. At breakfast that morning there was little conversation. There was no mention of Donnel's blimp. We didn't discuss it until nearly a year later.

We were driving to a Cubs game and my cousin spotted the Goodyear Blimp and pointed it out.

While we watched the blimp, Donnel spoke up. He asked, "Hey, you guys remember last April? We were on the back porch and I saw that blimp go by? Remember, that crazy blimp with no lights?"

I said, "I think I remember." Everyone admitted to remembering it, but the details were fuzzy. There was an uncomfortable minute

*of silence until someone said something about the game, and the sub-
ject changed. I didn't think it was unusual at the time.*

*Weeks later I thought about it for some reason. I played the
whole thing over in my head in slow motion, like a movie. Our reaction
in the car on the way to the game too. When Donnel brought it up I felt
uneasy for some reason. The details were a blur at the time. I can remember everything clearly now.*

*Donnel and I spoke about it the next day. He didn't remember
it as a big deal. I pressed him, "Is there some reason you don't want to
talk about it?"*

*He got angry. He said, "Yeah, we saw a stupid blimp from the
back porch, what the hell's the big deal?"*

*I apologized and said, "All right, you're right. Sorry, no big
deal." I never discussed it with anyone else in the family. We never
asked neighbors if they saw anything that night. No one ever asked us.
This was urban Chicago, and no one noticed or cared. In retrospect it
just feels odd. It feels like maybe what we saw was not a blimp.*

ANALYSIS

I asked Tyrell if he or anyone in the house had memories of strange
events before or after. He said "no" and described the blimp sighting as
a "one-on." I thanked him for his story because it helps validate the
same thing we've heard before. Witnesses are reticent to talk about a
sighting, even among family members.

Case #21

Someone's in the House...

Mary

Omaha, Nebraska

Hi Mr. Lovelace,

My name is Mary and I'm writing you to tell about the bizarre things that happened in our family home when I was 13. These things happened now and then, until things came to a head and I left home to live with a relative who was not a Jehovah Witness. I am 39 now, and teaching 5th grade in an Omaha suburban school.

I never married or had children of my own. I enjoy children vicariously through teaching. I have never been treated for any form of mental illness except for mild depression following the untimely death of my brother. I've been taking a prescription antidepressant for years and my mood is stable. I do not drink or use drugs because they are contrary to my religious beliefs. I did not make up this story for attention, that's why I insist you not use my true name. The suburban area surrounding Omaha is a collection of huge districts pulling in students from farming communities all around Omaha. Just "Mary" is fine.

I finished your book and found it deeply unsettling. I am not exactly sure what it is regarding your book that made me feel so unsettled. But I think I know. It was my adolescence in a demonic home where my family had contact with what my parents believed were

270

"demons." We also experienced poltergeist activity in the home. It was a literal nightmare for two years.

There is a family dynamic at play here that is somewhat unique and relevant to my reactions and coping efforts. I was raised in a Jehovah Witness (JW) household. We were dedicated to Jehovah and the cause of bringing others into the Hall to worship with the congregation. That involved "door knocking" to hand out our magazine, the "Watch Tower," with the aim of saving people by bringing them into the congregation. Practicing the JW faith requires obedience to Jehovah and discipline to do his work.

Each family member knows his or her role and is expected to participate. It is a very structured upbringing. My social life was strictly limited to friendships with other JWs. Usually, socializing together at functions in the Kingdom Hall. Associating with people outside the congregation was frowned upon.

Post-secondary education was not a priority, but if you wanted a college education you could attend a JW institution that emphasized religion and did precious little to prepare you to compete in the outside world. I was fortunate to attend a small college not affiliated with any religion and obtain a teaching degree.

This began when I was an average 13-year-old JW girl, little different from any other. Dating was a complicated affair for us. You were expected to only associate with congregation members and your time together was always chaperoned. A boy and girl might date for five years and marry before ever knowing intimacy on any level.

Notwithstanding the rigidity, I was happy with the same prepubescent angst most feel at age 13. This was my environment when supernatural things began to happen. I guess they would be called "paranormal" today.

My experiences were frighteningly like yours in so many ways. I know this sounds strange, but when I read your book, I felt you were talking to me.

At home, I had a room to myself. I was the youngest, just like you, with two older brothers across the hallway. It mirrored your living conditions in so many ways.

My father was a window washer and my mother a homemaker. Both considered to be noble professions. Being a JW means preparing for the end of times by living a good life and personally spreading the news about Jehovah to others. JWs believe the end of the world is coming and we should prepare and be ready.

There was also great satisfaction in knowing the rules, living within the boundaries and having reasonable expectations about your future. That is the allure of JW, the simplicity of life that came from blind obedience.

I am not here to disparage JW. I still love Jehovah although, through no fault of my own, I eventually found myself shunned as an "apostate" by the congregation and everyone in it, including my own family. The word "apostate" simply means one that leaves their religion. Everyone that leaves their place of worship to become a JW is an apostate!

I was expelled from the Kingdom Hall as a result of what happened to me. I'm not asking you to harbor anger toward my former religion or my family. I have no anger. I was the focus of these events that disrupted my preplanned and orderly life, and I just want to share the facts. What I thought was demon activity in our home was actually extraterrestrial beings. I know that now.

One evening I went to bed at 10:00 PM. I was exhausted from a day of hard work, door knocking and handing out our literature. Afterward, we had fellowship at the hall and by 9:00 PM, I was exhausted and glad to be home with the day over.

It was the middle of a Nebraska summer and hot as blazes. We had no air-conditioning, but my father gave us all window fans.

We lived in the country. We had a five acre lot with a doublewide home that was comfortable and spotless. My bedroom faced the rear of the property. It was next to my parents, and my two older brothers were across the hall. I had never felt spooked before in this house, except for an occasional bad dream.

Less than a quarter mile behind us was an old cemetery. It hadn't been used since the 1920s and was so overgrown with weeds it was invisible from our backyard. It had been back there my whole life and I never paid it no mind. I certainly hadn't visited it.

This hot summer night I went straight to bed and fell asleep immediately. It was sweltering, so my window was wide open with an old box fan leaned against the widow screen. The white noise of the fan whirling was like a lullaby.

At 2:15 AM I woke up to lights outside my window. They were shining into my room like a searchlight or a bright motorcycle headlamp. There was just a single beam of light and I had no idea what it might be. It scared me and I thought someone might be trying to break in.

I went to Mom and Dad's room and knocked on the door. My dad opened the door. He'd been sound asleep. He rubbed his eyes and asked, "What is it Mary?"

I said, "Dad, I think someone's in the backyard! They shined a light through my window."

Dad didn't hesitate, he said, "Shut your bedroom door and wait in our bedroom with your mother." In his pajamas and slippers, he grabbed a flashlight and walked out the side entrance. We didn't own guns. But my dad was a strong man who did hard manual labor for a living. I think he could handle about anything.

He came back in a few minutes later. "Yeah, there must be some kids in the old cemetery because I can see lights down there."

Fortunately, he did not find any sign that someone tried to break in, but he called the sheriff's office and made a report anyway. They agreed it was probably just kids in the cemetery. They said they would send a car to check things out. We all went back to bed.

I wasn't satisfied. Something had been in the backyard and close to my window. Dad saw lights at the cemetery by the time he got outside, but I know they were in the backyard. My imagination ran wild with thoughts of being raped and murdered in my bed.

274

The next morning, I felt exhausted, like I hadn't slept. A week later the light came back and woke me up again. But it was different this time. I remember going to the window and just watching it. This time, it was about 100 feet off the ground and the light was blue and red sometimes, but mostly all white. I watched it for a while and went back to bed. This time I wasn't concerned or afraid and I didn't feel the need to wake anyone.

The next morning, my mother woke me up and asked, "Why did you go outside at night with no shoes?" She was angry.

"I don't know what you're talking about!" I told her, still in bed and not yet fully awake. I was angry for being woke up and accused of something I didn't do. I had no idea what was going on.

She was lecturing me about tracking mud and grass through the house. "You'll get a bucket and soapy water and clean these floors before you eat breakfast."

I pulled back my sheet and threw my feet over the side of the bed. I was shocked to see my feet were muddy and there was dirt and grass at the bottom of my bed. I was dumbfounded. At the moment, I had no memory of the light in the backyard that night, I wouldn't remember that until later that afternoon.

Mom added, "And you'll wash those sheets too!"

After I cleaned the floor and Mom had cooled down, we talked some more. She was worried and asked, "Did you meet someone last night? One of your girlfriends or some boy? What were you doing outside at night and why didn't you wear shoes? Did you even wear a

275

robe?" she asked. This conversation was more about concern rather than scolding me. I reassured her I met no one. But I thought to myself, "No one I remember anyway."

I had no memory of getting out of bed or ever going outside. I thought about it and the only thing that made sense was sleepwalking. My mother knew I didn't lie.

But soon, there were more strange things happening. Stuff inside our house was moving around all by itself. Either that or someone in the family was playing a horrible prank. That wasn't possible, not my family. We were obedient and loving. None of us would ever do such a thing.

My dad's wallet went missing. He found it two weeks later, it was on top of the hot water heater. I would leave things in my room and they'd be moved. Sometimes by a few feet and a couple times found in my brothers' room or the bathroom.

One night we were all at the kitchen table working on homework, Mom was sitting with us doing her reading. We heard a noise and we all looked up at once. A bowl of apples on the kitchen counter slid across the countertop. Over the edge and crashed on the floor. We all watched it, everyone except my dad who was in bed already. We watched this glass bowl slide four feet and right over the edge of the countertop. Seeing a bowl of apples move by itself as if pushed by an unseen hand scared all of us. It seemed such a mean and malicious thing. We prayed together. None of us slept well that night.

I began having awful nightmares about meeting tiny people in the backyard at night. They didn't hurt me, but they examined me medically and I obeyed them. I heard them tell me "don't be afraid" and I was in a different place like a strange office. The "little people" as I called them were nice to me, but I could never see their faces, they were just a blur. They told me things I could never remember. This was terrifying. I do not believe these were dreams. Not for one minute. This happened.

I finally told my parents and we all prayed. Things quieted down for a while around the house, but at the hall, things were headed out of control. These bizarre events had been happening for almost two years now and it was impossible to keep it secret.

I had a girlfriend at school who was a Baptist. I liked her and wanted her to bring her family to the hall and be our guests. She always refused. But she was always nice to me. Years later it dawned on me, "She pitied me."

Between classes one day we were talking in the hallway by our lockers. The hallway was packed with kids and we spoke louder than we should have. I told her what was going on inside our house and my "dreams." I told her I did not think they were dreams. She wanted me to talk to her pastor. I couldn't do such a thing; it would be a betrayal of my faith.

"Mary," she said with genuine concern, "I think you may have a demon in your home." My church has dealt with these things before. They can be driven out.

I gasped. The thought of our home being possessed by demons scared me. I wondered, "Were they possessing me?"

Regrettably, this conversation was overheard by a fellow JW who promptly told the elders I'd been discussing spirits with a non-believer and had even discussed consulting with their pastor.

JWs don't believe that ghosts exist as the disembodied spirits of the dead. Mom and Dad went to the elders for guidance. It's what good JWs do. They did an "investigation," which meant they spoke to all the other girls that knew me and wanted to know if I was involved in "spiritism" or if I read books about witches, spells and the like. We were all taught those things are "detestable to Jehovah."

During this investigation, someone falsely accused me of reading books about "witches and casting spells." Supposedly, I was seen reading this book in a corner of the library by myself. I would never have done such a thing and I was devastated to be accused.

While this was all coming to a head, my brother claimed he got up to use the bathroom in the middle of the night and saw a three foot tall "spirit" in the hallway. He screamed bloody murder and the whole house woke up. He was convinced "something" was in the house.

The next evening, I was at the Kingdom Hall with my parents. We met with two elders who wanted to "get to the truth." Their idea of the "truth" was for me to confess my sins, be contrite, beg forgiveness for allowing myself to be misled and perform an appropriate penance.

That was unacceptable to me. I told them the truth. I said, "I will not confess to a lie. I don't read such things and the Baptist friend is someone I hoped to bring into the congregation. I invited her and her family to come to the Kingdom Hall, she reciprocated and invited me to visit her church. I politely declined."

No one believed me. I was brokenhearted to leave my school, the congregation and my family. I was sent to live with an "apostate" aunt in Omaha. It was the best thing that ever happened to me. I quickly learned about the world outside the congregation. I was loved like a daughter. My aunt taught at a small college and I was able to attend for little money. I had a job, friends and enjoyed life. My aunt and I are as close as mother and daughter. We attend the Church of Christ together. I never hear from my family. I miss my brothers terribly.

I wish that were the end of it. It wasn't. "They" left me alone for a few years but now and again I'd see the lights outside my window at night. I'd be exhausted the next day and I knew I'd been taken by them. The Church also teaches that these things are demons from hell. I don't think so. Not at all.

Someday, soon I hope, the truth of their presence here on Earth will be known and they'll be accepted for what they really are, living creatures superior to us in intellect that come from a faraway solar system in a distant galaxy. But I don't believe they are supernatural in any way. Superior in some regards, but still the Lord's creatures.

ANALYSIS

I commend your courage and the ability to recover from that level of rejection. Your story is another reminder of the spiritual aspect to this phenomenon.

Your aunt must be an amazing woman. There is so much about world religions I'm just unfamiliar with. I almost left your story out of the mix because I was concerned about offending Jehovah's Witnesses readers. My wife was quick to point out that a book entitled "Devils Den" is unlikely to make the JW reading list. Many people have told me "there's a spiritual component to all of this." I think so too, but I don't understand it. I have had some poltergeist-like events myself and they are scary. Thank you for sharing your story and I wish you and your aunt the best.

Case #22

Never Accept a Ride From a Stranger

Delores
San Francisco, California

Hi Terry,

I enjoyed your book, but it was scary as hell. It brought back a memory from 1968 when I was 15 years old. I was hitchhiking from East San Francisco where I lived with my parents to Long Beach to attend a party.

It was a sunny Saturday morning around 9:00 AM. I'd had my thumb out for 20 minutes and was getting discouraged. My smile and my peasant blouse usually insured a pretty quick ride. We all hitchhiked back then. Unaware there were numerous murders up and down I-5 of young girls looking for a ride.

Finally, an older car, a silver car with white leather interior pulled over. It was odd, but not too unusual for California where cars are a big deal. It looked like a style from the late 50s. The ones with the fins. There were not a lot of silver cars around at the time. This was shiny silver too, almost like chrome.

I caught up to the car and sized up the driver from the open passenger side window. If anyone looked creepy or gave me a bad vibe I'd say, "Thanks, I'll catch the next one, my friends should be by any minute now," and walk away.

The driver looked like a slightly-built middle-aged guy. He was a small man, about the size of my younger brother. He wore jeans, a white tee shirt, sunglasses and slicked back hair. What we called a "greaser look" back then. A bit unusual, but he didn't look dangerous and he smiled. He asked, "Where you headed?"

I told him and he said, "I can get you close, hop in." The car was amazing on the inside. The front seat was a big bench style seat. I thought it was vinyl, but it was nicely stitched white leather. The car was big too, and the dash was all chrome and shiny. It looked like it just rolled off the assembly line. He had some country western music playing low on the radio.

I thanked him for the ride and told him, "My name's Dee. Man, this is a very cool car."

He said, "Thanks." That was it. He wasn't talkative and kept his eyes on the road instead of on me. That was a good thing.

I asked, "What kind of car is this? I don't see any emblem or anything to tell what kind of model this is. Is it a Plymouth?"

Without taking his eyes off the road, he just said, "It's foreign."

And with that, I immediately felt sleepy. Like he had slipped me something, but I didn't eat or drink anything and we were just five minutes into the ride. But I wasn't freaked-out, just tired. I just sat back on this comfortable seat and closed my eyes. I felt like I dozed off for just a second and he said, "We're in Long Beach, where do you want off?"

I was shocked because I had no memory of the ride. Nothing. Fortunately, I didn't feel like I'd been accosted in any way. The same tune was still on the radio and his eyes were still on the road and not on me.

I said, "The second traffic light would be cool, thanks!" That would place me just a half block away from my destination off a side street. My lucky day, or so I thought.

As I got out of the car, I noticed a bank on the corner with a clock outside. It read 11:38. He picked me up around 9:00, it must be wrong I thought. This was a much longer ride.

I intended to look at the backside of the car as he drove away to try to identify the model, but I was distracted by the clock. I felt spacey and tired again. I was a little unsteady on my feet but walked to my friend's house. He was glad to see me. I was supposed to be there early to help him set up things for the party and enjoy his company.

I told him I felt kind of "out of it." He offered me a joint and a cup of coffee. I settled for a cigarette instead and asked if I could lie down. I slept for a while and had the most peculiar dreams that I wish I had written down or told someone about. I can't remember them and that still bugs me.

When I woke up it was after 5:00 and the house was filling up already. I felt better and joined the party. I had a couple cans of beer and passed on the marijuana, I still felt disoriented.

I promised my mom I would be home by midnight and left the party early. I got a ride from friends and was home by 11:00 P.M. I

283

showered and checked myself to see if there was any sign I might have been messed-with in that car. I seemed fine. I went promptly to bed and slept nine hours with no dreams.

The disturbing thing was that the car and this guy were just so weird. Getting sleepy and dozing in a stranger's car is totally out of character for me. I always had my guard up when I was in a stranger's car. The ride took much longer than it should have; I have never been able to figure that out. The fact that this memory is so crystal clear in my mind after all these years is odd too.

My boyfriend at the time was really into cars. I told him about this weird car and the guy that picked me up. He didn't have a clue. Foreign cars of the day didn't have fins. It could have been 12 years old, but it looked so incredibly new. My boyfriend asked if it had "that new car smell."

I told him, "Yeah, kind of. The scent of the leather was really strong. Even with the windows down."

Lastly, I skipped my period the following week! I didn't think I could be pregnant. But I didn't know what may have happened in that car. I had my older sister take me to the doctor and I checked out fine. I had two pregnancy tests a week apart. Both were negative. I was examined and there were no tears or bruising that could be attributed to a sexual assault.

That was the last time I hitchhiked. I made my career in law enforcement as a dispatcher. Maybe that's what keeps this so fresh in my mind. I'm retired now. I doubt I could tell you more than one or two things about my life from when I was 15. But this memory is as sharp as the day after.

I always refer to this as my "Twilight Zone happening of 1968." Have other people had these things happen to them?

ANALYSIS

Yes Dee, other people have had similar experiences. Not identical, but very strange. I asked Dee if she ever considered hypnotic regression to try to recover the lost time. Her response was short and to the point:

If "he," or "they," suppressed my memory, as I believe they did, it was done for a reason. I can only assume it was done for my benefit. I'll leave well enough alone.

Case #23

Hypnotta

Doug Auld

Hoboken, New Jersey

I chose to write this in narrative form because Doug is reticent to blow his own horn. I met Doug earlier this year when he began a group discussion panel on Zoom. It was an eclectic collection of experiencers and researches in the UFO and related fields.

Our panel included Sev Tok who wrote an amazing book called, *You Have the Right to Talk to Aliens*. Her book is filled with wonderfully inspiring words. My favorite quote is on page 108, "When you are achieving your purpose for this lifetime, the entire universe aligns with you and provides a beautiful support system."

We also had Nancy Tremaine on our panel. Nancy is a speaker and author of *Symbiosis* and *Preordained*, both excellent books I highly recommend. We discovered Nancy and I share a great deal in common. Also, on our panel was the delightful Agnes from Austria who contributed so much, the well-read Albert Wacha, our friend "Aurora," me, and Doug Auld. Doug organized and produced the show. We had guests like Grant Cameron, Kathleen Marden and many others.

The second of four children, Doug Auld was born in Queens, New York, 1953. His family moved to a rural New Jersey town when Doug was a young child. He had a natural passion for nature and animals, often visiting the lakes and stream behind his house.

Doug was a resourceful kid who enjoyed tinkering. He liked taking apart and reassembling things. He learned to solve mechanical problems. By the time Doug turned 17, he began attending a technical high school for auto mechanics. His goal was to someday take over his dad's car dealership and follow in his footsteps. His education and experience taught him to think creatively and solve problems by logic and by troubleshooting mechanical things.

Surprisingly, these skills led Doug down another path, away from automobiles and toward an outwardly contradictory path toward his true passion. Doug discovered his instinctive ability for fine art and music.

A 1973 concert by The Doors was Doug's catalyst into the world of music. Doug began to study classical music on the piano and discovered his innate ability to discern pitch. So finely-tuned was his ear that he became a piano tuner with minimal training. His teacher called him "a natural."

Doug and his brother Greg formed a band called East Agony and performed their original music in the NY, NJ area. The band lived on through the 80s in various incarnations. Doug wrote the music and Greg was lead singer.

In 1976, Doug visited the Salvador Dali Museum with his brother Greg, who also painted with oils. The surreal images of Dali were extraordinary, and they haunted Doug. He was intrigued by the technique, style, and story of the paintings. It became a near obsession.

Inspired by Greg, Doug bought his own brushes and paints and decided to "give it a go." Doug's first painting was a portrait of the pop singer Cat Stevens. On seeing his finished painting Doug's family could not believe their eyes. On his first attempt Doug discovered he was an artist with a gift for oil painting. He intuitively captured images with paint as skillfully as a photographer captures images with pixels. Doug had found his true purpose. The would-be auto mechanic was a renaissance man.

As Sev Tok said, "He began achieving his purpose for this lifetime … and truly the universe aligned and provided the needed support." Doug began his art career as a representational painter. He produced 6 distinct series of works to date. His paintings are much sought after, and he hopes to hold a museum exhibit in 2021. I encourage you to visit his art website and judge his talent for yourself at dougauld.com.

In a book devoted to aliens, UFOs, and the otherworldly experiences of everyday people, what does a piano tuner, songwriter and classical painter have to do with the paranormal?

As long as he can remember, Doug has always been drawn to the paranormal. He grew up on Rod Serling's *Twilight Zone, The Outer Limits* and all the UFO and sci-fi movies of the day. He began following the UFO community and its many witnesses and whistleblowers in military and government circles. Doug also became an avid sky watcher, who captures amazing objects with his camera in the night sky. After years of study, eyewitness encounters and research, Doug became convinced the phenomena is real.

He used his creative gifts of art and music to express his passion for the paranormal in a screenplay. Doug just completed a stage musical, "Hypnotta," a fictional story, with an amazing plot based on true events.

It is interesting that Doug had never heard the word Hypnotta before. He explains, "It was a gift, given to me when I woke one early morning." It was a rare moment when an idea manifests from a sleep state to become something profound. The use of the word Hypnotta in Doug's show refers to the twinkling of conscious between the states of asleep and awake. It is not a new concept.

Consider...

Nine ideas that manifested in the sleep state:

- Google. As a student, Larry Page had an irrational fear that he'd been accepted into Stamford University by mistake – which triggered an anxiety dream. ...
- The sewing machine. ...
- DNA. ...
- Einstein's theory of relativity. ...
- Frankenstein. ...
- The periodic table. ...
- The structure of the atom, and undoubtedly Doug's favorite,
- Salvador Dali's Persistence of Memory.

Inspired by experiencer Nancy Tremaine's real-life encounters, Hypnotta tells of the struggle between two 10-year-old friends, Nectar and Jilly. Together, they witnessed an incredible UFO event while at school one day. It was a profound and life-altering event for them both. It caused them to question their belief systems. Because they dared to be truthful, they dealt with the pain of being doubted, even being called liars by their parents and peers. The ridicule drove them to seek to comprehend why people who profess to love them cannot accept the truth. The lines between black and white blur as they try to discern where truth begins and ends.

The show then brings you into the present day, 12 years later. It recounts Nectar and Jilly's journey to reconcile all they saw and experienced and process the consequences. They attempt to find peace and achieve harmony with their past. Their efforts take them to the airwaves and digital media with their blog they call, "Hidden Truths." They investigate, research, interview witnesses and experiencers, spreading the word that this stuff is real and that too many suffer in silence for fear of scorn, but hope exists.

Through their work they seek validation, as well as vindication for themselves and others. They work to expose corruption and conspiracy. They seek to shed light on the darkness of lies and coverups by powers that want to suppress the truth.

It's dangerous work. But the friends know, the more visible they are, the more vocal they are, the safer they are. They experience triumph and tragedy so truth and justice may just prevail. Despite the drama, Hypnotta is free of violence and foul language. It is not needed to tell their story.

Hypnotta is about hope. It was created to entertain, inform, and bring to light the hidden realities of the spirit world. It's the light that illuminates the darkness of misconception regarding the paranormal. In doing so, it frees us from fear.

Hypnotta is uplifting and inspirational much in the tradition of *ET* and the *Wizard of OZ*. It's Judy Garland and ET on a voyage to see the Wizard. It's just fun.

Join us and become a part of the production, please contact Doug Auld at dougrauld@gmail.com

Please visit his art website www.dougauld.com

Case #24

That's My Boy . . . Ugh, Girl?

Timothy

Mobile, Alabama

Dear Sir,

I'm about your age. I lived in Mobile all my life except for two years in the US Army, 1969–1971. My family has a furniture business started by my granddaddy back in 1940. I've had a solid upbringing; I don't drink or use drugs and I've been married to the same woman for 38 years.

This story is going to sound way out there. It happened in 1986 – 1987, beginning in early summer. We lived outside the city in a semi-rural area. We'd rather I not mention the city by name. My wife and I are both members of a Baptist Congregation that we love.

I wouldn't want this experience to harm our relationship with the church we consider family or be seen as demon contact with a member of the opposite sex or such. It was not a demon. It was not a woman either. But its gender was 100% feminine. That at least is not debatable.

It was a really warm summer night. I was ready for bed and I went outside for a quick smoke. I lay down on our porch swing, which is just as comfortable as our bed and I was catching a little breeze to help with the humidity. I remember lighting up a smoke, but I don't remember finishing it or putting it out.

I must have fallen into a deep sleep. The next thing I knew I was in an examination room of some kind, but different. The exam table was built to accommodate one very large person or two people comfortably. The table was padded plastic and soft. I don't recall anything else besides white walls. A small grey man with a human face came into the room carrying some kind of grey canister like a fire extinguisher. I could never get a good look at his face. I couldn't see it clearly. He just seemed like a little generic guy.

He told me to stand up and undress, and I did so without a second thought. When I was naked, he sprayed me down with some sort of aerosol from this canister he held under his arm. I was fine with this too. Whatever this thing was it had a smell like acetone, and it dried almost immediately. He turned and walked out of the room.

I never once had an aggressive thought. I could have easily beat this guy and got the hell out of wherever I was. But I didn't. That's unusual for me, I'm not that passive, usually.

I sat back down on the exam table and felt, I hope it's okay to say this, "sexually aroused." I didn't understand it. I thought, "that man sprayed me with something to make me feel like this."

As I finished that thought a tall blond woman came into the room alone. She was dressed in a white robe that went to her knees. She looked human and about 20 years old and was a very healthy girl, if you get my drift. She had green eyes and made eye contact with me while she took off her robe. She never changed her facial expression or broke eye contact. She let the robe drop to the floor.

She was gorgeous. Looking back at it, she was like perfect. I'd say she was my idea of a perfect woman from her head to her toes. She had shoulder length blond hair. It was weird that she had absolutely no body hair. She did not have eyebrows or hair around her genital area or on her arms. Her skin was very white. She didn't appear to be wearing makeup. She didn't need it. We embraced, and as I held her, I noticed there wasn't a mole or a blemish anywhere on her body.

It's so unlike me. I'm a religious man. I love my wife and can't imagine how this could ever happen to me. I tried to convince myself it was a dream. That worked, but just for a while.

She climbed on top of the table with me. She was just as aroused as I was, I'd say she was the aggressor. And well, we "did it" in the missionary position. She was wonderful, except she never opened her mouth. She just moaned loudly throughout the experience. That was unnatural. If it had not been for her eye contact, I'd been concerned she was in pain. I guess moaning from pain or pleasure sounds about the same. Her eyes were the deepest green and seductive I'd ever seen.

As soon as we finished, she got off the table and picked up her robe and just walked out, carrying the robe in her hand. The little man came in and handed me my tee shirt, shorts, and slippers. That's all I was wearing when he picked me up. I can remember getting dressed, but after that, nothing. I woke up in our bed beside my wife. It was so real. In a way it felt like a dream. But at the same time, I felt violated. I was used somehow against my will.

It was not how people usually have sex. It's not how I would act unless I'd been under the influence of some drug. It was crazy. I never told anyone. But the memory's still with me, and I'm ashamed to admit parts of it are a pleasant memory.

I slept very well that night. In the morning I checked my shorts for any sign of discharge and there was none. I'm married and what I did was a sin. But I don't feel the slightest bit guilty. It wasn't my doing. Not all of it anyway. The cannister of gas the little man held was maybe some kind of disinfectant? Maybe it was something to make me excited? What happened was outside my control.

About eight months later in 1987, I went to bed with my wife as usual. This is going to sound hard to believe. I woke up around 4:00 AM and the little man was in my room again. I was in a haze or twilight-like place. I levitated off the bed by about a foot and floated down the hallway and through the front door. I don't mean an open front door. I went through the damn thing feet first about three feet above the floor. Ten feet from my front door was a silver, metallic egg-shaped thing the size of an RV. I don't know how I got into it, but I found myself in my night clothes sitting on a padded plastic cube in a white room again.

Looking around, I never saw the little man again. The room was empty except for my chair. A woman walked in. I don't think she was a real human being; I think she was an alien of some kind. I'm no expert in these matters. Maybe you can tell me? She was grey and three feet tall. In her hands she had a swaddled infant in a little white cotton blanket. She had a face that was almost human, except it was flat and her eyes were black. She seemed to be casual and friendly enough.

She spoke to me but never opened her mouth. I swear I heard her inside my head, just as clear as if you and I were in a room having a conversation. She held the child out to me, and I took it from her. I was blown away by how little the thing weighed. I thought, "Is this child sick, what am I supposed to do?" She spoke to me telepathically again and said, "This is your child. She needs to see you, smell you and feel your touch."

I pulled back the blanket that was hiding her face. I broke down in tears. Surely, this was my child. She had the most beautiful dark eyes. There was intelligence behind those eyes. Though she never spoke to me. But she communicated with me by her facial expression. I was blown away by the love I felt from her.

Concerned, I asked the matron, or whoever she was, again out loud, "Is she sick, she's so frail?"

The matron responded telepathically again and said, "The child is healthy and well. She will mature into a beautiful being. You'll see her again. Know that she is well and that we thank you."

I kissed her forehead and handed her back to the matron. The little man came in and walked me down a short ramp onto my walkway just a few feet in front of my home. As soon as my foot hit concrete, it flew away.

I was locked out of the house, but I knew where to look for the spare key when needed. Key in hand I laid back on the porch swing and fell asleep. I woke up at dawn and let myself back in the house. My wife was sound asleep still. I lay down and joined her. I experienced mixed emotions of happiness, satisfaction, and a sense of loss. I wondered, "Where will she grow up?"

ANALYSIS

I've heard this story from both genders. It's common. But how would we know if they have the ability to erase our memory or supplant reality with a screen memory? Just for argument's sake, what if this has happened to millions or billions of people? Toward what end? In our next case a sane, solid, former military intelligence analyst with 16 years of active duty military experience recounts a sexual encounter with a blue lady in his own bed. In place of her head was a computer monitor.

Case #25

Intelligence, A Hero's Journey

Matthew Roberts is a former active duty US Navy, and former Office of Naval Intelligence service member. Matthew was on board the USS Roosevelt during the Gimbal event. His book, *Initiated,* is available on Amazon and it's highly recommended.

As told by Matthew:

I first contacted Terry after reading his first book "Incident at Devils Den" in 2018. The reason I decided to reach out to him was because of the multiple subtle similarities between what he experienced and what I experienced. What struck me about his story was his credibility. He had an impressive resume, so I knew in reading it he had to be serious because he was putting all that on the line. At the time I was writing my own book about my experiences. Like Terry, I understood that all of this is much bigger than myself. I understand how all of our experiences are stories worth telling. Individually, they may not tell us a lot but when taken in the entirety, they start to paint an undeniably credible picture of the phenomenon. Collectively, the weight of the evidence over the last 100 years is undeniable proof of the phenomena.

I knew some people would never believe my outrageous story. There were times in my life when I wouldn't have believed it either; until it happened to me. Even a few of the people closest to me, friends who recognized me as the most levelheaded and trustworthy person they had ever met, would change their opinion. I soon discovered who my true friends were.

I realized that I had to share my experiences because I knew what happened to me was very real, it was happening to others, and there needs to be voices out there to share all of this. When my experiences began, I was not okay for quite a while. Like so many others who've shared the experience, it's difficult to process an encounter with the inconceivable without questioning your sanity.

There was no one to talk to, and no way to make it stop. These experiences catch you off guard and turn your life upside down. I told Terry he could choose an experience from my book to include here and I'm glad he chose the one he did because it seems to be the most unbelievable and yet the most deeply personal aspect of the truth of the phenomenon. In talking about this aspect of the phenomenon, we reduce the stigma. When all of this started for me, I was not a spiritual person. I thought religion was nonsense. In looking back at that now, I realize how completely ridiculous that is. The truth is that there is indeed a spiritual component to all of this.

Human beings have long believed in some aspect of the consciousness surviving the death of the human body. Evidence of this belief is supported by archeological data found in funerary sites in ancient Egypt, and as far back as burials dating to 100,000 years ago. Archeologists have unearthed entombments of early humans where personal items and even floral arrangements were placed in the graves of the deceased to take with them. They interred their loved ones with material object that would be useless to a soulless corpse. It's proof that they wanted the cherished and respected members of the community to face the unknowns of the afterlife adequately equipped. They believed their loved one's essence, consciousness, and identity were immortal. That meant that one day they would be reunited on a different plane of existence or return to this realm anew.

Mythology and religious accounts from cultures the world over validate our experiences. Still, many completely dismiss it because we live in a world ruled by peer review. I challenge you to show me a belief system that humans held over the past 100,000 years that had no basis in fact. Something drives these beliefs, otherwise they would have never become so deeply embedded in the human psyche. Today, as I write this, I would take all of the religion, superstition, paranormal, mythology, and lore and I would tie it up in a nice little bow under the quite normal and natural title of "consciousness."

Once, just to take my mind off things, I decided to go to an after-work get-together with some coworkers. In the haze of not getting enough sleep, I forgot to bring civilian clothes to work with me, so I had to go home and change. I came home from work in a rush and changed quickly. I got dressed but didn't like the shirt I chose, so I changed it. Feeling rushed, I threw it over the closet door. It's not something I ever do because I like to keep the closet door closed and you can't do that if there's something hanging on it. It's sloppy, I'm meticulous and averse to clutter and disorder in my bedroom. Like so many other people who've had encounters with the paranormal, I must sleep with my closet door shut.

I got home late that night and recall being exhausted, so I took a shower and went to bed. I was too tired to bother with hanging up that shirt that still hung on my open closet door. "I'll take care of it tomorrow," I thought to myself as I looked up from my bed at the open closet door. This wasn't the type of thing I would normally do. It was out of character for me. I had adopted this philosophy about life. Whenever I was tempted to procrastinate, I took that as my cue to take immediate action. Nonetheless, I threw my head into the pillow and fell asleep rather quickly.

At some point that night I woke up. I could feel a hand touching my arm. I opened my eyes. The first thing I saw was my window off to the left. I was in my room, in my bed, on my back. I was looking at the trim around my window as I thought about how I must have snored myself awake. I inevitably do this when I sleep on my back. I am a stomach sleeper because of that. I then noticed that my vision was slightly blurry. I could not see the detail in the trim around the window anymore. I tried to raise my hand to my face to rub the sleep out of my eyes and realized that it just flopped there at my side. I couldn't move. I glanced down toward my hand and noticed that I was no longer under my comforter. My body felt very heavy.

I then woke up fully because I felt a hand on my right arm just below the shoulder. I should have been scared out of my wits, frightened that there was someone in my room and they had their hand on *my arm. But my thoughts and emotions were inappropriate to the events that unfolded. I felt no fear. It was as though my emotions were also paralyzed. I fought to turn my head to the right. As I did, the room became even more blurred and the grip on my arm became tighter. I turned my head slowly and scanned the room. I saw my shirt hanging on the open closet door. By the time I was able to get my head turned to the right, my vision shifted from blurred to completely out of focus. I squinted and saw a dark shadowy outline of someone standing over me bent slightly at the waist. They moved closer, looking into my face. I saw two arms, a torso, and a head. As soon as I processed what I was seeing, the very tall shadowy figure began to slowly light up with this golden glow.*

I saw the being lean back and away from my face. I saw the golden glow reflect on the walls behind this figure. It was as though this figure had a light source on its back that became more luminous as it slowly began to warm up. The figure began to turn its head toward my window. Soon, the light became blinding and then became organized into rays of golden light that were extending out of the indistinct dark head of this being standing over me. All the while its hand was on my arm. I saw the being turn its head back in my direction. Abruptly, an image appeared over the face of this being. It was the image of a face. It was as though there was an extremely high definition screen, similar to a computer monitor. It covered the beings face and displayed benign images of people I knew. I was aware these were projected views and not the genuine individuals portrayed.

The faces were so sharp and well defined that it occurred to me I had never seen a device with this type of clarity before. I never imagined a device capable of such precision existed. It stopped on a picture of an ex of mine from 20 years ago. It wasn't as though I could have thought this image was this person in any way. While it was crystal clear, it was plain to see it was not the true face of the person I was seeing. It was fake, a projected image to deceive me. You can't hold a tablet up to your face with an image of someone else and be deceived or even pretend that it's actually the person. In looking at this scene and taking this all in, I thought to myself, "What is going on?!" I drifted back to sleep. Just before I lost consciousness, I felt the heavy weight of a large being crawling onto my bed.

I began to have a sexual dream with me and my ex from 20 years ago. In the dream, it was me and my ex surrounded by nothing but complete darkness. There was no floor, no bed; there was nothing. I was barely asleep. The dream seemed so real, as though I was actually feeling the things that were happening in the dream. I opened my eyes as I started to regain consciousness.

I could see that there was a female on top of me. I was back in my room out of the dream. This female had blue skin. I could see her legs were straddling me. My hands were on her legs and I could feel her skin. It was not like human skin. It was clearly thicker and felt tighter than ours. I could see a belly button. I remembered seeing that there was even a slight layer of fat under her skin because I could see the cellulite dimples even though she was thin and had an amazing body. She was wearing a top. The top had red and silver stripes in a vertical zigzag pattern and appeared to be made of the most impossibly tiny beads. It appeared handmade, and of the finest craftsmanship. The way her top glistened in the light of my TV made me think that the beads may have been tiny rubies and actual silver beads or perhaps some other precious metal.

As I scanned up toward her face it was a blur, although much clearer than before. It was obvious that she did not want me to see her face. I could only see the outline of her face and a very large black mass around her head. I couldn't make out what this black mass was. Maybe she had a lot of black hair on her head? Maybe she was wearing something on her head and perhaps that mass on her head is some kind of technology? Maybe it was the technology she didn't want me to see? Perhaps her face is very alien and would be shocking if I saw it? Maybe she had giant black wings? Or it's a combination of all of that. I wasn't really sure, but as I write this now, I know what it was. Whatever was going on up there she wasn't going to let me see it. I was in and out of this dream state several times as the experience wore on.

At one point, I felt her breath on my face. I remember thinking that I couldn't believe this was happening. I knew even in this state that she was not human. I knew there must have been some craft parked in the backyard. In my dream I did climax, obviously. She wasn't going to leave without that I'm sure.

The next thing I remember was waking up the next morning. I was once again looking at the window when I woke up and daylight was coming in through it. I went downstairs in a daze, went out to my truck and stood there dry heaving. I wanted to vomit, but there was nothing in my stomach. I climbed in my truck and lit a cigarette. I was confused. I was angry. Most of all I was terrified. I was raped and there was absolutely nothing I could do about it. I had zero recourse. It was sinking in that there was nothing that I or anyone could do about it. I couldn't even tell anyone. I found all of this very, very, deeply disturbing. I felt devastated. I wanted to understand all of this. I was just raped and denied any empathy or meaningful communication.

I began to unwrap the experience in my mind. How could this being have known about an ex and the intimacy we shared 20 years ago? Why was there a complete disregard for me in this encounter? What does this mean for humanity? I may have a child or countless children somewhere in the universe that I will likely never know or even meet. The thought occurred to me that this has been going on a long time.

Religious art and even cave paintings have always depicted deities and divine beings with golden halos around their heads. Golden rays of light extending from the head. It was exactly the same light show I had seen as this being stood over me. The whole story of fallen angels having sex with the daughters of men went rolling through my head. This is a fucking nightmare!! Were we just fuel for some kind of slave race and didn't know it yet? What - the - f**k - is - going - on?!!

I began to comb through the entire experience. My mind was racing. Lying there paralyzed...that feeling of heaviness...feeling like my body weighed a thousand pounds. This was what medicine would

describe as "sleep paralysis." The dream state surrounded by noth-
ing... I've experienced that before... This isn't the first time this has
happened to me. Tears began rolling down my face as I recalled an-
other time when I felt the same heaviness. I started shaking. I was ter-
rified as I recalled these experiences, I thought were just weird dreams
in my past. Now I know better.

For a long time after this experience I was not okay. I was a 39-
year-old man that slept with the lights on like a small child. The dark
terrified me because it was a place where the comfortable reality to
which I was accustomed no longer existed. The nighttime terror was
exhausting and at times I couldn't bring myself to go to sleep because
the second I did; the darkness would creep in. Reality would crumble
like the deteriorating walls of some old, dark haunted mansion and
come crashing down around me. Whether it was waking up to a room
of beings that were clearly not human or some night terror where I
woke covered in so much sweat that it looked as though I had been
standing in the shower, sleep was not something I looked forward to.
The emotional crisis and terror I felt saw to it that I spent the next sev-
eral months curled up in a ball on the floor of my bedroom with my
teeth chattering, shivering, and crying like a baby.

As I sit and write this to be included in Terry's book, I want
readers to know that I have never been better than I am right now. I am
reminded of my favorite bit of Greek mythology in the form of "The
Homeric Hymn to Demeter." In the hymn the goddess Demeter wan-
ders the earth disguised as an old woman. She decides to repay the
Lord of Eleusis and his family for their kindness toward her. To repay

them, she decides she will turn their youngest son into an immortal god. To accomplish this, she begins delivering the boy sacred rites by coating his body in ambrosia and placing him in a fire to burn like a log every night, burning away his mortal soul. The boy's mother discovers this one night and screams. Demeter is enraged by her reaction. Demeter throws off her disguise and chides the boy's mother, "Silly mortal, unable to tell the difference from good fortune and bad." Soon Demeter is standing enveloped in her immortal beauty as her divine light shows like a bolt of lightning illuminating the entire palace.

These days, I can see the truth of these experiences in all the world's religions, mythology, art, movies, and music. It's everywhere. I see it in the works of ancient Egypt, Greece, and Rome. I found it most recently in the humanist art and Neoplatonism influenced perennial philosophy movement of the high Italian renaissance. Know that if you are experiencing these things associated with the phenomenon that you are going to be alight. Once I worked past the fear, I realized that "I AM," and that this is the most powerful phrase ever spoken. It can be found in two of my favorite songs, "Heaven" and "The Adventure," both by Angels and Airwaves. In the wise words of William Walker Atkinson, one of my favorite authors on the subject of the phenomenon and the associated pain, "All Life follows this plan—the pains of labor and birth ever precede the Deliverance. Such is Life—and Life is based upon Truth—and all is well with the world."

ANALYSIS

Matthew's restrained by law from telling us his complete story. I'm not a psychologist, so I can only imagine how difficult it must be to carry this burden. I kept mine secret for 40 years. Matthew is still a young man. Entanglement with US Naval Intelligence or the FBI could be a disaster affecting his future career, peace of mind and emotional health. It might also hinder his ability to heal from a traumatic sexual assault.

There's also the lingering question. What was the purpose of this entity's encounter? It was likely to produce a partially human hybrid. It's painful to wonder if your child, even if only half human but your flesh and blood none the less, exists on some other plane of existence. A problem many more women than men report, but the true numbers will never be known.

Case #26

Another Veteran's Story

Gregory Perkins

Huntington Beach, California

Dear Mr. Lovelace,

Greetings to you, hopefully all is well! Thank you for sharing your deeply personal story regarding the strange events, which have seemingly greatly impacted you and Toby throughout both of your lives. Please accept my condolences regarding the loss of Toby. I understand that you lost touch after the incident, according to your book, but I would not think that would make his passing much easier, considering the events you shared. Aside from that, speaking from experience, losing brothers-in-arms (those with whom we served in the military)—irrespective of how much time passes—is always impactful. Thank you for your service, sir. I have served 14 years and 2 months in the U.S. Army as an enlisted non-commissioned officer (1994-2007).

I have experienced events of "high strangeness" which I would like to share; I am hoping you will not mind. I have had a fascination with paranormal topics for most of my life specifically because of events I experienced beginning from when I was approximately four years old.

I will share what I think was the most impactful to me from that time. I believe around late spring-early summer of 1980; I was playing outside in my maternal grandparents' garden. This was not a small garden; it took up roughly a quarter of their property. They lived in a residential area in a section of California known for its many vineyards and wineries. My mother's side of the family were agrarian and blue collar laborers. My grandparents grew mostly grapes with a decent-size patch of vegetables.

I remember playing in the dirt in their small corn patch one day. The sun was shining, and it was warm. Suddenly, something fell out of the clear blue sky and bonked me on the head. It hit hard enough to cause me to cry but not hard enough to cause any serious damage. It was a small dark object with a filament type line attached to its center. It did not touch the ground; the small object was dangling just above the ground by this line. I traced the line up into the sky where it appeared to come from nowhere. There was no visible source. The line appeared to literally come out of the clear blue sky.

I remember running into the house to tell my grandma that something hit me on the head in the garden. She comforted me, but also said that's what I get for being disobedient; the garden was supposed to be off limits. She sent me back outside to play.

Of course, I went straight back to the garden. I climbed over the small fence and loitered at one end of the garden. Somehow, I knew that whatever it was that bonked my head was still around. I took off running through the garden as fast as my little legs could carry my disobedient little butt towards the other end. The objects were dropping out of the sky one by one attempting to bonk my head again. I moved just fast enough that the objects would miss and fall behind me. I was looking over my shoulder and could see them miss me which made me squeal with laughter. I ran clear across the garden out maneuvered three attempts to bonk my head. I glimpsed the first two objects being retracted back up into the sky as I ran on. After the third object fell behind me, I turned around and grabbed a hold of the filament. I pulled myself up and set my little feet on top of the object dangling at the end of the line. I swung on the line, waiting for it to pull me up to wherever it came from. It never did. The line stayed stationary as long as I was hanging on to it. I remember feeling some bounce as the filament stretched some with me playing on it. After a while, I became bored and let it go.

As soon as I let go, the object retracted back into the sky. I never saw the source—or, perhaps better stated, I do not remember ever seeing the source. Mr. Lovelace, I personally know there are things all around us that we cannot see. However, "they" watch us for sure.

As far as I can remember, I was never approached by "monkeymen." They did not approach me in that form. When I was young, they would take the form of clothes on a hanger. A set of clothes or a jacket would approach me, with no visible body or limbs. Just the clothes, with the hanger sticking out as the head. I called them the "hanger heads." I'm sure the monkeymen were scary but try to imagine your reaction to empty clothes on a hanger coming to get you. In retrospect, I do not think they meant to frighten me. They were trying to appear as something benign and non-threatening. Dude, big fail.

311

To be completely honest, as far as I can recall, I never actually saw "them." At least not their true physical forms. A very small part of me wants to see them at least once so that I know I'm not crazy. But perhaps I'm fortunate to not have seen them or to not remember seeing them.

My wife and kids were recently on a long trip to visit her family back in Iowa. She decided to make the long drive with our kids to save on airfare, and to avoid the hassle of air travel in the current COVID-19 environment.

Unfortunately, I could not go. I had just started a new job and had no vacation time accrued. So, I stayed home with the dogs. We have three large, male English setters. We generally do not let them in our bedroom—even though they are house trained—because their hair gets everywhere.

One night, they were running around the house and back and forth up and down my bedroom hallway half-heartedly barking every few moments. As if there might be something there to bark at but not totally sure. They kept me up because I kept getting out of bed to see if I could figure out what was antagonizing them. I could find nothing. It could have been a deer or stray dogs on the property. I reassured myself it was probably nothing, but I still felt a bit spooked. I chalked it up to being alone.

The next night, they started the same behavior after I went to bed. This time was different though. I could feel myself being forced to sleep. I could feel the familiar tingles running down the back of my neck. As I fought it, the tingling would intensify. I went from wondering, "Is there something weird going on with my neck?" to, "Yep, there is definitely something happening." I wasn't necessarily afraid, but damn if I did not fight it anyway. You can feel their annoyance when you do not fully cooperate. Instead of feeling worrisome about their annoyance, for some reason, it eggs me on. Their agitation makes me do it even more. They finally got me into that place between awake and asleep.

At this point, I felt something or someone crawl onto my bed with me. I tried to move but was completely immobilized. I fought incredibly hard and managed to start breaking their immobilization. I moved my arm, but it was extremely difficult. It was analogous to moving through soft clay. The harder I fought the more they turned up the juice on whatever it was that they were using to keep me still. I was able to move regardless.

As soon as they realized I was breaking free, they sent a person into my dream to talk to me. It was a light-skinned Black lady. I said to her, "So this is the form you appear in."

She did not respond. She just started to walk away. I asked, "Since you're here, can you run your fingers through my hair?"

She stopped, turned to look at me inquisitively, and said, "Yes." I could feel fingers stroking my hair. She then knelt down beside my side of the bed and said these exact words: "We would love it; it would be very helpful to us if you could bring home moon focus."

Immediately afterward I woke up and was able to move freely again. I picked up my iPhone and searched for "moon focus" but did not find anything I felt was relevant. This happened only a few weeks ago. I have no idea what "she" was talking about. Mr. Lovelace, do you by chance know what is meant by "moon focus?"

Anyway, after that night, my dogs slept in the bedroom. The largest dog slept in bed with me. They didn't come back while our dogs were with me. I know they have wild technology and can do crazy things, but I'm not convinced they can safely deal with me and the three dogs together. Although, I could be wrong. Also, I sense that they are concerned that their technology was not 100% effective on me. It was 90% – 95% effective so it may as well be 100% for all the good fighting being retrained did me. But they find that 5% – 10% concerning. That 5% – 10% difference may account for the fragments of memories most of us carry.

There is a lot more, but I think this is enough for now. I want to conclude by thanking you again for sharing your story. Your book was well-written and informative.

I am taking you up on your offer to reach out to someone. I don't talk about this mess with people generally. I keep this all to myself. Somehow, that seems counterproductive. But if I say anything, people think I'm nuts, I lose credibility, people laugh and joke, etc. I talk to my wife about it and she is understanding. But her understanding only goes so far because she's also very pragmatic. She tends to only concern herself with things over which she has control. I've reached out to

MUFON about my experiences. They sent me a form to fill out. Unfortunately, they only care about those experiencers whose experiences meet very specific criteria. In other words, they gravitate towards those who have the most sensational stories. My tale is definitely weird but by no means is it earth-shattering. If I do not hear from you, I wish you all the best. I'm glad your ordeal is over, Mr. Lovelace.

Most Sincerely,

Gregory

ANALYSIS

I emailed Gregory back immediately. So much of his story hits home with me. As earlier discussed, people have reported entities appearing to them in their childhood as benign beings. For me, it was little circus monkeys. For my cousin Gerald, it was clowns. People have reported bunnies, orbs, racoons, Disney characters, owls, "little grey men," and on and on.

I asked Greg's permission to share his story because I thought it was important on several levels. We're both veterans, and like Matthew Roberts in the previous case, we both have military service in our history and experiences in our home with a female non-human entity. Both of us experienced disguised beings as young children.

His experience at his grandparent's property with the filament of line dropping down from a clear sky reminded me of my own backyard encounter in 1963. Was he abducted? I can only speculate, but I would say it's likely.

I asked Greg if there was more to his story he'd care to share with us. The following is his kind reply:

Hi Terry,

Thank you for responding to my email. I didn't think I would get a response so quickly. I don't mind if you use my story for your book, if you think it's worthwhile to include. I'll share whatever details I can remember. I do agree with you that "they" follow us for a lifetime. I know that they are always there. I can occasionally feel their presence—they make it known. As far as I can remember, though, I have never actually physically seen them.

As to your questions: Have you woken with weird wounds or bruises in the past six months?

Short answer, no. That's a detail that seems critically different from many encounter stories. I do not ever remember waking up with or otherwise receiving unexplainable wounds, bruises, or marks; not in the last six months nor throughout my entire life. Aside from no unexplainable marks or no memory of unexplainable marks, my encounters seem to be similar to those that others experience. Why? Good question.

Have you suffered from a vague anxiety that "something big is coming?" I do have a feeling that "something big is coming." But I don't have anxiety about it. Oddly, the feeling doesn't worry me or bother me in the least. It's not ambivalence, I do care. I'm not sure how else to explain it.

I don't mind sharing more information. The encounter in my grandparents' garden is not the weirdest event. A lot of my memories as a child are with my grandparents. I was born in 1976 and spent a good bit of my early childhood with my grandparents in California. This is why my experiences were centered around my grandparents.

One evening, I was lying on the couch watching TV. The set was an old-school, box color TV with the rabbit-ear antenna, on-off pull switch, and UHF click dial as well as a VHF click dial.

Grandma was sitting on the end of the big couch doing her crossword puzzles under the table lamplight. My grandpa was in the kitchen. I heard his footsteps in the kitchen coming towards the living room. I sat up and twisted partially around to ask him a question as he was coming through the doorway between the kitchen and living room. However, my question was never asked because I immediately recognized something bizarre was happening.

As I turned and looked at Grandpa, he was completely frozen in place, in mid-stride. One foot in the kitchen, the heel of the other foot planted in the living room with toes off the floor. His mouth was wide open as if he were speaking. Despite his mouth being opened, his lips and eyes were crinkled in a way as if he were amused. It was the same effect as looking at a single frozen frame of movie film.

I looked over at my grandma. She was frozen in place under the lamplight with her pen, still and unmoving, pointed into her puzzle book. I looked back and forth between them trying to reconcile what was happening.

317

A few moments later, they vanished in the darkness as the lights and TV went off. I was left sitting on the couch in complete darkness whereas just a moment before, my grandparents were fully animated and into their evening routine.

I was terrified. I didn't know what time it was when this first began and when all the lights went out. I have no idea if there was missing time—I suspect there may have been, but my position on the couch hadn't changed. Aside from cowering underneath the afghan in paralyzing fear, I don't remember anything else from that night. I also don't remember asking my grandparents about it. I remembered it happening at some later point in my life.

Unfortunately, I couldn't say how long before or after the garden incident this took place. I've had unbelievable things happen to me throughout my life.

Another example. My dad's parents had a four-foot above ground swimming pool. One day I was there, I don't recall my exact age, but I was a kid. Not knowing how to swim and having very little experience with water outside my routine bath, I jumped into water that was over my head.

I sank like a stone to the bottom; my feet were on the pool floor. I turned around to try to get to the ladder but couldn't reach it. I was struggling to get to it.

But I wasn't panicked—because I was breathing the whole time while submerged underwater. One of my uncles (my Uncle Joe, I believe) eventually lifted me out of the water. There I went, taking off to the next thing as if nothing happened.

Another incident occurred when I was a little older. I was walking home from a friend's house when it was stormy. I stepped off the curb to cross the street when I suddenly, immediately, and uncontrollably jumped back to the curb. My body reacted before I even knew the catalyst for my actions. I was back on the curb in a split-second and a bolt of lightning struck the exact spot where I had been standing less than a second before.

That was nutty. My entire life in some respects has been charmed. I haven't been immune to bad things or bad luck, but I seemed to escape potentially major life-altering events unscathed. Not only do these things follow me, they intervene a lot on my behalf.

I don't know why, Terry. Why are some folk terrorized by these things and others treated well? Not everyone is affected by them or treated the same. Some people are treated with disdain, some with ambivalence, and others with kindness and respect. Many, many people are not treated any way at all because they are completely ignored and left alone. I don't think I'd be here, Terry, if they weren't watching and intervening.

I'd be more than happy to answer any questions you may have and help you fill out other details you think are pertinent to telling the story. If you want to interview me or otherwise talk about this, I'm more than happy to oblige. My story is all over the place and it's hard to make sense of it all. Our children have all had weird experiences too.

They were all different from my experiences and from each other. My oldest saw a "shadow person" watching him from his bedroom door-way. My middle one said he floated out of his bedroom down to the basement where he was surrounded by men with laptops. My youngest had interactions with what he called, "the monsters in the woods." They are all otherwise healthy and generally well-adjusted youngsters. Our middle one now swears it was just a dream. Perhaps it was.

Let me know what you need, Terry. I'll accommodate as best I can. Thank you for taking an interest in my experiences.

All the best,

Greg

ANALYSIS

Greg's email was one of the best I received, not only because of its authenticity, but the variety of his experiences are incredible. I also find military witnesses to be some of the most credible.

His story demonstrates this phenomenon is a familial experience. They tend to be a family affair involving multiple generations. His description of the filament line from above and the stoppage of time while visiting his grandparents are both unique. His stories underscore how diverse these experiences can be.

In a subsequent email Greg assured me his children are fine and don't seem to have suffered trauma from their encounters. I asked him to please keep me informed of future developments.

Case #27

Mt. Diablo Abduction

Tony

Northern California

Dear Mr. Lovelace.

As we discussed in our telephone conversation these events happened, or should I say began, in November 1996. It occurred at Castle Rock Park in California on the foothills of Mt. Diablo. My experiences began with solo excursions, but ultimately my cousin and best friend would be drawn into a shared experience. It changed our lives and sadly altered the nature of our relationship.

It started with a visit to a hill atop Castle Rock and the discovery of a special place. What I knew as "my spot." Visiting that spot morphed into an inexplicable compulsion to travel to Castle Rock Park at night and enjoy some time there. It became a strangely satisfying nightly excursion. I felt inappropriately possessive of my little spot. My visits to the site became a nightly ritual that took on the feel of an obligation.

I made the journey to "my spot" almost every night. In retrospect, I was being controlled by something. Whatever was driving this compulsion was outside of my ability to perceive it. It made no sense to me then, and it makes no sense all these years later. I was obligated to make the trip and stand vigilant. But for what? Beyond the compulsion it was a mystery. I should add there was nothing wrong with my state of mind or mental health. I wasn't suffering from OCD in any other area of my life.

I recognize now that I was to there to make myself available to "them," but I had no conscious awareness of that at the time. My spot was a meeting place, and my appointment date would come soon. I always made a campfire as my beacon. On some level I knew they didn't need a beacon to find me, but the fire gave me a little light and the warmth was comforting.

This night, as I stood next to my campfire, I just enjoyed the magnificent view of Mt. Diablo in the glow of the moon. I felt at peace with the woods around me. I'd been there for about an hour or so and everything had been serene and peaceful. It was mostly silent except for the occasional hoot from a nearby owl or the quiet rustling of a raccoon or possum in the tree line. Nothing was out of the ordinary. Just another quiet night in the hills, just me and nature, subconsciously waiting for my rendezvous.

Then I heard the footsteps. They were easily distinguished from the other forest sounds. We're the only bipedal animal on the North American Continent, the only bipedal animal on the planet for that matter. I heard the unmistakable crunch of footfalls from no more than 25 to 30 feet away. I heard each foot meet the ground and twigs crunch under the weight. I squinted and strained my eyes to see beyond the dim light of my campfire, but whoever was there chose to stay hidden in the shadows at the tree line. It was unnerving. This didn't feel right. Something was off.

I shouted into the darkness, "Hey, who's there? I'm just enjoying my fire and chilling. No problems man."

Silence. I waited but there was no reply. By now, the footsteps had moved closer. When they were within 15 to 20 feet away, I tried again, "Hey, what's up? You better let me know who you are. I'm warning you! I'm armed."

I questioned myself, "Another hiker?" That hardly seemed likely. I wished I'd had a firearm. I did have a decent knife, long enough to be lethal, but it worried me I might be taking a knife to a gunfight. Still, it was all I had. I felt my heart pounding as the adrenaline kicked in. Balancing the fight-or-flight impulse, I stood determined to hold my ground.

Whoever was there wasn't intimidated. Their failure to respond turned the whole encounter adversarial. The last thing I wanted was a confrontation. I still couldn't make out a figure in the distance. It continued to get closer and I held my knife at the ready to defend my position, what I saw as "my ground." The footsteps were now just 10 or 12 feet away. I could clearly hear them, but no one was visible. It made no sense. I took some comfort in that they didn't make the pounding sound of heavy steps taken by something or someone much bigger and heavier than myself.

It was now nearing eight feet from where I stood. Defensively and instinctually, I backed up a few feet. By the dimming light of my *fire, I could see dust rise and the leaves move with each disembodied footfall. I started to call out again but stopped myself. I reasoned, "Whatever this was, it wasn't human, or it would be visible by now." My mind raced with possibilities, "ghosts maybe?" I wish it had been. I'd been better prepared mentally to encounter the spirit of a deceased Native American or some long-deceased explorer.*

The footsteps abruptly halted just six feet in front of me. Still, I saw no one. This whole encounter lasted just thirty seconds, but time is hard to measure when I'm under stress. My knife was at the ready and I stood in a defensive posture. I was afraid but dared not show it.

I then became aware of a static electric-like charge in the air. I also had that feeling of eyes on me. I was aware that I was being watched by something invisible. I froze in place. Terrified, I realized I couldn't move as I tried my best to take a step back. I felt a numbness come over me, my fingers tingled. Unable to maintain my grip, my knife dropped to the ground. Now I wanted to flee for my life. Only able to move my eyes, I strained hard again to focus on what was now nearly in front of me.

Then I saw it. Well, I almost saw it. It was a transparent but distorted silhouette. I could distinguish its blurred outline against the background of the trees behind it. It was a humanoid figure about four foot tall with a disproportionate large head, spindly limbs and torso. This was not the image of a human being. I sensed that somehow, we locked eyes, even though its eyes were invisible.

Either from shock or terror I felt I was losing consciousness. I wasn't fainting. There's a difference. I felt like I'd been anesthetized and was drifting into a sedated state. I can recall that his figure reached out to me and took me by my arm. Firmly but not forcibly, it guided me back toward the campfire. I was unsteady on my feet and staggered as he walked me back. I was unable to resist. The thought of resisting never really entered my mind.

That's when I heard the others approach. They were also invisible, but I was aware of the presence of three or four other beings around me. I felt other hands on my back, head and arms to steady me. They gently helped me to the ground by the fire. The one cradled my head and placed it on top of a rotten log. The others straightened my legs. I was stretched out by the fire with the impression they wanted me to relax. I felt reassured that everything would be okay. My fear ebbed and I began to relax as the sedated feeling intensified.

I never heard them audibly or telepathically, but I knew their intention. They controlled my perceptions and actions so I would comply with their instructions.

It was suddenly silent. No more sounds of motion, but I knew they were there watching. I was in a calm state, relaxed but still conscious. Without warning I saw a blinding flash of light visible through the closed lids of my eyes. It was like a bomb went off in front of my face. I heard nothing and felt nothing. Quickly, everything went black and I lost consciousness.

I figure I was out for about six hours. When I came to, it was dawn. The sun was just up. It was about 6:00 AM. My campfire was cold. Glancing around my campsite I could see nothing had been disturbed. My backpack was in place and even the ground looked undisturbed. My clothing was fine except for a little dirt from being on the ground.

When I sat up, I realized I hurt. I was sore and groggy. Confused, I had no memory of what transpired that night. My mind was blank. All I could recall was being overwhelmed by sleepiness and lying next to the fire. I assumed I'd slid into a deep sleep, tired from the hike and the late hour.

In September of 2019 something unexpected and dramatic happened. I woke up. After years of nightmares and flashbacks my memory returned. At least partially. I could now remember what happened up until that silent explosion of light. It would be just a glimpse into the totality of my journey.

ANALYSIS

Mt. Diablo has a long and haunting history. More so than Devil's Den. Here again we see someone drawn to a location by an uncontrollable compulsion. Tony did not send me his account of the actual abduction, all I have is bits and pieces from a telephone call. In that call, he spoke about an abduction event where he and his friend and a cousin were taken together. He remembers an exam room and a being similar to what I saw in 1977, an entity I call "Dr. Bug."

326

He also uses a phrase I've heard used often lately. In the last year or so, people tell me they, "woke up." Memories come flooding back in what some refer to as a "download." Is this reality, fantasy, or confabulation? I believe this is real and a global phenomenon leading us to a global shift in human consciousness. But I don't expect change to occur overnight.

Case #28

The Billy Hallmon Story

By Billy Hallmon

I met Billy Hallmon at a Dallas MUFON meeting in 2018. I spoke for roughly two hours. I ran into Billy in the hallway afterward and in 15 minutes he told me the most incredible story.

Billy is a credible man and a keen observer. I'll defer to Billy and allow him to tell you his story personally:

Photograph of Billy displaying his recreation of the UFO he saw over Dallas, Texas. Photographs are property of Billy Hallmon and shared with his kind permission. It's worth noting here that Billy is a talented artist and can "draw what he sees."

A UFO over Dallas had two operational phases, which I observed—slow-speed and fast-speed. During the slow-speed phase, it
looked and sounded material, and acted within Newtonian laws. Con-
versely, during the fast-speed phase, the UFO appeared to be non-material and moved outside of Newtonian physics. I visually and audibly
witnessed my UFO change its physical state so that it could act at either
slow-speed or fast-speed. Understanding this phase change is paramount because in order for humans to achieve interplanetary and interstellar travel, we must first learn how to alter the physical state of
our space vehicles—from obvious material to apparent non-material—
like this and other UFOs have done. UFOs do not simply zip silently
through the air and water at hypersonic velocities while in a material
state because they would burn up. No, they obviously phase change first
and then achieve a non-material condition. Of paramount importance,
this UFO phase change offers an insight into how we must engineer
our own spacecraft in order to achieve interstellar travel.

On two nightly walks, I observed what was obviously the same
UFO over northeast Dallas on two different dates that were six months
apart. About 9 PM CST on December 11, 2013, the sky was clear and
there was a waxing first-quarter moon to my southwest. Visibly under
the moon and above the horizon, a tiny dark silhouette swiftly rose upward against the luminous night sky from ground level. This appeared
to be about three miles away and airplane-sized. At first, I thought it
was a swept wing jet interceptor taking off from Love Field, which lay
eight miles westward to my right. However, there were no lights as required by the FAA and the thunderous roar of afterburners never

materialized. The shadow had peculiar transparency that was unfamiliar. It climbed almost vertically at a slight angle towards me, traveling about twice as fast as a jetliner, which would be over 1,000 mph. When it reached the glare of the moon, I lost it. The silhouette never reappeared above me on my side of the moonlight, so I now assume that it continued upward into space. I was not sure that I had actually seen anything material so I did not tell anyone about it, including my wife. On subsequent walks, I would scan the sky for a repeat performance. Six months later I was to bump into this thing again in a surprise visit.

On Friday night, June 13, 2014, at 11 PM CDT, I had just left a gym at Buckner and Northcliff and was walking northward on Northlake Drive through a tree-lined residential neighborhood, approaching Peavy Road. The sky was clear and there was a full moon to my southeast, lighting up the streets below. I was approaching two 40-foot overhanging oaks on my right, or east side, when a brilliant sky light quickly moved in from the east and instantly stopped about 1 mile directly above me. By now I had walked under the trees and saw that this was not an airplane, so I spun to my right and carefully stepped into someone's front yard under the foliage for cover. Things were happening in microseconds and I instinctively realized that my December silhouette was out hunting and had stalked me immediately before I had walked under the trees. It lingered overhead for a few seconds and then moved back eastward to impatiently search back and forth above the neighborhood there. Visualize standing on the bottom of a deep clear lake watching the underside of a motorboat, which was searching from the flat water surface above, and you get the picture.

The thing was garishly-beautiful like a fairground ride contraption. It was about half the size of a 737 and appeared rather wedge-shaped. The body was not visible because of the glare, but I infer from my earlier 2013 sighting that it was solid. There were two strings of green lights in a V-shape along its sides. Knock off the point of the V and string red lights across the gap to understand its full makeup. The green lights were steady, but the red lights pulsed together on a 2-second cycle—there was no 1-2-3 sequence. The pulse was uniform and not keyed to any movement, so I assume they were ornamental or had some external function. At their maximum, all of the lights, both green and red, were of equal size and intensity. The red lights appeared to be the front; it always moved in this direction, it never moved sideways nor backward. To change direction, it would always pivot, so I assume that it was unidirectional. It seemed to be on an impatient commando get-in-and-get-out mission. The entire appearance throughout was strange, cartoonish, and almost comical as the craft frantically went back and forth, repeatedly. I would have laughed if I had not been so shocked and apprehensive.

There was an almost imperceptible sizzle emanating from the UFO, which sounded similar to an electric generator brush or bacon frying. This sound varied in intensity, either from a load put on machinery inside the UFO or from electrostatic around the shell as the craft moved around. The sound drifted down, much as from a hot-air balloon or migrating geese. Here I had visual and audible proof of a nuts-and-bolts machine and of its apparent distance one mile above me. There was nothing vague about my 2014 UFO; it was as real as your car. During the six months between the December silhouette and this ambush, I had researched UFO experiences and knew not to mess with them. Anyway, I was cowardly sucking up to my tree trunk and became a certified tree-hugger. Thankfully, the full moon bathed the treetops above and made visual penetration into underneath difficult. I kept under the wooden tree limbs to help block my bodily infrared heat radiation from detection.

After the longest three minutes of slow-speed searching, the mile-high UFO stopped at a periphery. Then, it suddenly shot downward like a meteor at a slight angle away from me. I thought, "So that is what you have been up to!" I later calculated that it "landed" around Lochwood Park. It traveled one mile in five seconds in a straight line from its mile-high perch to the ground without revving up against inertia or slowing down against momentum. When I saw it go behind the eastward housing, I instantly confirmed its size and distance with the visually-familiar background reference. Throughout all of this movement, the UFO remained about the same distance from me because it maintained the same apparent size, never greatly swelling nor shrinking. During its dive, the UFO's appearance to me became transparent, artificial, and surreal. It looked like a ghost of its former garishly-bright searching form, now being about one-third as bright. It was completely silent; there was no sound, either emanating from the UFO or from its estimated 720-mph dive through the air. I have never witnessed anything like this five-second alteration during my now 80 years, except perhaps for the vague 6-second upward-moving dark silhouette of 2013.

To visualize this slow-speed to fast-speed phase change, pretend that you are attending a drive-in movie theater. A Boeing 737 flies overhead about one mile up, plowing through the air and emitting that wonderful jet noise. You can see and hear that this is a hard material machine, which you could rap on with your knuckles. Then, over on the movie screen, the projector sweeps across a silent photographic image of that 737—same apparent size, shape, and color. You instinctively see that this is only a transparent light projection, which you cannot touch. That was essentially the difference in appearance between my UFO when it changed from slow-speed to fast-speed. Throughout the second phase, the UFO looked transparent and ghostly, as though behind a screen.

Confirming that there was an actual physical barrier of some sort between the diving UFO and I were these six factors:

1. Screening and transparency in the UFO's direct visual appearance.

2. Total cessation of its previous operational "electrical" sizzling sound.

3. An absence of inertia against starting and of momentum against stopping.

4. Inferred nullification of fatal G-forces from hovering to instant Mach-1.

5. The absence of compression or friction noise against the atmosphere.

6. Continuation of a 2-second blinking red light cycle with no time-change.

A very acceptable hypothesis that I have seen, which would explain my UFO's operation, comes from Robert L. Schroeder's book,

"Solving the UFO Enigma: How Modern Physics is Revealing the Technology of UFOs," Schroeder illustrates how the UFOs may be defying our understanding of Newtonian physics and I highly recommend his book because it fits my case perfectly. UFOs are particle accelerators that generate gravity and according to relativity, "gravity shrinks distance and stretches duration." For example, I saw a one-mile dive while the UFO only felt one yard. I estimated five seconds while it experienced a long one minute.

Based on my observation and logical inference, I believe the 2013-2014 UFO was a utility vehicle, which was directed to snatch people off the streets of Dallas and take them up into near space for unknown reasons. The UFO was possibly unlit in 2013 because commercial airline flights were at a peak at 9 PM. Then, the lit up 2014 version at 11 PM might have been because flights had already quit by 10 PM. I have never seen a UFO described like mine, with seemingly non-functional ornamental lighting. Perhaps this was designed to attract a sucker to stand still and gawk? In retrospect, I later noticed that there was no automobile traffic when the UFO had me pinned under the tree. Maybe the thing had scoped out an area where there was no vehicular activity. My beliefs are inferred from—

Its takeoff from a NE Dallas neighborhood near the White Rock Lake spillway on 12-11-2013.

The sneaking up on me as I walked home from the gym at 11 PM CDT on 6-13-2014.

Its subsequent three-minute search above the Old Lake Highlands and Lochwood neighborhoods.

The Mach-1 dive to the ground, which I could trace to around the Lochwood Park area.

After my experience, I soon ran into an equally-bizarre phenomenon—the solipsist UFO debunker, who knows more than the witness. Having myself been oblivious to any paranormal existence for 73 years, I know that folks need some personal background information, so here it is. I was born in 1940 and had my first UFO sighting in 2013, although I have never been successfully abducted nor met an alien face-to-face. In 1957, at age 17, I joined the United States Navy and served 4 years as an interior communications electrician and scored in the 99 percentiles on the GED science test. (There is no 100 percentile.) I graduated from Texas Christian University in 1968 with a Bachelor of Fine Arts Degree. In 2009, I retired from AT&T with a total of 44 years in the graphic arts field and can draw what I see. During both UFO sightings my vision and hearing were good, as there were no restrictions on my driver's license. As of today, I have attended about 25 consecutive air shows with my daughter and have much experience viewing things that fly—both manmade and otherwise.

Billy Hallmon
November 17, 2020

Billy and daughter Elizabeth

ANALYSIS

There's very little I can add of value. Billy does such a spectacular job of telling his story. I would like to add a note of thanks for sharing his photographs and sharing his experiences.

Case #29

Dirty Little Secret

An excerpt from
Dirty Little Secret: Confessions of an Alien Contactee
by Erin Montgomery
Roswell, New Mexico

I first met Erin Montgomery at Roswell's Annual 4th of July UFO Festival. If you've never been, it's a lot of fun with a street festival vibe and a kid-friendly venue. I recommend it. Erin and I hit it off immediately, as so often happens when abductees first meet one another.

Erin wrote a very candid book entitled *Dirty Little Secret*. It's on Amazon. I was honored that she asked me to write the introduction. Yvonne Smith wrote the prologue. It's a book that is at times hard to read from the sense of loss and heartbreak that accompanies this phenomenon. But, especially for some women, it will reverberate loudly. It's a relatively short but intense read. Below is an excerpt.

***

As a contactee, there are many different aspects of being in contact with extraterrestrial or extradimensional creatures. Some of these experiences are very loving and kind, often full of important lessons and information. However, there is no denying the trauma that contact with these non-human entities causes on the human brain. It cannot be ignored that people who are taken at night from their beds are forever changed by these experiences, and often, they are changed in ways that takes work with a professional to fully heal.

Even as a clinical therapist, and even though I have spoken about my experiences over and over again on paper and on many radio and video interviews, sitting down to explain the trauma that comes with contact is something that I have waited until the last minute to do. The avoidance of the feelings that come up around these moments is palpable and it is taking everything I have to not get up and start scraping paint off the walls in the bathroom, anything just to not to have to do this.

This desire to avoid remembering what happened is one of the symptoms of post-traumatic stress disorder (PTSD). I experienced it with the writing of my book "Dirty Little Secret: Confessions of an Alien Contactee." Not only did I struggle to recall information, but the act of reliving the experiences created a mental anguish that is common in people who have been traumatized. I wrote:

So many nights have consisted of me curled in a ball with my back to the wall, the light on, long past midnight. "Please don't come. Just leave me alone. Go away. Oh God, just leave me alone." It certainly wouldn't be every night—it ebbs and flows like waves of contact times. I always seem to have a warning or a message before they come. A cold feeling washes over me, my heart races. "No not tonight." And there I would be, balled up in bed. I certainly don't sleep. This often lasts several days until I can no longer keep both eyes open and focused

338

on the door and windows: sleep overcoming me regardless of my protests.

The real question here is—how many of those nights that I spend in terror are really nights in which I was visited? How much of this anxiety is due to PTSD? In the process of becoming a therapist, these symptoms look very familiar to me. I see it often with my clients, many contactees, and certainly myself (as I wipe sweat off of my upper lip while I type). Yes, even the act of writing this book is causing me serious mental distress.

What is PTSD? Post-traumatic stress disorder (PTSD) is the re-experiencing of a trauma that one has endured in varied and often surprising ways with acute stress symptoms that accompany those triggers. Months, even years, after the initial trauma, a person may experience disturbing memories, nightmares, flashbacks, psychological distress, and physiological reactions such as sweating, pounding heart, rapid breathing, possibly even chest pains (DSM-5, 2013). Those suffering from PTSD will do what they can to avoid these memories, etc., which may include avoiding the people, places, or activities that remind them of the trauma. There may be some blocked memories around the trauma, exaggerated negative beliefs, some distortion around blame, persistent negative emotional states such as fear, anger, or guilt, a loss of interest in others and activities, and other depressive symptoms (DSM-5, 2013). A person with PTSD may be easily irritable, be hypervigilant, have an exaggerated startle response, lack of concentration and may suffer from sleep disorders (DSM-5, 2013).

There is no doubt that alien contact can be traumatic, especially when contact starts as a child. So far, I haven't found a way to stop the contact, however, I can treat the PTSD. I don't have to be afraid to go to sleep. I don't need to negatively impact my family by being irritable and withdrawn. I know my husband suffers as well. He startles awake so easily and so dramatically that I must be very careful not to wake him. But who do you go to for this? Many counselors are trained in dealing with PTSD, and many of those are also trained in hypnotherapy. But making the decision to see a counselor isn't so simple for a contactee. One cannot just spring this information on just any ol' counselor. Well, I mean you can, and some counselors may be receptive, but this isn't anything I have personally wanted to talk about in therapy. No way.

As mentioned in the preceding blurb, these moments of trauma symptoms come and go. Sometimes there are no issues, but at others the levels of paranoia and fear can take over one's life. And then something happens to remind one of why they are afraid in the first place. After attending my first UFO Festival in Roswell in 2012, I had a reality shifting experience that challenged everything I thought I understood and knew about being a UFO contactee. I had been coming to terms with the fact that I have been contacted by aliens since I was a child and was having experiences off and on throughout my adulthood. But then this happened:

Things got really intense that night as I tried to go to sleep. I had to fight with paranoia for the first time in a long time. This feeling of anticipation creeps in, causing my heart to race, I breakout in a cold *sweat, and my mind repeats, "They are coming, oh God, they are coming tonight." I can't close my eyes, I can't turn off the light, I can't turn my back to the door or windows, and I pull myself into a tight ball trying to logic away the inevitable. "This isn't happening. I am crazy. I have totally lost it. Oh my God, what was that?"*

Next thing I was aware of was being wrapped in a sheet type of gurney, folded snug in the material and was carried right through the wall of my bedroom! I remember feeling a sense of awe as I watched the barrier between inside and outside pass over my head. I reached my hand out for comfort. How did I know I would find comfort like this? My hand was grasped by a warm, reassuring being. I gazed into her (Her? How did I know her gender?) eyes and knew her. She was...how does one describe an alien? She had large expressive eyes in an overly large head, small mouth that seemed to smile, and wrinkly grey skin on her too-thin limbs. She was a sweet being, one that I feel I have known since I was a child; one who knows just what to say and do to keep me as docile as possible.

She stayed by my side. I must have been put down, to sleep, knocked out, made unconscious, lost memories or something because the next thing I remember is feeling excruciating pain ripping through my lower abdomen. I screamed and tried to sit up but found I was restrained across my chest. I was on a cot or medical bed. A surgical barrier was up across my stomach so I couldn't see the lower half of my body. Again, the pain tore across my mid-section. My handler, for lack of a better term, patted my shoulder and clucked calming sounds. Taking a deep breath, I looked at what surroundings I could see. There

341

were many other cots in rows around me—all filled with women in the same predicament. We appeared to be in a cave or underground as the walls were rough-hewn stone. Military green cabinets lined the walls. Two taller grey aliens were near my feet, doing whatever it was they were doing to me.

A human male in a military uniform covered by a white lab coat, a grey buzz cut, and a clipboard of papers he was sifting through walked by me. He glanced down at me, looking directly into my eyes. I tried to sit up, call to him, ask for help. But he blinked and looked over me as if I didn't exist. My own species, regarding me as no more than cattle. I felt my heart sink in my chest. My tenuous hold on hope crumbling through my fingers and my only sense of comfort coming from a being who has, as far as I can tell, been with me only to keep me calm when scary things are happening.

Swiveling my head to look at the cots nearest me, I finally understood what procedures were being performed. We were being harvested! Tiny fetuses, smaller than the palm of my hand were being taken from all the women around me. And me! That is why it hurt so bad. Induced labor! But I wasn't pregnant—was I? How could I be? I was single then, with no sexual partner. Why isn't there something more sophisticated happening with the harvesting? Why did it have to be a—cynically called—natural birth? And why did that human not care? I started to scream in an ever-desperate crescendo, "What are you doing? These are your own people! What do you need us for? Why are you taking babies? Why did you take my baby?" The buzz cut man

342

turned back around and looked over me. My handler reached forward and placed her hand over my face. I disappeared into darkness.

I woke up back in my bed. Under the covers. Curled up in a fetal position. I stretched out my legs only to feel aches and cramps around my midsection. The memories trickled back, and I threw off the blankets. Three fingerprint bruises laced each inner thigh. When I looked in the mirror my eyes were swollen, and tiny broken blood vessels dotted my eyelids as they always do when I have cried a serious cry during moments of extreme emotional hurt. It wasn't a dream.

It was at this point that my mental health took a drastic turn to the south. How could I process the fact that not only was I dealing with being a life-long contactee with alien entities, I was having fetuses harvested from me, and there were human military personnel who were observing the process?! I started missing more and more work. My ability to take care of myself and my children was beginning to diminish. I definitely was not sleeping, at least not well, and not for many hours at a time. But what was I to do? Who could I talk to about this? Several years went by before I could not stand it any longer and decided I needed to take my peace of mind into my own hands as contact was not going to stop:

I was very lucky to have met Yvonne Smith at the Roswell UFO Festival in July of 2012. It was through her I joined Close Encounters Research Organization International or CERO (cerointl.com), her support group and was able to go through a hypnotherapy session with her. My paranoia and inability to sleep was beginning to impact my

343

ability to work, care for my family, or even take care of my own basic needs. I knew that Yvonne was going to be back in Roswell for the UFO festival, so I made an appointment to meet with her in the afternoon of July 4th, 2015.

I was very nervous going into this session. I had never been hypnotized before. I had no idea what to expect and so I brought a friend with me to drive just in case I was a zombie or something after the session. I was imagining myself driving into the little alien lamp posts that line Roswell's Main Street. Yvonne put both of us at ease quickly and we discussed the process of hypnosis and what it was we were aiming to accomplish.

I was determined to pull the moment that had caused me the most trauma. I felt like I needed to go right to the source so that I could finally get some sleep! Yvonne took me back to the home my father built for the family. I was seven years old and could even remember the nightgown I was wearing. I saw a light coming through my window. It was so bright. I thought it was the moon. I became aware of a small being with a very pointed face standing next to the head of the bed.

I had the impression this was a female figure, and I was comfortable with her. She touched my arm which felt like electricity. She told me that we were going to go for a ride. It was then that I noticed two other beings in the room. They looked just like her, but I knew they were boys. One was standing by my bedroom door, which was open. The other was at the foot of the bed. He reached out and touched my foot.

344

Together the two held me aloft. This was fun! I felt like I was flying! They directed my body, floating out of the bedroom door. When they had me positioned in the hallway, we began to rise up towards the ceiling. To my amazement I phased right through the ceiling, into the attic and out through the roof! It was like my atoms were slipping between the atoms of the wood and other building materials as we ascended. Did I know how to explain that at seven years old? No, but reliving it, I was able to put that sensation to words.

That bright light that I thought was the moon became visible as it came from the bottom of a circular craft that hovered above the house. In the beam of light, we as a group ascended higher and higher. We entered the ship through an opening on the underside, where the light was being generated. The interior of the ship is smooth and rounded and metallic like the tank on a milk truck. It felt so sterile.

I was floated down a hallway and into a room that looked like an exam room. There were cabinets in the room and a chair that looked like a dentist's chair. They placed me in the chair and secured me into place. The female being stayed near me, calming me. A few minutes later a taller entity entered the room. He was much taller than these smaller beings. His limbs, torso, and even fingers appeared so long and thin. I had difficulty focusing on his face at this point, but he felt insect-like as he had moving mouth parts, like mandibles. He was wearing a black jump suit with red piping around the edges.

As he approached me in the chair, I began to panic. The female did her best to reassure me. He produced an instrument that was like a two-pronged mental fork. He inserted something biological, pink and wiggling, into the fork area. My head was restrained, my mouth opened, and the fork instrument inserted the mass into the roof of my mouth.

He left quickly after, and I was released from the chair. I remember the female entity showing me the stars outside the window and pointed out Earth far, far below. She led me back to the center of the ship, we descended back into my bedroom and I was placed back in bed.

I left the session feeling dazed. It wasn't that I was still in a hypnotic fog—it doesn't work like that. I was fully awake. And I was aware—more aware than I have been perhaps ever in my life. I had witnessed the memories of my childhood self. Defining memories that have essentially made me the person I am today, trauma and all. I had my own truth, the proof of my contactee status. I really had experienced being taken onto a spaceship by alien beings. And from the familiarity of the handler being, it obviously wasn't the first time.

That night, I was able to sleep without vigilance. I could turn out the light and sigh with relief as sleep overcame me. After this session, I understood that I needed to follow in Yvonne's footsteps. I needed to help others like me.

Three years later, I had an intriguing memory pop up when my husband at the time accidentally shone a light in my eyes while heading to the bathroom in the middle of the night. Soon as the light hit my eyelids, I had a memory of standing outside as a child, surrounded by these non-human entities, large head and eyes, naked, chattering to-gether, and I was a part of the group like a friend and we were so ex-cited about something coming. It was approaching July again, and so I made another appointment with Yvonne to dive into this memory. I wanted to explore this possible moment of joy and happiness. I wanted my trauma experiences to be redeemed by remembering something fun and positive. However, while the information that came out of the re-gression wasn't all negative as I was taught how to manipulate gravity and how to access chakra centers in the body, it also highlighted the beginning of the "hybrid program" that I was to participate in from then until now:

I remembered being outside in a group of people, several chil-dren and small grey-type aliens around me. There was a sense of ex-citement in the air, anticipation. There were adults at the front of the group, and I remember seeing my father among them.

The excitement grew and I saw the lights of a ship as it de-scended toward the group. There were many tall trees around us and I heard the awful screeching sound as the ship penetrated into the tree line, shattering the trees around it. The ship landed and we slowly walked on board. I remember my feelings of fear increasing as I got closer, and I wanted to be closer to my dad, but he is quite far ahead of me in line.

I was lead in a room off to the left as the rest, including my father, continued ahead. There were three beings with me, as I seem to most often recall. I was stripped naked and my anxiety skyrocketed!

347

They helped me onto a table and there were straps placed across my belly and chest. They placed a strange cone shaped cap onto my head that seemed to have electrodes coming from it. I could feel my scalp being manipulated by the energy inside. Then I felt hands on me, spreading my legs apart. Apparently, I was having my very first pelvic exam! I was at the beginning of puberty, so I can understand why, now, they were interested in my reproductive health. After the exam, I was helped off the table, was able to dress, and was escorted into a different part of the ship.

The harvesting of fetuses has become a constant in my adult life. Dream after dream of giving birth to these very small babies, no bigger than the palm of my hand, naming them, introducing them to other children, bonding and loving them, and then leaving them. How does a human make sense of this? Men and women both endure these procedures, the creation of hybrid children using their DNA. I am part of a multiple generation family of contact, and now my children are having experiences as well. They have the tell-tale signs of being part of this breeding program themselves with bruises on their thighs and pregnancy symptoms with no possible way they could be pregnant.

The emotions of a person dealing with the fact that they have these experiences is compounded when they find out their children are also being harvested. And a heavy despair settles in because.... what can we do? Nothing. Not a thing. There is no way to stop this. It has been happening for generations and it will continue to happen in generations to follow. One of the most disturbing emotions that crosses through my perception is that of disconnect. I shut down. I stop feeling, become devoid of emotion, in regard to knowing my children are suffering now, in regard to knowing there are children on ship that I have little to no contact with. The guilt of feeling nothing weighs heavier than the sight of a scary being with moving mouth parts inserting an implant into the roof of my mouth.

I do not have full recall of every experience I have had with these beings. Little bits and slips of memory come to me, sometimes at very unexpected and inconvenient times. After the publication of "Dirty Little Secret," I started to do promotional radio shows and podcasts. One show I did was with a couple who are fellow therapists. They wanted to explore my moment of trauma when the implant was placed in my mouth. They thought that perhaps I was so terrified of that being because I had run into him before. I wanted to explore this idea as they were suggesting to pretend, I had met him before, but a wall came down and I felt like I slammed face-first into it. My mind was not going to allow me to access that information. It was so abrupt that I was startled, but the couple easily steered the conversation in a different direction. That week was a grueling week of shows, and I found it more and more difficult to sleep, get up, and do what I needed to for work, and I was becoming more and more irritable. Then, one day while at work between clients, talking to a fellow experiencer friend, we had simultaneous recall of a moment when we were children.

In a circular room, a small bench along one wall, and two round doorways at 45 degree angles from each other across from the bench, he and I found ourselves remembering being on that bench. Red light emanated from the ceiling, and an impenetrable darkness rose *from the floor. At about the age of 6, long braids down my back, and wearing only underwear, I clung to this boy of about ten with blond hair and also in his underwear. Our feet were tucked up close to us to keep them away from the blackness. Abject terror filled us as we felt into the moment. Why were we in this room? How did we get here? Why are we so afraid? Why are we naked? Then, two beings, so tall and so thin, in black jumpsuits entered, one through each doorway. They approached us quietly, arms pulled tight to their chests, triangular heads and large dark eyes intent on us. They had mandibles. These must be the mantid beings people talk about, and so much like the creature who placed the implant into my mouth. They reach us and we were picked up by the two entities. We began screaming and reaching for each other, desperate to be able to touch each other for comfort. We were taken out of the room and that is where our memory stops.*

Shaking, breathing heavily, tears squeezing out of eyes that have seen fresh new horrors, my friend ended the phone call, and I was left to compose myself before I had to call my next client. Questions still swirl in my mind. What happened with us that night? Were we hurt? Why were we so scared? And why were we in our underwear? How do I pull myself together enough to help the next client on my schedule when I just had the rug pulled out from under me, again? Weeks later I still fight with the resurgence of my PTSD symptoms. Time to call for another hypnotic regression. I believe it is.

"Dirty Little Secret: Confessions of an Alien Contactee" was written in order to map my journey as I processed these traumas, and as has been recently experienced, they are never fully put to bed.

However, it is important for all of us to come to terms with our traumas in order to face these entities with clear heads as to more easily assess why they are among us, because among us they are. Through this process I have followed in Yvonne Smith's footsteps, have begun work as a clinical therapist, and begun training to be able to do hypnotic regressions myself in order to help others who have suffered as I have. The lives of contactees are irreversibly changed by this contact. We feel different than other humans, we experience things other humans don't, and are able to perceive on a level that can only be explained as psychic. We can choose to stay in these symptomatic states and fight with our fate, hide from reality, and slip into depressions so deep that we may turn to substances or worse, or we can choose to rise above the fear, heal the trauma, and find ways to discern what is happening to us so we can share with the world. I choose to embrace this challenge. What do you choose?

ANALYSIS

Compare Erin's experience to the facts in Case #14. In total I received seven emails from women who claim to have "lost" a fetus. I included a story from a man's perspective in Case #24.

Erin's story resonates with me on so many levels. The fact that she recognized her "handler" and felt an odd affection for her reminds me of my maternal feelings toward Betty. When Erin reached out for comfort, her handler was there to hold Erin's hand when she needed comforting. Erin's story of moving through a solid wall was almost identical to my April 16, 2019 event where I went through my own ceiling.

Erin, as a trained and licensed therapist, recognizes the psychological and emotional dilemma of choosing whether to suppress these events, or accept them as fact.

It's interesting that she can recall the extraterrestrial maternity ward. This is a memory you'd think ET would have screened to save her the trauma. As I've said before, "We remember what we're allowed to remember." In hindsight, this memory may have been an act of kindness because it allowed Erin to process what was happening to her and her body.

Case #30

Rita and Richard's Childhood Encounter

Orchard Park, New York

Dear Terry,

I grew up in Orchard Park, NY, a wealthy suburb of Buffalo with a population of under 3,500. Everyone knew everyone; it was a safe and bucolic environment for kids. Orchard Park had a lot of wooded areas, orchards, meadows, etc. throughout the town.

The second house my family owned was built in a new development on Henning Drive. It was a beautiful place with a couple miles of forests behind the house. We lived there from when I was four or five-years-old, until about 1974 when I was 10, and my brother Richard was 13.

The two of us spent many a day in the little forest behind our home. It was our playground. We spent hours in those woods doing all the fun stuff kids our age loved to do. We ran, built forts, swung on huge vines and smoked our first cigarette.

My cousins lived in a neighborhood about a half mile away from us. It was adjoined to our development by back roads that were only trafficked by the residents who lived there. My favorite grandmother lived about two miles away, close to the center of town. We rode our bikes or walked to our cousins' or Grandma's house all the time, coming home only when called for dinner. There were miles and miles of fields and forests behind our cousins' house too. It was a second playground.

I was the youngest in the family. I had two brothers, Richard and Arnold. They were three and four years older than me, respectively. My parents and my brothers were pragmatic to a fault. If they couldn't personally touch, smell or taste something, it didn't exist. Esoteric things like ghosts and UFOs did not exist for them. For Richard and I that would change, at least on one night.

In the Henning Drive home, I had a lovely bedroom. I recall that I slept on my stomach. For as long as I can remember while living in that house I would every so often wake in the middle of the night. My back would be arched, and I felt a sensation like someone had run something up my spine. It almost tickled in the way, like someone ran their finger up your foot or tickled your sides. It caused me to stay in an arched position as well as in a state of temporary paralysis. I can't tell how long it lasted. I sensed a presence in my room and somehow, I knew it was not human. It was the cause of my paralysis. I couldn't roll over or sit up to see what was there. I could only lie on my stomach and search the room with just my limited peripheral vision. I came to dread bedtime; always afraid it would happen again. I knew there was some-one or something scary in my room.

I would have Dad check under my bed and in my closet to help allay my fears so I could get to sleep. Dad still remembers me asking him to do that for me, to help me feel safe enough to close my eyes. I'm told I would sleepwalk and talk in my sleep at times too. There were two windows in my bedroom that faced our backyard and the forest. At times I sensed someone, or something was staring at me from one of my windows at night.

Around 1973 or 1974, I had what I thought was a very vivid dream one night. It was a dream that never faded from memory, as most dreams do. In it, I was drawn to my bedroom window facing our neighbor's yard. It was the same window that I believed they used to watch me at night. I saw a saucer-like craft with a bright white light from underneath descend into the neighbor's yard. I walked into my brother Richard's bedroom and saw him standing at his window staring at the same descending craft. Without a word spoken between us, we climbed out of his window onto the roof of the enclosed sun porch below. Together, we walked through the grass toward this craft as it was still descending. I clearly recall a lot of bright white light shining underneath and within the craft. We watched as it came to stop about four feet above the grass and a door opened as we approached. While we stood in front of the craft neither of us felt the slightest bit of fear. In fact, we felt euphoric, nearly jubilant. It felt like a reunion. We felt like we were getting together with old friends. That was the last thing I remember about that "dream." When I try to remember what happened next there's nothing but a blank slate.

The next morning, I bolted into my brother's bedroom and screamed excitedly, "You won't believe the dream I had last night!" I told him all the details of what happened in my "dream." Richard was shocked and exclaimed, "No way, I had the same dream!" I think we were too young and possibly too influenced in some way that kept us from processing what really happened. Rationalizing, we just chalked it up to being a coincidence that we had the same dream, and then locked that memory away and never spoke about it again until we were in our 20s.

Right after my brother and I had our "dream," there was a perfectly circular area burned into my neighbor's lawn approximately 15–20 feet in diameter. God I wish I had thought to photograph it. My neighbor called my mom over to see it. He and my mom were both avid gardeners. He told Mom he had no idea what could have caused it. In the weeks afterward he would complain that nothing would grow there. It was just a bare patch of dirt. My mother would later corroborate that fact when we were together discussing our experience. Then we realized it was not a dream.

I still have no conscious memory of what happened after we approached the craft. I hope to find out through hypnotherapy in the coming months. After all these years I still need to know exactly what happened to us that night.

In 1974 we moved to a larger house, about a mile away from our Henning Drive home. I don't recall having anymore UFO experiences at our new house. I never again woke up in the middle of the night to a presence in my bedroom. I suspect our new house was not conducive to a visit or maybe they had everything they needed from us already, and/or maybe they just tracked us from afar.

I had several incidents where odd wounds on my skin would show up out of the blue. For instance, I had a bulbous cyst under my left ear which was the size of a BB from an air rifle. I eventually had it removed in my late 40s, but the surgeon failed to biopsy it. It was simply discarded, so I'll never know if there was a tracking device embedded inside it. But I suspect there was something embedded in it to track me or monitor me somehow.

Also, once as a kid, I felt something sticking out of the top of my head. I kept picking at it and finally was able to grab it with the tips of my fingernails and pulled out what looked like a 1.5-inch-long thorn. I regret not saving it, but the thought never crossed my mind. As an adult, there have been times where I woke up and there would be a small spot of blood on my white pillowcase. I would diligently check my face and head, inside my ears, mouth, nostrils and feeling all over my scalp but I could never find a trace of residual blood. It made no sense.

When I was in college at University of Rochester, my parents moved to the Southwest. They divorced, and my mom moved to Albuquerque, NM with her second husband. My dad moved to El Paso, TX with his new wife. Mom thought she was sparing me from the sadness of leaving my home, so she insisted I not come home from college while she packed up the house. Her good intentions failed. I ended up having recurring dreams for the next decade that I went back and bought the old home, so that my family could be together again.

A few years later, my brothers eventually moved to NM too. During Christmas break of my second or third year in college, I flew out to visit my mom. She asked me to go through all my boxes that she had moved from our house in Orchard Park so I could keep what I wanted. They rest we'd use for a garage sale and donate the leftovers. While going through my childhood toys, jewelry boxes and such, I came across a piece of orange construction paper I had saved. Amazingly, I dated it and drew an image of the UFO landing in my neighbors backyard. I was stunned to see it again. I had completely forgotten it. I had no conscious memory of ever drawing it. But the instant I saw it, memories of what happened in my childhood came flooding back into my mind. It's important to know I was never a sci-fi buff. I had no interest in science either. My passion was in the area of fine arts. I embraced drawing, painting, writing, and sports.

Something else I used to do when we lived in the Henning Drive house, at night I would sometimes take a blanket to the backyard and lay it on the grass. I'd lie there in peace and stare up at the moon, trying not to blink to keep it in focus, looking for the slightest movement on its surface. I was sure there was life on the moon, despite hearing in the media that it was barren and supposedly no life could possibly exist, given the harsh conditions.

To this day, I have a fascination with the night sky. I love to gaze at the stars and constellations, keeping an eye out for any anomalies. Before the memories of the encounter my brother and I shared resurfaced, I bought glow-in-the-dark stars and constellations and stuck them to the ceiling of my first apartment bedroom. Somehow this was very comforting to view at night.

It might have been that trip to Mom's in NM when I found my UFO drawing that spurred the whole family conversation about the

358

"dream" that Richard and I shared. There was also the issue of the strange, burned area in my neighbor's backyard. My mom witnessed it and remembered it well. No one questioned what happened that night. Odd that it wasn't discussed in depth as my family was pragmatic and we all knew this to be fact.

Years later my brother told me about a camping trip he made with his wife and daughter to Elephant Butte, NM. The campground was situated around a large water reservoir where people could boat and swim. After Richard's wife and daughter went to sleep in the camper, Richard sat on the tailgate of his truck and enjoyed a drink. He told me a UFO hovered in front of him for some time. But he never said a word about what may have happened after that. Rich always partied and eventually he slid into chronic alcoholism. Sadly, the disease progressed until he died of a brain aneurism when he was just 53 years old. I don't know if his alien encounters contributed to his drinking, but I would like to know.

I was living in Philadelphia right after college when these memories resurfaced. I read practically every book Whitley Strieber and Budd Hopkins ever wrote about UFOs and ET encounters. I wrote to Budd and laid out all the odd things that happened to me that couldn't be explained as anything other than alien encounters. Surprisingly, Budd wrote me back and said he thought I may have been abducted. He validated my suspicions and invited me to meet with him and a colleague who used hypnosis to recover repressed memories.

Budd explained that through hypnosis, I might recall what really happened that night. I could possibly recover that missing piece of the events past the point where my memory abruptly ends. I might finally know what happened after my brother and I were standing in front of the UFO in our neighbor's backyard.

I tried a hypnosis session but could never quite get "under." It may have been a trust issue with his hypnotist. I tried; I just couldn't do it. In retrospect, I don't think I was ready. I was also working on a lot of other issues that were turning my world upside down. Perhaps unconsciously I knew I couldn't handle uncovering a possibly terrifying extraterrestrial encounter at that point in my life. I shelved it for the next three decades.

Over the last 10 years, I've spoken with a few trusted friends and colleagues who've also experienced encounters like mine. It's not as rare as many people think. Among other things, I discovered that people who've experienced an abduction tend to also be very intuitive. I don't know if that's true across the board, but it would be interesting to find out.

I'm considering working with a hypnotherapist to help uncover my unconscious memories of what happened when my brother and I approached that craft in our neighbor's backyard. To this day my memory abruptly ends as I reach the craft. I also need to know what happened to me at the hands of the entities that entered my bedroom all those nights. I am hoping it may shed light on my brother's issues too. I want to know if "they" were the cause of his struggles and contributed to his untimely demise. I miss him. Lastly, I need to know if the issues still plaguing me today are a result of my encounters. Hopefully, uncovering the truth will allow me to heal and grow.

ANALYSIS

I chose this case for last because it succinctly states all the commonalities in so many cases. They are:

- A childhood experience involving aliens and a UFO.
- Bedroom childhood visitations.
- Repressed memories.
- Inexplicable wounds discovered upon waking.
- Reluctance to openly discuss the issue between family members. In this case there where multiple witnesses including Rita, her brother Richard, their mother and a neighbor.
- Physical evidence burned into the neighbor's yard. Rita's mother and her neighbor were both "gardeners" but never investigated the mysterious circular burns that manifested immediately following Rita and Richard's "shared dream."
- One of the witnesses, Rita's brother, was plagued by substance abuse, likely due to his inability to fully process and integrate his experience at age 13 or before.

EPILOGUE

First, thank you so much for reading my book. If you'd like to get into contact with me regarding any topic or to share your story, I would really appreciate hearing from you. You can contact me at:

lovelace.landpope@gmail.com.

I promise your anonymity will be preserved. I am not a therapist and can offer little by way of answers, but I promise to reply to every email I receive.

My parting message is aimed at those of you who have ever contemplated writing a book about their life and experiences, paranormal or otherwise. My advice is to write and accept responsibility for the effort and not concern yourself with the outcome.

Gone are the days of laboring to send submissions to various publishing houses and waiting for a response and hoping for the best only to be rejected. We've all heard the stories of great books being rejected by a hundred publishers before finally being accepted. Amazon may not be Simon and Schuster, but it's a forum, a platform that will accept your book, post it, and give you a voice. But success is usually not that easy. It usually requires hard work to market your book. It's a competitive world. Fail or succeed, all you can do is your best and just write.

In recent years the level of consciousness with regard to paranormal phenomenon has been growing. Increasing numbers of people are identifying experiences regarded as anomalous and most are without explanation. This leads not only to questions but also to a need for further support of some kind. This support should be based on the individual's experience and reaction to the phenomenon. This is why OPUS has been organized; OPUS…The Organization for Paranormal Understanding and Support. The mission of OPUS is to educate and support people having unusual /anomalous personal experiences. Such experiences may include extraordinary states of consciousness, spiritual or parapsychological phenomenon, close encounters with non-human entities, and/or UFO activity. The sometimes disturbing, difficult-to-believe, or spiritual nature of anomalous experiences might lead an individual to seek professional help, but because these experiences often fall outside the realm of what is considered "normal," there is often a lack of professionals willing or able to work with these issues. OPUS has recognized the need for a clearinghouse where an experiencer can receive assistance in locating and choosing a professional who is knowledgeable about a particular experience in question.

When appropriate, OPUS refers experiencers to physicians, licensed mental health practitioners, consultants, investigators, and alternative health assistants. OPUS also refers to support groups of all kinds where experiencers can share feelings and concerns without fear of ridicule or embarrassment, while learning to understand, bridge, and integrate what happened to them into daily life.

Recently, in addition to our Zoom, and face-to-face support group, OPUS has created an international "on-line" support group which can only be accessed by the members and is available 24/7. For UFO matters, OPUS networks with many like-minded groups and organizations such as Yvonne Smith and CERO (Close Encounter Research Organization), Dr. Leo Sprinkle and ACCET (Academy of Clinical Close Encounters Therapists, Inc), Barbara Lamb, MS, and previously with the late Dr. John Mack (JEMI) and Budd Hopkins (Intruder Foundation). For psychic issues, we refer to Lloyd Auerbach of the Paranormal Network and for Kundalini, to the Kundalini Support Network and Kundalini Awakening Now. For spiritual emergencies, we refer to June Steiner PhD and the Spiritual Emergence Network. Co-founded in 1994 by Les Velez and Dr. Eugene Lipson we seek to understand and support people having paranormal experiences. OPUS, through its educational services and position of neutrality, provides a safe and caring meeting place for people and groups with the intention of working together to further our overall knowledge in these areas and better support people to integrate their anomalous experiences into everyday life. You can read more about this on our Experiencer Support page.

OPUS is a non-profit tax-exempt corporation formed for the public good and is recognized by the I.R.S. under section 501(c) 3. Its activities are guided by an executive council around which is created the larger network of volunteers, mental and medical practitioners, and experts in various fields. Please contribute whatever you can by sending your tax deductible check to the mailing address listed and donate through PayPal. Volunteers are welcome and encouraged to participate. OPUS can be found at http://opusnetwork.org where the website provides information on clinical discussions and contact information. Our snail mail address 2701 I Street, Sacramento California 95816

A white box over roof at high speed. October 2019. Property of Terry Lovelace.

Implanted device discovered 2012, above right knee.

X-ray property of Terry Lovelace

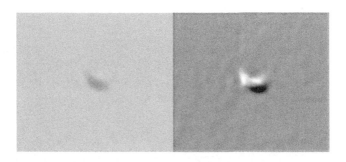

Rotating globe over landscape, September 2018. Property of Terry Lovelace.

Unmarked military helicopter followed Terry from Methodist Hospital to the VA
Clinic and home, April 16, 2019. Property of Terry Lovelace.

Unmarked helicopter and straw hat-shaped UFO in pursuit.
Property of Terry Lovelace.

Rotating crystal-like structure, June 2019. Property of Terry Lovelace.

Saucer photographed over author's home April 29, 2019. Note the sun on top, reflective surface and underside in shadow. Property of Terry Lovelace.

Made in United States
Orlando, FL
27 August 2022

21507392R00232